# The Master Chefs of Britain Recipe Book

# The Master Chefs of Britain Recipe Book

250 recipes from
the Great Chefs of Britain

A Publication of The Master Chefs Institute
Sandy Lesberg, Director

**DAVID & CHARLES**
Newton Abbot  London

**British Library Cataloguing in Publication Data**
The Master chefs of Britain recipe book.—
   Rev. ed.
   1. Restaurant, lunch rooms, etc.—
Great Britain
I. Master Chefs Institute
641.5′0941        TX725.A1

   ISBN 0-7153-8629-8

Illustrations: Judy Parensis and Jonathan Doney
© The Master Chefs Institute 1984

Typeset by MS Filmsetting Limited, Frome
and printed in Great Britain
by Butler & Tanner Limited, Frome
for David & Charles (Publishers) Limited
Brunel House Newton Abbot Devon

# Preface

There can be no doubt that the following work, for which I have the honour of being asked to subscribe a preface, will turn out to be both a tangible and an invaluable aid for the lady of the house, the gourmet, and also for the professional.

It is a great pleasure to discover throughout this book chefs of different nationalities carrying out their chosen profession in all kinds of restaurants scattered all over Great Britain. They offer a wide selection of international yet personalised dishes, ranging from the most simple to the most sophisticated and from the most economical to the most sumptuous.

The wealth of colour and variety herein is reminiscent of an artist's palette from which the pupil can indulge either his own tastes or exploit the possibilities of the moment, to choose his master, and to cook in the knowledge that what he has cherished and pampered will always receive the acclaim that it rightly deserves, and that very often he will be agreeably surprised by the final result. Could there be any greater satisfaction than witnessing the hum of conversation around a dinner table being brought to a sudden halt by the presentation, the colours, the texture, and the sophistication of a culinary creation?

The British chefs included in this work deserve a special and encouraging mention. They have no reason to be envious of their European counterparts, as they too are truly masters of their trade. The public is only too often either unaware of them or adopts a disdainful attitude towards them. Let us hope that, one day, measures at government level will restore the former professional prestige to this hard but noble vocation. If this were to happen, we could well one day see British chefs in action, not only in their own country, but all over the world.

My culinary philosophy and my everyday working attitude since the age of fourteen have led me to certain positive conclusions and have given me a great deal of satisfaction. Without a certain amount of sacrifice and a constant striving towards new goals, however, life would be empty and meaningless. My brother and I have understood this, and without doubt, the most concrete and the strongest vindication for us lies in the strength of our "association." It is this, and this alone, that constitutes the success from which I draw my faith, my respect, and my love.

The Master Chefs Institute is an association that will serve to strengthen the bonds between professionals. Let us hope that as many chefs as possible understand its significance and decide to join, lending their strength to its purpose. Its aim is the further promotion of our splendid profession, and this can be nothing but an advantage for the discerning public.

This book is a splendid initiative and provides us with an important and much needed glimpse of the serious side of gastronomy in Great Britain.

Michel Roux
Director, Roux Restaurants, Ltd.
Life Fellow of The Master Chefs Institute

**Publisher's Note:** To avoid any possible diversion from the precise intentions of the chefs we are printing the recipes exactly as they were written. "Spoons" in the list of ingredients usually mean "tablespoons," but do use your own judgment. You must decide for yourself what liberties, if any, you will take. I strongly recommend that you stay fairly close to the chefs' instructions for at least the first try at any of the recipes. There is much to be said for freedom of action in the kitchen but with a collection of pedigree recipes such as these a modicum of conservation would, I suggest, stand you in good stead.

# Contents

# Introduction

The Master Chefs Institute is an international affiliation of important chefs and restaurateurs whose primary function is to provide a bridge between the professional working chef and the public. THE MASTER CHEFS OF BRITAIN RECIPE BOOK represents the finest cuisine in the country presented by her greatest chefs and restaurateurs. Through their membership in the Institute they share with you the secrets of their speciality recipes, some more challenging than others, but all worthy of your attention and eminently adaptable to your household kitchen.

You will note that after the names of some of the chefs there are printed the letters M.C.G.B. They stand for the title "Master Chef of Great Britain" and while every chef represented in this book has, by dint of his or her membership in the Institute, achieved an unassailable position in the culinary world, the relatively few of these declared Master Chef of Great Britain are to be considered at the very zenith of their art and profession.

The Institute has a limited number of "Gourmet Memberships" available to the general public in each country where the Institute functions. These Gourmet Members receive special discounts for Institute publications (i.e. THE MASTER CHEFS OF FRANCE RECIPE BOOK, in French or English). From time to time receptions/demonstrations are held in various parts of Britain to which Gourmet Members are invited. The Institute food and wine magazine "THE MASTER CHEF" is sent free to Gourmet Members each quarter, who also are entitled to reduced tuition rates for our various teaching programmes both here and abroad. For further information write to our membership secretary:

Mrs. Melinda Renwick
P.O. Box 2
Shepperton
Middlesex
TW17 8JZ

Finally I would like to express my appreciation to the Steering Committee in Britain for the great support they have given to the Institute since the British Chapter was formed, and to pay tribute to our Hon. Secretary Clive Osborne for his devoted work in compiling the material for this book.

Here, then, is a collection of the most exciting recipes from the greatest restaurants of Britain. There are many wonders to be worked from these pages. It's time to begin!

Sandy Lesberg
Director, The Master Chefs
Institute

# L'Arlequin

**L'Arlequin** was opened in the summer of 1982 by Christian Delteil and his wife Genevieve, adding a further incentive for gourmets to cross the river to Queenstown Road in search of good food. The restaurant has already been awarded a Michelin star, an extraordinary achievement in such a short time.

The decor of this small but attractive restaurant reflects its calm, capable and friendly atmosphere: soft shades of cream predominate and there is nothing to startle, everything to soothe.

Before starting on his own Christian Delteil was chef at Chewton Glen Hotel in Hampshire, where he established a reputation for French cuisine with a leaning towards the *nouvelle*. This he has successfully carried on at L'Arlequin, where the food is as subtle as the surroundings.

Fish features strongly on the menu: the starters include several fish dishes, but you may if you wish order a half-portion of any of the fish *entrées* as a starter. Unusual among the main dishes are rabbit — the breast stuffed with chicken and the legs roasted — and duck *en deux services*.

There is a short but well-chosen wine list, and the friendly staff, supervised by Genevieve, are helpful and keen to offer advice.

*L'Arlequin*

**123 Queenstown Road
London, SW8**

**01-622-0555**

**Lunch: 12.30 to 2.30 p.m.
Dinner: 7.30 to 11 p.m.
Monday — Friday
Reservations**

**Proprietor/Chef: Christian Delteil**

# Blanquette de St. Jacques aux Truffes

20 g chopped shallots

1 glass Chablis

500 ml fish stock

¼ pt cream

knob of butter (extra for frying)

salt and pepper

5 live scallops in their shells

1 oz fresh truffles, thinly sliced

100 g cooked spinach

nutmeg

tomatoes for garnish

To make the sauce: make a reduction of shallots and Chablis. Add the fish stock, reduce to ½, add cream, butter and seasoning.

Prepare scallops as usual. Cut each scallop into 6 thin slices and place on a lightly buttered dish. Place truffles on top. Steam for 30 seconds. Meanwhile, sauté spinach in butter with a pinch of nutmeg and season well.

To serve: place spinach around edge of a plate, in small individual mounds. Place scallops in the centre. Nape with sauce, garnish with diced tomatoes.

Serves: 2

---

# Émince d'Agneau Basilic

1 fillet of lamb

oil

fresh thyme

½ green pepper

½ red pepper

1 aubergine

1 courgette

2 tomatoes, blanched

½ onion

1 clove of garlic

200 ml lamb stock

20 g chopped shallots

½ glass port

½ glass Madeira

knob of butter

4 fresh basil leaves, cut in julienne

Trim lamb, and marinade in oil and thyme for 20 minutes. Prepare peppers, aubergine, courgette, tomatoes, onion and garlic as a large brunoise and cook as a classical ratatouille with stock. Lightly sauté lamb (it should be very pink).

To make the sauce: make a reduction of chopped shallots, port and Madeira. Reduce to correct consistency, pass through a fine chinois, add butter and julienne of basil.

To serve: put ratatouille into two buttered moulds, and place in the centre of a dish. Slice lamb, arrange around the ratatouille, and nape with sauce.

Serves: 2

---

# Salade Fromage de Chèvre Chaud

feuille de chêne

endive

radiccio

3 large slices goat's cheese

1 beaten egg

bread crumbs for coating

butter for frying

walnut oil

salt and pepper

Prepare and wash first 3 ingredients for salad. Dip cheese in egg, coat in breadcrumbs and fry in butter. Toss salad in walnut oil and season well. Serve cheese on salad, on medium-sized plates.

Serves: 2

# Bagatelle

**Bagatelle** is a pretty and elegant restaurant situated in Chelsea, near the Kings Road that is renowned for its trendy clothes shops. The restaurant is now seven years old.

Daniel Marrocco, the owner, attended the École Hotelière de Paris, worked in the managing departments of different hotels in France, then moved to London where he worked as a cook for five years. Having gained full experience in both the management and the cooking side, he bought a two-storied restaurant with a vaulted cellar, fully refurbished and redecorated it, and opened Bagatelle. It is now a light and airy yet warm restaurant, accented with house plants, with a lovely garden at the back offering the possibility of having lunch or dinner under a trellis.

With his team of Japanese chefs headed by Osamu Ono, he produces a small regular menu of both very classical French cuisine as well as some *nouvelle cuisine*, together with a wide variety of daily specialities according to the availability of the day's market. The wine list is limited to 15 well selected French wines, and the cheese board offers a wide variety of French cheeses. Speciality recipes are presented on the opposite page.

## Bagatelle
RESTAURANT FRANÇAIS

**5 Langton Street**
**London, SW10**

**01-351-4185**

**Lunch: 12 to 2 p.m.**
**Dinner: 7 to 11 p.m.**
**Monday — Saturday**
**Reservations**

**Proprietor: Daniel Marrocco**
**Chef: Osamu Ono**

# Marinade de Filet de Boeuf

2 lb fillet of beef
2 oz salt
1 bottle red Burgundy wine
1 onion, sliced
2 cloves garlic
bouquet garni
3 shallots, finely chopped
juice of 2 lemons
100 ml walnut oil
30 ml *fond de veau* (veal stock)
salt and pepper
pinch of cayenne
30 g chopped chives

Salt the beef, leave it for 30 minutes, then marinate in the wine with the onion, garlic and bouquet garni for 24 hours.

To prepare the dressing: mix together remaining ingredients, adding chives at the last minute. Chill.

To serve: cut beef into very, very thin slices (like smoked salmon). Serve cold with very fine julienne of légumes (cucumber, carrots, celery) and chilled dressing.

Serves: 6
Wine: *Chablis Premier Cru*

---

# Saucisson de Loup de Mer au Beurre Blanc

6 × 4 oz sea bass fillets
8 oz monk fish
2 egg whites
½ pt cream
salt and pepper
cayenne pepper
a few drops of cognac
4 oz salmon fillet, cut into 6 pieces
1 sheet seaweed (dried)
tarragon leaves
sorrel leaves
3 cucumbers
2 shallots, chopped
¼ bottle white wine
6 oz unsalted butter
juice of ½ lemon
1 tomato, peeled and finely diced

Make 6 thin rectangular (5 × 8 inch) sheets with the cucumbers, then sprinkle with a little salt to soften. Cream the monk fish with the egg whites, cream, cognac, salt, pepper and cayenne to make a mousse.

Cut each sea bass fillet into 2. Put one half on the edge of a cucumber sheet, followed alternately by tarragon, monk fish mousse, seaweed, salmon, sorrel and remaining sea bass. Roll up into a large green sausage. Wrap the 6 sausages in tinfoil, and put them into a tray of hot water. Bake at gas mark 5 (375°F/190°C) for 20 minutes.

For the butter sauce, mix the shallots with the white wine and add the butter a little at a time. Stir in the lemon juice.

Decorate with the tomatoes and serve hot with butter sauce, boiled potatoes and French beans.

Serves: 6
Wine: *Meursault*

---

# Crème d'Ange au Fruit de la Passion

3 egg whites
50 g sugar
100 g double cream, lightly whipped
100 g full fat cream cheese, softened
10 passion fruits
¼ pt crème Anglaise
sugar to decorate

Beat the egg whites stiffly with the sugar. Mix in the cream and cheese gently. Put the mixture into 6 buttered 3 inch ramekin dishes, then stand in a tray containing hot water. Bake at gas mark 3 (325°F/170°C) for 30 minutes.

To prepare sauce: liquidise and sieve the passion fruits and mix with the crème Anglaise. Sprinkle sugar on top of creams and serve cold, with sauce.

Serves: 6
Wine: *Château Broustet*

# Boulestin Restaurant Français

**Boulestin Restaurant Français** was opened in 1925 by a French journalist called Boulestin. With the success of his cookery books and his knowledge of classic French cuisine, this man, who had also been an interior decorator and a Great War interpreter to the British forces, had a strong influence on British cooking and culinary taste. When he died during the 1939-45 war, the restaurant changed hands shortly afterwards and its standards dropped.

It wasn't until late 1978 that it reverted back to its original glory. It was bought by Grand Metropolitan Hotels, and Kevin Kennedy was put in charge. Kevin Kennedy is Chef de Cuisine et Directeur. He has been a professional chef for more than 16 years, is a graduate from the Westminster Hotel School, and is of the new school. One meal at Boulestin will tell you that he is a master of French sauces. In fact, such is his culinary background that he is a master of all departments.

Boulestin Restaurant Français is located in London's Covent Garden. The decor of the 1930s has been retained, even to the colour prints in the lobby: 1920s cartoons with archly-flirty girls, smooth men, and culinary captions. It has a truly friendly ambiance — the feeling you are walking into a friend's home.

**25 Southampton Street
Covent Garden, London, WC2**

**01-836-7061**

**Lunch: Monday — Friday 12 to 2.30 p.m.
Dinner: Monday — Saturday 7 to 11.15 p.m.
Reservations**

**Proprietor: Grand Metropolitan
Chef: Kevin Kennedy**

# Brioche d'Oeufs de Caille aux Girolles à la Porto

1 oz unsalted butter

1 oz wild girolle mushrooms

1 tsp chopped shallots

    salt and milled black pepper, to taste

2 fl oz port wine

2 fl oz thick dairy cream

1 round *brioche à tête*

1 tbsp duxelles of girolle mushrooms

1 tbsp spinach purée

4 quail eggs

To prepare sauce: heat butter, add girolles, and cook quickly over fast heat. Add shallots, season, and stir well until all is cooked. Add port and reduce by ⅔. Add cream, stir, and cook to correct consistency. Check seasoning. Hollow out the brioche and warm in oven. Heat the purée of girolles and purée of spinach together, mixing well. Check seasoning. Poach the eggs and drain onto cloth or kitchen paper. Fill brioche with purée, top with eggs, and coat with sauce.

Serves: 1

# Andouillette de Saumon en Habit Vert

3 tbsp finely chopped shallots

    butter, as needed

5 fl oz plus ¼ bottle dry white wine

    sea salt and freshly ground black pepper, to taste

15 fl oz thick cream

2 fl oz chicken stock

8 oz blanched watercress

1 tbsp chopped chives

4 fl oz water

1 tbsp lemon juice

8 oz salmon fillet

2 egg whites

4 × 4 oz fillets of salmon

    blanched spinach leaves, as needed

    fish stock, as needed

    watercress, to garnish

To prepare *crème de cresson* sauce: sweat ⅔ shallots in butter until translucent. Add 5 ounces wine, salt, and milled pepper and boil until reduced to 2 tablespoons of purée. Boil ⅔ cream with the chicken stock until reduced by ⅔. Let cool. When cold, put into a liquidiser with blanched watercress, chives, water, and lemon juice. Check seasoning and store, covered, in refrigerator until required.

To prepare mousse of salmon: pass the 8 ounces of salmon fillet through a food processor with egg whites, salt, and black pepper for 1 minute. Add remaining cream and run for 30 seconds. Allow to rest in refrigerator 1 hour.

Gently flatten the 4 salmon fillets into a rectangle by placing them between 2 sheets of cling film and gently tapping with a smooth meat hammer. Place onto a single layer of overlapping spinach leaves. Season the salmon and spread an ⅛ inch layer of mousse on the salmon. Roll up like a Swiss roll. Butter a heavy ovenproof dish and place the salmon on the bottom, sprinkle with remaining shallots, add ¼ bottle white wine, and enough fish stock to cover the sides of the salmon by ⅓. Cover and cook for 15 minutes in an oven at gas mark 5 (375°F/190°C). Drain and keep warm between 2 plates. Reduce the cooking juices by ⅔, add the prepared crème de cresson sauce, and boil to a thick but pouring consistency. Pour sauce onto warm plates and dress salmon on top with a small sprig of watercress.

Serves: 4

# Salade des Fruits Brouillés (Mixed Fruit Salad)

**ripe fruit, prepared for use: kiwi fruit, orange segments, strawberries, banana slices, grapes, etc.**

**a little liquor of your choice**

**whipped, unsweetened thick dairy cream**

**soft light brown sugar (Demerara), as needed**

Mix fruit together then sprinkle with only a little liquor. Fill china dishes (just a little larger than a tea cup) with fruit to within ½ inch from the tops. With a palette knife or plastic scraper, fill remaining space with cream. Level off at top. (May be refrigerated for up to 24 hours.) Coat the top liberally with sugar (about ⅛ inch thick) and gently flatten. Use a flattened kitchen serving spoon or a salamander (a long metal rod with wooden grip and a round, thick heavy metal disc attached) and place in a hot fire until red hot and tops of sweets burn to a golden brown. Serve.

# Capital Hotel

Brian Turner is the executive chef of the **Capital Hotel**'s restaurant. He was born and brought up in the West Riding of Yorkshire. His father owned and ran a transport café of a very high standard. Brian's interest in cooking stemmed from this, and at the age of 16, he enrolled at Leeds College of Technology for the Chefs' course and got his first job in London at Simpson's as a *commis tournant*. After 18 months, he went on to become *commis saucier* at the Savoy. After more schooling, a year working in Switzerland, and a year at Claridge's, he came to the Capital Hotel.

Chef Turner enjoys running the small attractive ten-year-old French restaurant at the hotel. It is modern and imaginatively decorated in quiet beige and brown, with well spaced tables. His kitchen is small but superbly organised and has a grill section. His staff is a happy group, all young English lads. He reports, "We have everything scaled down to what we can do, and we do what we can do best. We stay within the framework of our ability."

The quality and presentation of a meal at the Capital Hotel supports Chef Turner's philosophy, which is "You have to put a lettuce leaf on the plate as if you cared about it. The good Lord who made it cared, so you should."

CAPITAL HOTEL

**22–24 Basil Street**
**Knightsbridge, London, SW3**

**01-589-5171**

**Breakfast:**
Monday — Saturday 7 to 10 a.m.
**Lunch:**
Monday — Saturday 12.30 to 2.15 p.m.
Sunday 12.30 to 1.45 p.m.
**Dinner:**
Monday — Saturday 6.30 to 10.30 p.m.
Sunday 7 to 9.45 p.m.
**Reservations**

**Proprietor: David Levin**
**Chef: Brian Turner, M.C.G.B.**

# Salade de Coquilles St. Jacques

12 scallops

butter, to sauté

4 oz white button mushroom caps

lemon juice, as needed

seasoning, to taste

curly endive, to garnish

chives and parsley, to garnish

Sauté cleaned scallops in butter very lightly (with colour on the outside). Leave to drain slowly; collect the juice. Slice the scallops across the grain and lay them around the outside of a small plate. Slice the washed mushrooms thickly and marinate in lemon juice for 5 minutes. Drain, sauté in melted butter, season, and add the juice from the scallops. Be careful that the mushrooms do not cook but just warm through. Lay them on a leaf of curly endive, sprinkle with chives and parsley, and serve just slightly warm.

Serves: 4

# Noisettes d'Agneau à la Crème de Basilic

1 loin of lamb, boned and trimmed of fat and gristle

butter, to sauté

¼ pt port

1 bunch finely chopped fresh basil, reserve leaves for garnish

¼ pt white wine

½ pt veal stock

½ pt double cream

4 oz butter

seasoning, to taste

Tie lamb into a roll and cut into 12 slices 1 inch thick (3 per person). Sauté the noisettes in butter to a pink colour, remove, and leave to stand in a warm place.

Remove excess fat from pan. Add port, chopped basil leaves, and white wine and reduce until almost completely disappeared. Add veal stock and reduce. Add cream. Boil all these ingredients gently, skimming all the time, until the sauce has reduced enough to give correct consistency and amount of "body." Add knobs of butter and shake the pan until butter is absorbed by the sauce. Check seasoning and consistency. Pass noisettes through the oven to reheat. Put lamb onto a serving dish and nap sauce on top. Serve immediately.

Serves: 4

# Tarte aux Poires Bordeloue

1 lb puff pastry dough

¾ pt pastry cream

2 oz ground almonds

zest of 1 orange

10 × ½ poached pears, sliced

¼ pt whipped double cream

4 oz egg white made into meringue

toasted ground almonds, for topping

double cream, to serve

Line 10 × 3 inch tart moulds with puff pastry. Fill each ¼ full with ½ pint pastry cream mixed with ground almonds and orange zest. Leave to rest ½ hour. Fill tarts with slices of poached pears in an attractive design. (Half a pear should fill each tart.) Bake at 380°F (195°C) for 20 minutes. Remove from oven and let cool.

Mix remaining pastry cream with whipped double cream and spread on each tart. Crumble meringue over the top, sprinkle with toasted ground almonds, and serve with double cream.

# Chez Moi

**Chez Moi** is a small genteel French restaurant situated in one of the elegant Victorian houses in the exclusive London district of Holland Park. Fourteen years ago, it was taken over by Colin Smith, who now runs the restaurant with confident efficiency, and Richard Walton, who is now a widely acclaimed chef. The two men worked together at another establishment before venturing out on their own.

The restaurant is small, yet somehow seats 50. The à la carte menu is by no means extensive, yet it capably offers a goodly number of choices in each category. Several special dishes are always present and are changed every two weeks.

There is a fairly broad wine list available with many French regions represented, and there are also two fine house wines from which to choose.

Chef Walton is a native of Rhodesia who originally was interested in hotel management, but after a year in the kitchens of London's Savoy and six months at Lausanne, he decided his first love was cooking. It is to his credit that the food served at Chez Moi is imaginatively and always deliciously prepared.

### Chez Moi

**3 Addison Avenue
Holland Park, London, W11**

**01-603-8267**

**Dinner: Monday — Saturday
Reservations**

**Proprietors:
Colin Smith, Richard Walton
Chef: Richard Walton**

# Oeufs à la Pomme d'Amour

6 very firm tomatoes

1 tbsp olive oil

1 finely chopped onion

2 large cloves garlic, finely chopped

1 tbsp white wine

salt and freshly ground black pepper, to taste

6 egg yolks

grated Parmesan cheese, as needed

6 croissants

butter, as needed

Cut the tops off the tomatoes and scoop out the flesh. Turn tomatoes upside down on a plate to drain.

Heat olive oil, add onions and garlic, and sauté for about 1 minute. Add scooped out tomato flesh, white wine, salt, and pepper, and continue to cook until sauce is fairly thick. Cool.

Place a little sauce in the bottom of each hollowed out tomato. Gently slip an egg yolk into each tomato, add more sauce, top with grated cheese, and dot with butter. Put into a very hot oven at mark 7 (425°F/220°C) for 10 minutes (no longer or the tomatoes will collapse). Serve each on a croissant dotted with butter and gently warmed in the oven for 1–2 minutes.

Serves: 6

---

# Crêpes de Palourdes Chez Moi

1½ oz butter, and as needed

1½ oz flour

5 fl oz clam juice

5 fl oz double cream

juice of 1 lemon

1 oz gelatine

1 tbsp white wine

pinch of salt

5 fl oz dry champagne

2 × 10 oz tins baby clams

4 oz white button mushrooms, sliced

4 oz white grapes, peeled and pitted

1 finely chopped shallot

6 × 6 in crêpes

grated Parmesan cheese, as needed

Melt butter over gentle heat and add flour to make a roux. Cook the roux about 1 minute. Add clam juice, cream, and lemon juice and continue to whisk over gentle heat. As mixture thickens, add gelatine dissolved in white wine and a pinch of salt and continue cooking for 5 minutes. Remove from heat, whisk in champagne, and allow to cool.

Drain clams from the 2 tins, discard bits of shell, and mix clams together. Add mushrooms, grapes, and shallot. Divide mixture among crêpes, roll up, sprinkle with grated cheese, dot with butter, and place in a hot oven for only 5–6 minutes (no longer or champagne sauce will ooze out). Lift off with a spatula onto plates and serve.

Serves: 6

---

# Glace de Canneberge (Fresh Cranberry Ice Cream)

½ pt rosé wine

½ pt red wine

6 oz sugar

1 cinnamon stick

8 cloves

3 thick slices lemon

3 thick slices orange

2 drops vanilla essence

1 good dash Angostura bitters

¼ pt glycerine

2 × 7 oz punnets fresh cranberries

½ pt double cream

3 egg yolks

Make a syrup by reducing the wines with sugar, cinnamon, cloves, lemon and orange slices, vanilla, Angostura bitters, and glycerine to ½ original quantity. (Temperature should be 240°F, 115°C, or "Jam" on a cooking thermometer.) Strain syrup, add cranberries, and bring back to a boil. Continue to cook until about ½ the cranberries have popped (about 1 minute). Allow to cool, then refrigerate.

Whisk double cream with yolks. When thick, slowly strain in syrup from the berries. Finally, add berries, whisking only for a short period. (Mixture must be thick when berries are added.) Freeze.

### CHEF'S TIP

To make the ice cream a bit lighter, fold in 3 stiffly beaten egg whites last of all.

# Chez Nico

On 14 June 1973, proprietor/chef Nico Ladenis first opened the doors of **Chez Nico** on Lordship Lane in East Dulwich. According to him, "The only things going for us were low rent and total optimism." From the very first, he decided not to advertise, but instead, to rely on word of mouth. This was the longest road, but he believed it to be ultimately the best. To this day, even after a change of location (to the Queenstown Road address on 21 April 1980) and a break of five months, Chez Nico has retained customers who came in within a month of the first opening.

The restaurant's small interior is dressed in what Chef Ladenis calls "'feminine" decor. The colours are pretty pinks and apricot, the seating is snug but comfortable, and the lighting is subdued.

The menu, which features modern French cuisine, is small but well-balanced. Says the chef, "Our policy on food is to always get the finest quality regardless of cost. In fact, portion control and stock control are non-existent words for us."

Chez Nico is basically a husband and wife operation, with a small, but devoted staff that is most efficient. There is a short list of excellent French wines available.

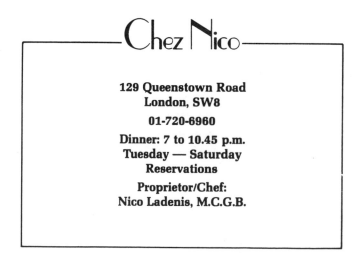

**129 Queenstown Road**
**London, SW8**

**01-720-6960**

**Dinner: 7 to 10.45 p.m.**
**Tuesday — Saturday**
**Reservations**

**Proprietor/Chef:**
**Nico Ladenis, M.C.G.B.**

# Les Filets de Sole au Beurre de Champagne

**fish fumet made from water, wine, butter, shallots, chives, bay leaf, and peppercorns, as needed**

4 × **10 oz Dover soles, skinned and filleted, cut in 4 pieces each**

2 **c fish stock (fond de poissons)**

2 **c Noilly Prat vermouth**

9 **oz butter**

1¼ **pt double cream**

1 **c water**

2 **chopped leeks**

½ **bottle good quality champagne**

**salt, as needed**

**chives, to taste**

Bring fish fumet to a boil. Roll the sole fillets and secure them with cocktail sticks. Drop fillets into fumet and remove from heat. Leave in a warm place.

Place fish stock, vermouth, 2 ounces butter, and 1 cup cream in one saucepan. Place water, 3 ounces butter, leeks, champagne, and a little salt in a second saucepan. Cook second pan's contents for 20 minutes, then place contents into first pan and reduce over fast heat until syrupy. Add remaining butter in pieces and remaining double cream, adjust seasoning, and cook very gently for 5 minutes to make a sauce. Add chives to sauce; stir together.

Pour sauce on each plate and arrange fillets, 4 on each plate, on top. Do not pour sauce on top of fillets.

Serves: 4

**CHEF'S TIP**

Oven temperatures and cooking times can be meaningless. Much depends on your own oven, how old it is, if it's gas, electric, etc. Know your own oven and plan accordingly.

---

# Mousse Glacée au Caramel, Sauce Framboise

2 **pt double cream**

1¾ **lb sugar caramelised without water**

1 **pt water**

½ **lb sugar**

18 **eggs, separated**

**Sauce Framboise (recipe follows)**

To prepare mousse: bring the double cream to a simmer, then very slowly mix in the caramelised sugar (very difficult), mix together properly and leave to cool. Prepare sugar syrup by heating the water with sugar. Beat the egg yolks in a mixer on high speed for 3 minutes. Slowly add hot syrup until yolks have risen and are hard. Mix this with the cream and caramel mixture. Whip the egg whites, blend into the main mixture slowly, then pour into 50 × 3 inch ramekins. Freeze for 12 hours. Serve with Sauce Framboise.

Serves: 50

## Sauce Framboise

¼ **lb sugar**

½ **pt water**

1 **lb puréed raspberries**

**lemon juice, to taste**

To prepare sauce framboise: mix sugar and water together to make a syrup. Strain the puréed raspberries to obtain maximum juice. Mix the syrup and raspberries together and add lemon juice to taste. Serve with mousse glacée au caramel.

# The Dorchester Grill Room

**The Grill Room** at the **Dorchester Hotel**, which opened in 1931, is an elegant comfortable restaurant with period Spanish-style decor and spacious positioning of the tables. The room has recently been made smaller and the kitchen modernised, so it gives Chef Anton Mosimann full scope to put into practice many of his own ideas for the international cuisine he considers suitable for the present day.

Anton Mosimann was born in Solothurn, Switzerland, and knew at the age of six that he wanted to be a chef. He became an apprentice at the Hotel Baeren in Twann at age 15 and was considered its best student by the time he turned 17. Later, he travelled the world, working in many hotels at all levels and, thus, gaining all his experience. He was the youngest chef ever to gain the "Chef de Cuisine Diplome," the highest culinary award in Switzerland.

Chef Anton was working at the Palace Hotel, Gstaad, as commis patissier ("the humblest role of the pastry kitchen, just to gain further experience in patisserie") when he was asked to come to the Dorchester as Maître Chef des Cuisines.

Simplicity, precision, and perfection are the basis of his art. "Take the ingredients, cook them to perfection and present them with simplicity. The whole secret of successful cooking — more, the very essence of culinary perfection — is, or should be, simplicity."

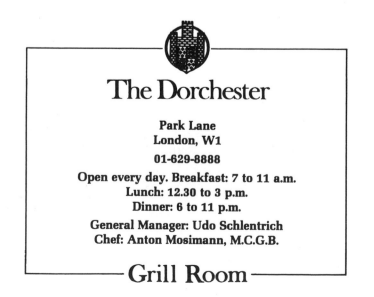

# Rendezvous de Fruits de Mer

60 g butter

30 g julienne of celery, carrot, and leek

60 g fresh salmon

60 g scallops

60 g lobster

60 g turbot

100 ml Noilly Prat vermouth

100 ml fish stock

400 ml double cream

10 g basil, julienne

seasoning, to taste

Place ⅓ butter into a hot pan and add julienne of vegetables. Cut fish into ½ inch cubes and add to pan. Swill with vermouth and cook for a few more seconds. Remove fish. Add stock to pan, reduce, then pour in double cream. Bring to a boil. Whisk in butter. (Make sure sauce is very thin.) Add julienne of basil, return fish to sauce, and heat but do not boil. Season to taste and serve.

Serves: 4

---

# Entrecôte Sautée Dorchester

4 × 180 g entrecôte steaks

well crushed white and black peppercorns, as needed

salt, to taste

50 ml peanut oil

40 ml cognac

200 ml brown veal stock

200 ml double cream

40 g butter

freshly ground pepper, to taste

3 g green peppercorns

3 g pink peppercorns

Season the well-trimmed entrecôtes with white and black peppercorns and salt. Sauté them on both sides in hot oil. Remove entrecôtes and keep warm.

Skim the fat, flame the cooking juices with cognac, add veal stock, and reduce to ½ original volume. Add cream and reduce to required consistency. Finish with butter and season with salt and pepper. Add the green and pink peppercorns just before serving or sauce will be too spicy. Cover the entrecôtes with the sauce and serve.

Serves: 4

---

# Bread and Butter Pudding

100 g butter

20 slices bread without crusts

100 g currants

5 egg yolks, whisked

2 eggs, whisked

200 g sugar

1200 ml milk

nutmeg, to taste

50 ml apricot glaze

Butter 2 oval pudding dishes and the bread. Cut the bread diagonally and place in layers with the currants in the dishes. Sieve the whisked eggs and mix with the sugar and milk. Pour mixture over the bread, sprinkle with grated nutmeg, and cook in a bain-marie in the oven until done. Brush the top with apricot glaze and glaze gently under a salamander.

Serves: 10

Wine: *English Adgestone or Lamberhurst Priory*

# Eatons Restaurant

**Eatons Restaurant** was opened in December of 1975 with a very clear aim: to establish itself as the neighbourhood good value "local." The location on Elizabeth Street was chosen because of its famed village atmosphere and its proximity to the large residential areas of Belgravia and Chelsea.

The restaurant was originally smaller than it is today, which worked to its advantage initially in establishing an intimate atmosphere. The floor space was subsequently enlarged, so Eatons now seats 40. More than a third of the dishes appearing on the menu are changed every week to give the long-standing regular customers some variety. This formula seems to have worked well as many of their clientele have been "regulars" since the restaurant's opening.

The menu features Continental cuisine prepared and, in most cases, created by Chef Santosh Bakshi, who was trained at the Savoy and served as head chef at several establishments. At one such appointment, he worked with Shayne Pope for seven years, just prior to both of them opening Eatons. Their relationship continues to be most rewarding because Eatons has indeed become a successful "local."

The wine list at Eatons is extensive, with imported wines in all price ranges, and a French house wine.

49 Elizabeth Street
Belgravia, London, SW1

01-730-0074

Lunch: Monday — Friday 12 to 2 p.m.
Dinner: Monday — Friday 7 to 11 p.m.
Reservations

Proprietors: Shayne Pope, Santosh Kumar Bakshi, Dieter Vagts
Chef: Santosh Kumar Bakshi

# Carré d'Agneau en Croûte

2 pairs of best ends of lamb

salt and pepper

10 oz butter

2 tbsp oil

2 tbsp flour (extra for sauce)

1 onion, chopped

1 carrot, chopped

½ glass of wine

1 tsp tomato purée

wild mushrooms, finely chopped and sautéed in butter

puff pastry

beaten egg for brushing

Bone the lamb and remove the 4 long fillets (reserving bones). Clean and trim fillets thoroughly, removing all skin and fat. Cut into 6 equal pieces (2 will be joined up). Sprinkle with salt and pepper. Melt the butter in the hot oil. Dip the lamb in the flour and fry gently in the butter and oil, then fry quickly until brown to seal. Leave to cool.

To prepare the brown sauce: chop the lamb bones and fry with the onion and carrot. Dust with flour. Add wine and tomato purée, and cook gently for 1 hour, until thick like a demi-glace. Pass through a sieve. Add mushrooms to make about 1 cup of sauce.

Roll out the pastry and cut into six 9 inch squares. Put 1 tsp of sauce in the centre of each square, place a piece of lamb on top, then more sauce. Cut out the 4 corners of the square to remove excess pastry, then fold over the sides, one on top of the other, brushing each with egg, to form an oblong parcel. Brush top with egg. Bake at gas mark 6 (400°F/200°C) for 20 minutes.

Serves: 6

# Smoked Salmon Soufflé Alariki

1 tsp butter

2 spring onions, finely chopped

4 oz smoked salmon, chopped

½ cup white wine

¾ pt water

4 oz butter

5 oz flour

6 whole eggs

½ cup double cream

3 tbsp sour cream

Fry the onions lightly in butter. Add smoked salmon and wine and reduce to a dry consistency. Refrigerate.

Warm the water and butter in a pan. Add flour, remove from the heat and whisk in the eggs and double cream. Add the salmon mixture.

Dust individual soufflé dishes with flour, pour in the mixture and bake in a hot oven at gas mark 7 (425°F/220°C) for 20 minutes.

To serve: top with sour cream.

Serves: 6

# Meringue Shambles

8 egg whites

6 oz icing sugar

6 oz caster sugar

2 slices of thin sponge cake

1 glass dry sherry

6 oz whipped sweetened double cream

4 oz dark chocolate, thinly chopped

Beat the egg whites until thick. Add sugar, put in a tray and leave to dry out. When dry, break it up into small pieces.

Line an 8 inch bowl with a slice of sponge. Soak with ½ of the sherry. Pipe in evenly ½ of the cream. Sprinkle with ½ of the chocolate then ½ the meringue. Repeat with remaining ingredients, finishing off with a layer of meringue.

Serve with good brandy only.

Serves: 6

# The English Garden

Eating at **The English Garden** gives one the impression of a leisurely meal outdoors in the sunshine. The decor, created and designed by Michael Smith, is light-hearted and pretty. The Garden Room on the ground floor is white-washed brick with panels of large stylised flowers. The attractive pelmets are in vivid flower colours with stark white curtains, chairs are rattan in a gothic theme and the table cloths candy pink. With the domed conservatory roofs and banks of plants the atmosphere is relaxing and happy.

Private parties of six or more can take advantage of the beautiful upstairs apartment with its restful flower-filled country house sitting room and elegant dining room complete with antique furniture, wooden oak fireplace and open fire.

An extensive menu includes plenty of seafood and salads. Starters and main dishes are interchangeable and patrons can decide to take exactly what they wish — even if only a bowl of soup. A comprehensive wine list is available with over 170 wines, including 30 fine clarets, and an excellent French house wine is always obtainable.

**10 Lincoln Street
London, SW3**

**01-584-7272**

**Lunch: 12.30 to 2.30 p.m.
Dinner: 7.30 to 11.30 p.m.
Sunday
Lunch: 12.30 to 2 p.m.
Dinner: 7.30 to 10 p.m.**

**Proprietor:
The English Garden Restaurant Limited
Chef: Paul Brooks**

# Vegetable Pâté

½ lb fresh leaf spinach

½ lb lean veal trimmings

1 small leek, chopped

1 medium-sized onion, chopped

2 celery stalks, chopped

2 cloves of garlic

¼ pt double cream

½ tsp of mixed freshly chopped rosemary, thyme and parsley

2 tsp brandy

salt and freshly ground black pepper

1 oz aspic jelly

Wash spinach thoroughly in cold water, and chop. Pass veal trimmings, spinach, leek, onion and celery through a fine mincer. Mix in all remaining ingredients, except aspic.

Place in double bain-marie of hot water and bake at gas mark 3 (400 ° F/200 ° C) for 45 minutes. Remove from oven, allow to cool, and press down lightly to remove excess liquid. Dissolve aspic in 1 fluid ounce boiling water. Pour over pâté and refrigerate for 2−3 hours to set.

Serve on a chilled plate with fingers of hot buttered toast.

Serves: 4−6

# Solomon Gundy

1 cold chicken (roasted or boiled)

4 oz steamed potatoes

1 lettuce

12 button onions

2 oz flaked almonds

2 oz stoned raisins

1 × 8 oz pkt whole frozen beans

1 × 2 oz tin anchovy fillets

¼ lb grapes, black and green

4 hard-boiled eggs

1 large cup oil and vinegar dressing, well seasoned

lemon juice and zest to taste

1 tbsp mixed chopped herbs

Skin the chicken and carve the breasts and legs into thin slices. Wash and shred the lettuce and arrange on a flat platter. Skin and boil the onions, leaving them somewhat crisp. Plunge the beans into boiling salted water for 5 minutes, rinse under cold water until quite cold and drain well on a clean cloth. De-pip the grapes. Shell and quarter the hard-boiled eggs.

Mix together the dressing, lemon juice and zest and herbs.

Arrange all the ingredients in atractive groups on the bed of lettuce. Pour over the dressing and toss everything together at the table.

Serves: 4−6

# Lemon Cheesecake

1 × 8 in sweet pastry case (1½ in deep), baked blind

10 oz butter

10 oz sugar

4 egg yolks

zest and juice of 8 lemons

4 oz fine white bread crumbs

3 large eggs

icing sugar to dredge

To make lemon cheese: whisk together 4 ounces butter, 4 ounces sugar, 4 egg yolks and zest and juice of 4 lemons in a bowl over boiling water until thick.

To make the filling: beat together remaining sugar and butter until white. Add bread crumbs, whole eggs and remaining lemon zest and juice.

Smooth a good layer of lemon cheese over the base of the flan and fill to the top with the lemon filling. Bake at gas mark 6 (400 ° F/200 ° C) for about 30 minutes. Serve while still a little warm, dredged with icing sugar.

Serves: 4−6

# The English House

**The English House,** located in the heart of Chelsea, is an elegant town house that has been stylishly decorated by interior designer Michael Smith. Its rooms are accented in rich, warm fabrics and are most conducive to enjoying a quiet, intimate, and first-rate repast.

The goal of proprietor Malcolm Livingston, who opened The English House five years ago, is to emphasize personal service and good taste and to foster a renewed appreciation of classical English cuisine. The recipes prepared in his restaurant are almost all drawn from historical cookery books; the remainder are contemporary dishes created by Chef Paul Rigby, aged 24, who trained at Southport Technical College and The Savoy Hotel. He tries to use mainly English ingredients, and only the finest that London's markets can provide. The excellent house speciality is Capon Stuffed with Saffron Rice, an old English recipe. Also offered is a broad selection of English and French wines.

From the moment the restaurant opened, the response from customers, both English and foreign, was extremely favourable. Today, The English House is renowned for its accomplishments.

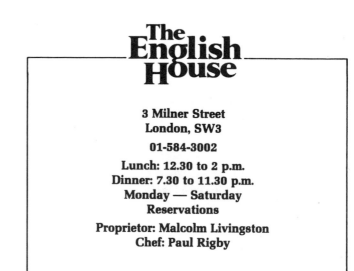

**The English House**

3 Milner Street
London, SW3

01-584-3002

Lunch: 12.30 to 2 p.m.
Dinner: 7.30 to 11.30 p.m.
Monday — Saturday
Reservations

Proprietor: Malcolm Livingston
Chef: Paul Rigby

# Tomato, Orange and Ginger Broth

4½ c chicken stock or tinned broth

½ c orange juice

    rind of 1 orange, julienne

2 tbsp drained stem ginger, julienne

1 tbsp tomato paste

4 tomatoes, peeled, seeded, julienne

¼ tsp ground ginger

    salt and pepper, to taste

chopped fresh mint leaves and orange slices, to garnish

In a large stainless steel on enamelled.saucepan, combine the chicken stock or broth, orange juice, orange rind, ginger strips, and tomato paste. Bring to a boil and simmer for 5 minutes. Stir in the tomatoes, ground ginger, and salt and pepper to taste. Heat the soup over moderate heat for 5 minutes or until heated through. Ladle soup into heated bowls and garnish with mint leaves and orange slices.

Serves: 4 – 6

# Leg of Lamb with Spinach and Apricot Stuffing

½ lb dried apricots

3 lb spinach

1 large onion, chopped

2 c fresh bread crumbs

½ c butter, cut in bits and softened

2 large eggs, lightly beaten

1 tbsp grated lemon rind

1 tbsp salt, and to taste

½ tsp ground mace

    pepper, to taste

1 × 6 lb leg of lamb, boned

    butter and vegetable oil, as needed

½ c brown stock or beef broth

To prepare stuffing: let apricots soak in enough cold water to cover for 4 hours, then drain and chop them. In a kettle of boiling salted water, blanch the spinach for 2 minutes, drain in a colander, and refresh under cold running water. Squeeze the spinach to remove as much water as possible, then chop coarsely. In a large bowl, combine spinach, onion, and apricots. In a food processor, grind the mixture coarsely in batches, then transfer to a bowl. Stir in bread crumbs, butter bits, eggs, lemon rind, salt, mace, and pepper.

Sew up the opening at the larger end of the lamb; leave the smaller end open. Sprinkle inside of lamb with salt and pepper, stuff it loosely with about 1½ cups stuffing, and transfer remaining stuffing to a buttered 1 quart baking dish. Sew up second opening of lamb with kitchen string; brush lamb with vegetable oil. Roast lamb in an oiled flameproof roasting pan in a preheated moderate oven (350°F/180°C) for 1¼ hours for medium-rare, or until meat thermometer registers 130°F (55°C). During the last 30 minutes of roasting, bake the stuffing in the baking dish covered with foil. Transfer lamb to a cutting board; keep warm and covered.

To prepare the sauce: skim fat from pan juices, add stock or broth, and deglaze pan over high heat. Season sauce with salt and pepper.

Cut lamb into ½ inch slices, arrange slices on a heated platter, and nap them with sauce. Serve lamb with the stuffing.

Serves: 6 – 8

# Flummery

2½ c double cream

¼ c sugar

2 tbsp grated lemon rind

1 tbsp unflavoured gelatine

¼ c water

1 tbsp orange flower water

    strawberries or raspberries, to garnish

In a large stainless steel on enamelled saucepan, combine double cream, sugar, and lemon rind. Heat mixture to just below boiling. In a small bowl, sprinkle gelatine over water and let soften 10 minutes. Set bowl in a pan of hot water and stir until gelatine is dissolved. Add gelatine to cream mixture, add orange flower water, and strain mixture into 4 × 6 ounce wine glasses. Chill until set, garnish with fruit and serve.

Serves: 4

# L'Escargot

**L'Escargot** is a cool green marble reincarnation of Soho's original *restaurant français*, L'Escargot Bienvenu, but it offers two distinct styles of eating. Downstairs, the brasserie offers inexpensive food at lunchtime and throughout the evening — anything from a simple grilled *crottin* salad to a hearty meal of mussel and saffron soup, Cumberland sausage with red onion and marmalade and rhubarb crumble — accompanied by an atmospheric cabaret.

The restaurant proper is upstairs, in three different rooms, one of which was the Duke of Portland's salon when this was his town house. Here the cuisine and clientele are distinctly more sophisticated. Eleni Salvoni (ex Bianchi's) presides as Maitresse d' — probably the most popular in London. The menu changes daily around a central *carte*, which is designed by distinguished Chef Martin Lam to utilise the season's best produce. Chef Lam joined L'Escargot in 1982 after reopening Le Caprice in Arlington Street. Before that he won fame at The English House, where he strived to promote the renaissance of English food.

L'Escargot's acclaimed wine list has fewer than 50 wines, but is probably one of London's most eclectic. Wine dinners are held regularly and parties are a speciality.

---

## L'ESCARGOT

**48 Greek Street**
**London, W1**

**01-437-2679**

**Lunch: Restaurant 12.30 to 2.30 p.m.**
**Brasserie 12 to 3 p.m.**
**Dinner: Restaurant 6.30 to 11.30 p.m.**
**Brasserie 6 to 11.30 p.m.**

**Proprietor: Nicholas Lander**
**General Manager: Nick Smallwood**
**Chef: Martin P. Lam**

# Seafood Sausages
## with cider and apples

1 lb pike or brill fillets

1 lb Dover sole fillets

3 eggs

1 tbsp chopped parsley

1 tbsp chopped chives

salt and freshly ground white pepper

1 pt double cream (½ pt lightly whipped)

natural sausage casings

court-bouillon to cook

clarified butter for frying

2 Cox's apples, sliced (extra to garnish)

¼ pt fish stock

¼ pt dry cider

lemon juice (optional)

sprigs of chervil to garnish

Mince the fish (or chop in processor) fairly coarsely, retaining some texture. Chill. Add the eggs, herbs and seasoning. Carefully fold in the whipped cream.

Fill the sausage casings with the mixture, using a sausage filling attachment to a food mixer, or a large funnel. Poach the sausages in the court-bouillon for 7–10 minutes. Then fry them in clarified butter with the apples.

To prepare sauce: reduce the fish stock and cider to ½. Add remaining ½ pint of cream and reduce again by ⅓. Season to taste, adding a little lemon juice if desired.

To serve: pour sauce over the sausages, garnish with chervil and apple slices.

Serves: 6

---

# Collops of Lamb
## with morels and young turnips

3 lb best end of lamb, cleaned of all bone and fat

olive oil (for marinade and frying)

fresh thyme

salt and freshly ground black pepper

3 shallots, chopped

2 oz unsalted butter

8 oz fresh (or 4 oz dried) morel mushrooms

½ pt Sercial Madeira

¾ pt veal glaze

1 lb small young (or turned) turnips

1 oz Demerara sugar

Marinate the lamb in olive oil, fresh thyme and seasoning overnight.

To prepare sauce: sauté the shallots in 1 ounce butter until softened, add the morels and sauté for 2 minutes. Add the Madeira and reduce by ⅔. Add the veal glaze and simmer for a few minutes to amalgamate flavours. Blanch the turnips and sauté in sugar and 1 ounce butter until glazed.

Sauté the lamb whole in a little olive oil for about 5 minutes, which will leave meat nicely pink. Slice the meat into rounds (collops) and arrange round the plates alternately with the turnips. Spoon the sauce over the meat and serve immediately.

Serves: 6

---

# Orange Creams with Tropical Fruits

½ pt milk

½ pt single cream

zest of 1 orange (extra for ramekins)

1 vanilla pod

4 oz cane sugar (or white)

4 eggs, beaten

4 passion fruit (and juice)

3 oranges, in segments

2 limes, in segments

2 bananas, cut obliquely

¼ pt fresh orange juice

¼ pt dark Jamaican rum

Bring the milk, cream, zest, vanilla and sugar very slowly to boiling point to infuse, then let it cool slightly. Strain the liquid onto the beaten eggs. Put a little extra zest into six 3 inch ramekins, then pour the mixture on top. Bake in a bain-marie at gas mark 4 (350°F/180°C) for about 25 minutes or until the custard is just set. Allow to cool in the bain-marie, then chill for 4 hours.

To serve: unmould the creams onto the centre of dessert plates and surround each with symmetrically arranged fruit. Mix the passion fruit juice, orange juice and rum together and pour over the creams. Serve with a *tuile aux amandes*.

Serves: 6

# Le Français

In March 1967, two French gentlemen, Jean-Jacques Figeac and Bernard Caen (respectively chef and headwaiter at a well-established restaurant), left their employ to open their own French restaurant in Chelsea, an area of London that became fashionable in the Sixties. In establishing **Le Français,** their aim was to promote the cooking of the various regions of France on a weekly basis. That is to say, each week they would prepare a different menu representing one particular part of France served with the wine of that same region.

Mr. Figeac, who has been a chef for more than 30 years, and Mr. Caen, better known by the customers as "Mr. Bernard," have been most successful in the endeavor.

The room space of the restaurant had 45 seats at the beginning, but after being extended, it now offers at least 75 seats divided into two sections. Two years ago, the entire restaurant was again altered, and now it offers a full length bar counter with the two dining sections becoming a restaurant room and a bar lounge. Furnishings have all been imported from France.

The staff employed is exclusively French "upstairs and downstairs," and the ingredients used in the cooking are imported from France. Both of these facts are a great source of pride for the owners of Le Français and is reflected in the service they bestow on their customers.

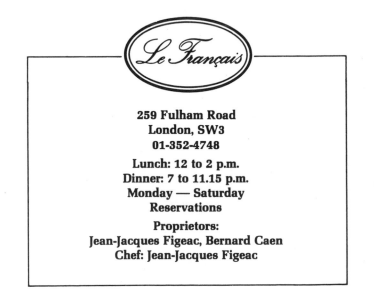

**259 Fulham Road
London, SW3
01-352-4748**

**Lunch: 12 to 2 p.m.
Dinner: 7 to 11.15 p.m.
Monday — Saturday
Reservations**

**Proprietors:
Jean-Jacques Figeac, Bernard Caen
Chef: Jean-Jacques Figeac**

The Marquee

The Chelsea Room, Hyatt Carlton Tower Hotel

# Stewed Lobster Provençal

2 × **800 g lobsters**

**oil, as needed**

4 **medium-sized onions**

4 **cloves garlic, well minced**

10 **g flour, to sprinkle**

8 **medium-sized tomatoes, peeled and chopped**

4 **wine glasses dry white wine**

1 **wine glass water**

1 **liqueur glass cognac**

Cut the lobster in pieces, cook them in oil, and keep hot.

In a separate pan, sauté the onions and garlic until onions are clear. Add flour and tomatoes. Dilute the mixture with a mixture of wine and water and let reduce. (The sauce should be well thickened.) Add the pieces of lobster. Before serving, add cognac.

Serves: 4

---

# Partridge with Cabbage "Limousine"

4 **partridges**

**seasoning, to taste**

2 or 3 **white cabbages**

4 × **30 g slices lean bacon**

2 **tbsp oil**

4 **medium-sized carrots, sliced**

4 **medium-sized onions, sliced**

275 **g sausage meat to make 8-10 meat balls**

**bouquet garni, as needed**

**broth, as needed**

**bacon or pork rind, as needed**

Season the partridges and roast for 10 minutes to brown them. Keep warm.

In a separate pan, blanch the white cabbages for 20 minutes, then cool them, drain, and grind them coarsely, pulling back the leaves that are too large.

Put slices of lean bacon in a large stew pot with oil, carrots, and onions. Add part of the cabbage, meat balls, and bouquet garni. Lay a layer of cabbage in the pot, then put partridges on top. Cover with the rest of the cabbage. Dilute some broth, bring to a boil, rectify the seasoning, and cover with a large slice of bacon or a piece of pork rind. Cover the stew pot and cook on moderate heat for at least 2 hours, then serve. Serves: 4

---

# Crème Bretonne

1 **pod vanilla**

500 **ml milk**

500 **g chocolate**

60 **g butter**

50 **g cream of rice**

Put vanilla in the milk and heat milk to bubbling stage. Melt the chocolate in the bubbling milk. Keep warm.

Put the butter and cream of rice in an earthenware pot. Beat the mixture with a wooden spatula, in a warm place, until very smooth. Gently add the warm milk and chocolate mixture, stirring gently. Pass this mixture through a cheesecloth or muslin into another casserole. Place back on heat and cook for about 10 minutes. Refrigerate and serve cold.

# Frederick's

**Frederick's** was originally a public house built in 1789 and called "The Gun." Upon its rebuilding in 1834, it was renamed "The Duke of Sussex" in honour of George III's sixth son, Prince Augustus Frederick (1773-1843), from whom Frederick's takes its present name.

Frederick's, as we know it today, is now 14 years old. Its proprietor is Louis Segal, who has been associated with the restaurant since its opening. Kitchen operations are supervised by Chef Jean-Louis Pollet, who enjoyed extensive experience in many hotel and restaurant kitchens before joining Frederick's five years ago.

Frederick's is a smart, pleasant restaurant that is surprisingly large. It has separate dining areas providing for various moods. The dining room is split-level and overlooks a white-walled conservatory that leads out into a garden room. The gardens are extensive and patio dining is offered in the summer.

The menu shows a varied range of starters (soups, duck terrine, taramasalata), with fish, poultry, and game represented in mainly French-style main courses. Carefully cooked vegetables and sweets from the trolley are all prepared to a high standard, and everything is attentively served.

## FREDERICK'S

Camden Passage
Islington, London, N1

01-359-2888

Lunch: 12.30 to 2.30 p.m.
Dinner: 7.30 to 11.30 p.m.
Monday — Saturday
Reservations

Proprietor: Louis Segal
Chef: Jean-Louis Pollet

# La Queue de Boeuf en Gelée aux Échalotes

2½ kg large fresh oxtails, trimmed and cut

beef bouillon

2 large onions

3–4 carrots

3 stalks celery

2 bay leaves, sprig of thyme

5 g fresh parsley

50 g shallots, finely chopped

150 g carrots, boiled in oxtail stock and diced

250 ml aspic jelly

salt and pepper

vinaigrette sauce flavoured with chopped parsley, shallot and finely diced gherkins

Boil the oxtail in the beef bouillon with next 5 ingredients until the flesh falls off the bone. Dice the largest pieces of meat and place in a large stainless-steel bowl (while still warm). Add the parsley, chopped shallot, diced carrot and aspic, mix well, and check seasoning. Pour the mixture into a mould and leave overnight to set.

Turn out and cut into thin slices (using a slicing machine or by hand). Arrange slices on each plate and coat with vinaigrette sauce. Serve with brown bread and unsalted butter.

Serves: 8–10

Wine: *Muscat de Beaumes de Venise (Rhône)*

---

# Les Médaillons de Veau
## à la crème de rhubarbe

150 g fresh early rhubarb

50 g unsalted butter (some melted)

20 g sugar

100 ml double cream

3 × 50 g veal medallions, cut from prime milk-fed fillet

salt and freshly ground black pepper

3 small bunches of fresh redcurrants

1 sprig of fresh mint

Dice the rhubarb into small chunks, roll in melted butter and sprinkle with sugar. Simmer very gently, covered, for a few minutes. Blend until a very fine purée is obtained. Add the double cream and boil for a few seconds to obtain a light pink sauce; check seasoning. Add a small nut of butter.

Season the medallions, fry in clarified butter, and drain. Place on a hot plate and pour the sauce over.

To serve: garnish each piece of meat with a tiny bunch of fresh redcurrants, and add a couple of fresh mint leaves.

Serves: 1

Wine: *Chiroubles 1981*

---

# La Terrine de Fraise avec son Coulis

1 sheet of thin sponge

800 g best-quality firm strawberries

1 litre double cream

100 g caster sugar

2 measures eau de vie de framboise

6 gelatine leaves, dissolved

2 tbsp golden syrup

150 ml Chantilly cream to decorate

mint leaves to decorate

Line a terrine mould (30 × 7 × 10 centimetres) with cling film, then cover sides and base with sponge. Fill the sponge terrine with selected strawberries, standing upright (reserve a few to decorate). Refrigerate.

Put 750 millilitres double cream and the caster sugar in a pan and bring to the boil. Allow to cool. When nearly cold, add the eau de vie de framboise, 100 grams of strawberries and the gelatine. Liquidise thoroughly. Whip remaining cream and add gently with a wooden spatula. Pour this mixture over the strawberries, filling the terrine to the top. Cover with a thin layer of sponge, then cling film and refrigerate for about 6 hours.

To prepare coulis of strawberries: liquidise the remaining strawberries with the golden syrup.

Remove the terrine from mould by turning it over and gently pulling on the bottom layer of cling film. Cut a few fairly thick slices from the terrine, arrange on a serving plate, and pour a spoonful of the coulis over it. Decorate with a rose of Chantilly cream topped with ½ a fresh strawberry and a mint leaf.

Serves: 8–10

Wine: *Lanson Brut Rose N.V.*

# Le Gavroche

**Le Gavroche,** opened in 1967 and run by the Roux brothers, features outstanding French cuisine. It is the only Michelin three-star restaurant in Britain.

The restaurant is divided into three main areas: the bar and reception lounge, decorated in moss green with deep green sofas and brown chairs; the large dining room, situated on the lower-ground floor and tastefully decorated, predominantly in green with circular tables and bronze-coloured chairs; and the coffee area, adjoining the dining room, furnished with coffee tables and deep red sofas. The atmosphere and service in the large dining area are formal. There are fresh flowers, crystal glasses filled with Malvern water, and handsome cutlery on each perfectly damasked table.

The menu offers a choice of carefully selected classical French specialities prepared by the celebrated chef Albert Roux. Appetizers include Papillote de Saumon Fumé Claudine and the genuine foie gras frais made by the Roux brothers. The main courses, such as Rognons de Veau aux Trois Moutardes, pot au feu sauce Albert, and Côtes d'Agneau au Vinaigre d'Estragon, are served with crisp and perfectly prepared vegetables. Then comes the excellent cheese board, the sable framboise, or the soufflé à l'orange.

The extensive wine list includes an impressive number of estate-bottled Burgundies and clarets.

*le Gavroche*

**43 Upper Brook Street
London, W1**

**01-499-1826**

**Lunch to 2 p.m.
Dinner to 11 p.m.
Monday — Friday
Closed Bank Holidays and
24—30 December
Reservations**

**Proprietor: Roux Restaurants
Chef: A.H. Roux, M.C.G.B**

# Caneton Gavroche

2 × 1¾ kg oven ready ducklings
400 g carrots with leaves
600 g turnips
300 g butter
water, as needed
salt, as needed
50 g sugar
6 shallots
1 dessertspoon white wine
bouquet garni
pepper, to taste
200 g chicken liver, chopped in large pieces
100 g foie gras, goose or duck, must be fresh
1 tsp thyme
2 tsp cognac
4 slices white sandwich bread

Roast ducklings, without fat, in an oven at 465°F (240°C) for 20 minutes. Remove and keep the fat and juices. Let duck sit 10 minutes. Remove legs and breast. Set aside. (Reserve legs for a second meal.)

Slice ⅔ carrots and turnips in oval shapes; reserve carrot leaves. Place sliced vegetables in separate deep frying pans, each containing 50 grams butter, a little water, pinch of salt, and ½ the sugar. Boil down liquid, remove vegetables, and set aside. Slice remaining carrots and turnips julienne with a shredder. Put another 50 grams butter in a deep frying pan, add julienne carrots. When half-cooked, add turnips. Keep julienne separate.

Mince remaining bones and meat from ducks. Put in oven tray and place in oven for a few minutes, then add 4 shallots and carrot leaves and put all into a casserole. Deglaze baking tray with white wine, reduce by ½, mix with minced bones, etc. Add enough water to cover bones, add bouquet, and boil. Leave for 1 hour on low heat but use skimmer frequently over surface. After 1 hour, strain through muslin. Put juices in pan over medium heat, reduce to syrup consistency, mix in another 50 grams butter, salt, and pepper.

In a frying pan, on medium heat, add 4 soupspoons duck fat, remaining 2 shallots, duck livers, and chicken livers. Add foie gras in large pieces, thyme, salt, and pepper. Flambé with cognac. (Do all this very quickly to keep livers medium rare.) Put all into a sieve and grind with a pestle, place in a bowl, put in a bain-marie, and mix for 1 minute.

Cut bread into 4 duck shapes with a pastry cutter. Melt ½ remaining butter in a frying pan and fry bread on both sides.

Remove skin from breast. Cut 4 slices from breast and place on a plate, one on top of the other. Cover with greaseproof paper and return to oven at 375°F (190°C) for 5 minutes to reheat.

Remove the mixture from the bain-marie, add 2 tablespoons duck stock, and spread on each breast. Put breast on plate. Place oval-shaped vegetables, julienne vegetables, and duckling-shaped bread around breast on each plate. Pour ⅓ duckling stock on bottom of plate. Serve remaining stock in a sauce boat.

*Serves: 6*

---

# Roule Marquis (Raspberry Cake Roll)

3 egg yolks
175 g icing sugar
4 egg whites
50 g cocoa powder
15 g potato flour
1 tsp butter
pinch of flour
300 ml fresh cream
250 ml thick sauce of red fruits or Melba sauce
2 tbsp raspberry eau de vie, optional
250 g raspberries
120 g coffee beans in alcohol

Mix yolks with 80 grams sugar until fairly stiff. Beat whites. When hard, add 45 grams sugar and mix well for 1 minute. Mix yolks and about ⅓ whites and, when smooth, carefully add remaining ⅔. When smooth, sift in cocoa and potato flour and mix well. Spread on greaseproof paper coated with butter and flour in a rectangular shape of 12 by 20 centimetres about ¾ centimetre thick. Bake in 375°F (190°C) oven for 8–10 minutes. Put upside down on cooling tray, remove paper, and let cool 5–10 minutes.

Beat cream with remaining sugar. Mix fruit sauce with raspberry eau de vie and coat cooled cake mixture with ⅓ this mixture. Spread beaten cream on cake, then raspberries, then coffee beans. Roll cake into shape of a roll. Refrigerate 2–3 hours before serving. (Will keep refrigerated 24 hours.)

To serve: slice roll. Serve on cold plates with remaining red fruit sauce in a sauce boat.

*Serves: 6*

# Gavvers

**Gavvers** is in the old premises of Le Gavroche and it too is owned by Albert and Michel Roux — but there the similarity ends.

Gavvers is a large and popular restaurant with a bustling, cheerful atmosphere. The chef is Denis Lobry, who was at another of the Roux brothers' restaurants, Le Gamin in Old Bailey, before coming to Gavvers. The food at Gavvers is similar to that at Le Gamin: largely French provincial, with a few small concessions to *nouvelle cuisine*. There is a set price menu which includes VAT and service, and for which you get a kir and a dip, soup or *hors d'oeuvre*, an *entrée* of fish or meat, cheese or dessert, and a half bottle of wine. There are several choices for each course, and the menu changes daily. It is undeniably very good value for money.

The menu is fairly short, thus enabling Chef Dobry to keep his standards high. Among his specialities are Boudin Noir aux Pommes, Calamars à l'Américaine and Langue d'Agneau à l'Échalote. The cheese, which comes direct from Maître Fromager Philippe Olivier in Boulogne, is particularly recommended.

There is a short, moderately priced wine list, which includes a particularly fruity Beaumes de Venise.

*Gavvers*

**61 Lower Sloane Street
London, SW1**

**01-730-5983**

**Dinner: 7 to 11 p.m.
Monday — Saturday
Reservations**

**Proprietor: Roux Restaurants
Chef: Denis Lobry**

# Aiguillettes de Saumon Carole

| | |
|---|---|
| 300 | g pike or sole flesh |
| | salt and a pinch of cayenne pepper |
| 2 | egg whites |
| 200 | g double cream (plus 1 cup for sauce) |
| 2 | tbsp fresh tarragon, chervil and fresh coriander, very finely chopped (plus extra for garnish) |
| 1 | tbsp very finely chopped shallot |
| 1 × 1½ | kg fresh salmon, the fillet cut into thick slices and each one slit through to make a pocket |
| 2 | tomatoes, peeled, sliced and seeded |
| 150 | g white button mushrooms, sliced and sautéed in butter with salt, pepper and a few drops lemon juice |
| 100 | g cucumber, peeled, sliced and blanched |
| 50 | g French beans, sliced and blanched |
| 100 | ml dry white wine |
| 100 | ml sweet white Martini |
| 100 | ml reduced fish *fumet* |
| 120 | g butter |

To prepare fish mousse: put pike or sole through mincer, then press through a fine sieve. Spoon into a bowl placed in a larger container filled with ice. Season with salt and cayenne pepper.

Add the egg whites one at a time, working each one in vigorously with a wooden spoon. Fold in the cream in the same way, working it in little by little to obtain a light well-blended mousse. Add fresh herbs.

To cook the salmon: spread a layer of chopped shallot over the bottom of a well-buttered dish. Lay the slices of salmon on the shallot using a knife, then fill each one with a good layer of the fish mousse. Put a layer of tomato, mushroom, cucumber, and French beans on top.

Pour in the white wine, Martini and fish *fumet*. Heat on top of the cooker until the liquid starts to 'shudder' then transfer to a preheated oven gas mark 5 (375°F/190°C) for 10 minutes.

Carefully drain the salmon slices and arrange them on a long dish. Cover with a piece of greaseproof paper until ready to serve.

To prepare sauce: reduce the cooking juice from the salmon to a *demi-glace*. Thicken this with the cup of cream and finish with a knob of butter.

To serve: coat the salmon with this sauce and garnish with fresh herbs.

Serves: 4–6

Wine: *Riesling, Puligny Montrachet*

---

# Tournedos Belle France

| | |
|---|---|
| 4–8 | slices white bread |
| | unsalted butter |
| | salt |
| 800 | g fillet beef, sliced into 8 small tournedos of 100 g each |
| 4 | round slices of foie gras (the same size as the tournedos) |
| 4 | extremely large and thin slices of Parma ham |
| 100 | ml red port |
| 50 | ml cognac |
| ¼ | pt unthickened veal stock |
| 70 | g tinned truffles, cut into julienne strips (juice reserved) |

Cut the slices of bread into the same shape as the tournedos. Fry bread in butter until golden brown. Drain on absorbent paper and sprinkle with salt. Arrange in an oval metal dish and keep warm.

Fry the tournedos very lightly in a very little butter over a strong heat. Keep warm. Sandwich each slice of foie gras between two tournedos, then wrap in a slice of ham. Fry them on a high heat until done to taste. Remove from pan and keep warm.

To make the sauce: drain the butter from the pan and deglaze with the port and cognac. Bring to the boil and strain into a good heavy saucepan. Add the veal stock and reduce by a third, skimming off the impurities. Add the truffle juice and reduce again. Finally add the truffles and a knob of butter.

To serve: place the tournedos on the fried bread at the last moment and coat with the sauce.

Serves: 4–6

Wine: *Château Margaux or Red Bordeaux Saint Emilion*

# Hotel Inter-Continental Le Soufflé Restaurant

**Le Soufflé Restaurant**, located in London's **Hotel Inter-Continental**, is a luxurious art deco dining establishment that opened in July of 1975. It offers exquisite, unusual soufflés and French speciality dishes which are highly complemented by pastries and other desserts of distinction. Emphasis is placed on soufflés, as the name of the restaurant implies, and most are the creation of Executive Chef Peter Kromberg, whose experience includes an apprenticeship in Germany followed by many years working for hotels and restaurants in Switzerland, Greece, Thailand, and other countries before he joined the Hotel Inter-Continental in 1971.

The restaurant is warm and relaxing and very classy. Skillful service is provided by a team of young waiters, all most competent and helpful. They are supervised by a manager, A.C. Belment, who previously worked for several hotel organisations before coming to Le Soufflé some years ago.

Week night diners can choose from an extensive à la carte menu. On Saturday evenings, the restaurant puts on a dinner dance with live music and a special menu. Sunday brunch is a family affair, and it too offers live music.

An extensive wine list featuring more than 200 choices is available at your table, and there is also a luxurious cocktail bar on the premises.

## HOTEL
## INTER•CONTINENTAL
### LONDON

**1 Hamilton Place**
**London, W1**

**01-409-3131 x 261**

Lunch: every day except Saturday
12.30 to 3 p.m.
Dinner: every night 7 to 11 p.m.
**Reservations**

Manager: A.C. Belment
Chef: Peter Kromberg, M.C.G.B.

# La Chartreuse de Grouse au Foie Gras

1 × 100 g chicken breast, finely minced

salt and pepper

50 g butter

50 ml double cream

1 egg yolk

nutmeg

1 medium-sized carrot

50 g French beans, cleaned

1 medium-sized turnip

2 cock grouse (oven ready)

30 ml vegetable oil

50 ml port wine

500 ml chicken stock

100 g foie-gras parfait, finely sieved

To prepare chicken mousse: mince the chicken, add salt and pepper. Place with 30 grams butter, cream, egg yolk and nutmeg in a food processor and mince very finely until the pâté is smooth. Refrigerate.

Cut the vegetables into batons 5 centimetres long, blanch in boiling salted water, then cool in cold water. Keep to one side. Roast the seasoned grouse in the vegetable oil for about 15 minutes (the grouse must remain pink inside).

To prepare sauce: remove grouse from roasting tray, strain off the excess fat and add the port wine to the tray. Cut off the grouse breasts and legs, but keep the thigh part of the legs only. Chop the bones into smaller pieces, add to pan with port, simmer until reduced to ½, add the chicken stock and reduce again to ⅓. Strain, add ½ of the foie-gras parfait, season and keep to one side.

Butter 4 ramekin dishes. Arrange the vegetable batons in an attractive colour sequence at bottom and sides of the dishes. Refrigerate for 10 minutes. Remove from refrigerator and spread the chicken mousse in a thin layer on and around the vegetables.

Cut the grouse meat into slices which fit around and inside the ramekin dishes, then place in dishes with remaining foie gras. Add some sauce to keep meat moist. Cover with remaining chicken mousse and bake in a bain-marie at gas mark 7 (425 ° F/220 ° C) for about 20 minutes.

Remove from oven, turn chartreuses out of ramekins, arrange on dinner plates, pour the remaining sauce around the chartreuses and serve with boiled new potatoes.

Serves: 4

# Le Soufflé au Citron Vert en Croustade

(Lime soufflé in a short-pastry case)

60 g granulated sugar

125 g strong flour

60 g butter, softened

1 small whole egg

4 egg yolks

60 g caster sugar (extra for dusting)

2 tbsp lime juice

1 tbsp grated lime zest

6 egg whites

20 g butter

20 g icing sugar

To prepare pastry shells: mix the granulated sugar and flour together, rub in the softened butter, add the whole egg, knead lightly, and leave to rest for 1 hour. Roll out the pastry to 3 millimetres thick and cut into 125 centimetre diameter rounds. Brush the *outside* of four 2½ inch ramekin dishes with butter, dust with flour and place upside-down on a baking sheet. Cover each one with a pastry round and mould into a shell. Cut away excess pastry. Bake in a hot oven at gas mark 7 (425 ° F/220 ° C) until crisp and brown. Keep to one side.

To prepare soufflé: beat together the egg yolks, ½ the caster sugar, ½ the lime juice and ½ the zest over hot water (a bain-marie) until the mixture reaches the ribbon stage (sabayon). Whisk together the egg whites and remaining sugar. When stiff, add remaining lime juice and zest. Carefully fold the egg whites into the sabayon.

Butter the inside of the pastry shells and dust with caster sugar. Fill shells with soufflé mixture and bake at gas mark 7 (425 ° F/220 ° C) for about 10 minutes. Dust with icing sugar and serve immediately.

Serves: 4

# Hyatt Carlton Tower Hotel

Bernard Gaume, who has been executive chef at the **Hyatt Carlton Tower Hotel** for 15 years, was born into the restaurant business. He comes from Vichy where his family owned a hotel, and he served his apprenticeship in some of France's best restaurants, as well as a number of hotels around the world. His talents have been largely the reason for the success of **The Chelsea Room** restaurant, which has won a Michelin star.

Mr. Gaume is an expert of *la nouvelle cuisine*, which he introduced to the Carlton Tower in 1976. All of his ingredients are fresh, and each dish is cooked to order. Many of the ingredients and delicacies, such as goose livers, are delivered daily from France, straight to the restaurant.

Each year, Mr. Gaume and Jean Quero, Maître d'Hôtel, make a journey to France to observe their fellow professionals in Rennes, Lyon, and Valence. In this way, new dishes find their way onto the Chelsea Room menu, which changes with the seasons.

It's not just the food that Messrs. Gaume and Quero are concerned with, it's the total ambiance of a restaurant, the way the food is served as well as how it's prepared. Jean Quero and his staff ensure that the service is first class, while Chef Gaume continues to receive accolades for his superb cuisine.

This elegant restaurant has been completely refurbished in classical style with mahogany and oak furnishings, and new picture windows overlooking the attractive gardens of Cadogan Place. There is soft lighting, an intimate atmosphere, and background music from the resident pianist. The quality wine list features several house wines.

HYATT CARLTON TOWER LONDON

**2 Cadogan Place
London, SW1**

**01-235-5411**

**Breakfast: 7 to 11 a.m.
Lunch: 12.30 to 3 p.m.
Dinner: 7 to 11.30 p.m.
Sunday to 10.30 p.m.
Reservations**

**Chef: Bernard Gaume, M.C.G.B.**

THE CARLTON TOWER

# Huîtres de Whitstable Chaudes

24 **Whitstable oysters**

2 **medium shallots, chopped**

    **butter, to sauté**

1 **oz shredded sorrel**

1 **oz green peppercorns**

2 **oz white wine**

2 oz **double cream**

    **shredded and slightly cooked leeks,
carrots, turnips, and mushrooms,
enough to cover oysters**

2 **oz butter**

Open the oysters and remove from shells. Put washed shells in a warm place and keep hot.

Toss shallots in melted butter in a wide, shallow pan for 2 minutes. Add oysters and poach them for 1 minute only over low heat. Remove oysters and ½ cooking juices. Put sorrel, peppercorns, and wine in the pan and reduce the rest of the cooking liquor. Add cream and reduce again until only ¼ cooking liquid remains (should yield enough sauce for 12 oysters). Pour remaining juice of cooked oysters into sauce, add shredded vegetables, and cook for a few minutes. While sauce is simmering, add butter, a few small pieces at a time.

Put oysters back in hollow, hot shells. Cover 12 oysters with vegetables and 12 oysters with sorrel sauce. Serve at once.

Serves: 4

---

# Filet d'Agneau au Basilic et au Tomate

2 **best ends of lamb**

75 **g butter**

2 **chopped shallots**

2 **medium-sized Dutch tomatoes, peeled and roughly chopped**

1 **bunch fresh basil**

100 **ml dry white wine**

100 **ml lamb stock made with the bone and strained**

Cut lamb meat from bone and trim off all fat. Put ⅓ butter in a pan, add lamb fillets, and cook very slowly (lamb should be served pink or medium pink). Remove fillets and keep warm.

Strain off fat, add shallots and cook for a few minutes. Add tomatoes and basil. Add white wine and let reduce a little, then add strained lamb stock. Bring sauce to a boil, then finish it with the remaining butter cut into 4 pieces and added a little at a time.

Pour the sauce onto a serving dish, cut the fillets of lamb diagonally and lay them on top of the sauce, and serve.

Serves: 4

Wine: *Louis Tadot Réserve Couent des Jacobins, 1978*

**CHEF'S TIP**

Herbs such as chervil and basil should be fresh and cut at the last minute using scissors.

---

# Flan aux Pruneaux (Prune Meringue Pie)

180 **g flour mixed with pinch of salt and sugar**

150 **g unsalted butter**

2 **egg yolks**

1 **tbsp milk**

100 **g sugar**

900 **g dried prunes, soaked then cooked in port and stoned**

250 **g double cream**

4 **egg yolks**

6 **egg whites**

250 **g sugar**

4 **tbsp hot apricot purée**

Prepare short pastry with the first 5 ingredients, then line 2 flan rings with it. Bake at 375°F (190°C) for 10 minutes. Fill the bottom of the rings with the cooked prunes.

Mix the double cream and 4 yolks together to make an egg custard and cover prunes with the mixture. Bake at 350°F (175°C) until set.

Prepare meringue by beating egg whites with remaining sugar and cover the flan with meringue about ½ inch thick. Return to oven at 350°F (175°C) to set the meringue.

Coat the meringue with the hot apricot purée and serve.

Wine: *Tattinger Comtes de Champagne Rose, 1971*

# Interlude de Tabaillau

**Interlude de Tabaillau** was opened in 1979 by Jean-Louis Taillebaud, who came to England nine years ago to work for the Roux brothers at Le Gavroche; for six years he was their head chef. He is an advocate of classical French cuisine, and the choice of dishes at this establishment range from a simple fish and leek tart to perfectly cooked fricassee de canard au Beaujolais.

The decor of this restaurant is "thirties-as-seen-by-the-eighties." The walls are stippled salmon pink with a blue line as a decorative feature. The low ceiling is covered in rough-textured tiles, and the windows are obscured with bamboo blinds.

The menu offers specialities of the house or a choice from the daily menu. The first course specialty is Feuilleté d'Agneau Sauce Moelle or, from the daily menu, a choice of consommé with port, Venison Mousse with tomato, or Ragout de St. Jacques et Huître au Sauternes. The main course specialties are Barbue Karpinski (brill),and Supreme de Caneton Juliette. The daily menu has a choice of a further half-dozen dishes.

The cheese board is excellent, offering a choice of about 25 different cheeses, all in peak condition. The desserts are mouthwatering, which makes the choice difficult. The service is smooth, professional, and friendly.

### Interlude de TABAILLAU

**7–8 Bow Street**
**London, WC2**

**01-379-6473**

**Lunch: Monday — Friday 12.30 to 2 p.m.**
**Dinner: Monday — Saturday 7 to 11 p.m.**
**Reservations**

**Proprietor/Chef:**
**Jean-Louis Taillebaud**

# Feuilleté d'Agneau Sauce Moelle

250 g lamb meat, middle neck

50 g fresh goose liver

2 egg yolks

salt, pepper, port, and Madeira wine, to taste

300 g double cream

puff pastry dough, as needed

egg yolks, as needed

To prepare filling: pass lamb meat, goose liver, 2 egg yolks, and seasoning through a cutter and *tamis* (strainer). Add double cream, make it quite firm, check seasoning, and refrigerate about 1 hour.

Roll out the dough to a thickness of 2 millimetres, then cut 12 rounds of 10 centimetres in diameter. Lay down 6 rounds and coat with some yolk. Put 2 soupspoons of filling in the middle of each round then cover each with a second piece of pastry. Make sure sides stick together well. Cover tops with egg yolk and decorate with scraps of dough. Cook in the oven at gas mark 7 (425°F/220°C) for 10–15 minutes.

Serves: 6

Wine: *Côtes du Ventoux Rouge*

# Barbue Karpinski (Brill Karpinski)

6 × 150 g fillets of brill

butter, as needed

2 sliced shallots

100 g chopped chives

4 chopped tomatoes

150 ml Noilly Prat vermouth

500 ml fish stock

250 g cream

50 g butter

2 medium-sized carrots

200 g French beans

200 g turnips

18 small tartlets

Cook the fillets gently in butter without colouring them. Cook the shallots, chives, and tomatoes together with vermouth and fish stock until it is reduced ⅓. Add some cream and let it boil for about 5 minutes. Finish sauce with butter, pass it through a strainer, and add tomatoes and chives.

Make 3 kinds of purées with carrots, beans, and turnips. Put a fillet in the centre of each plate, cover with sauce, and put 3 tartlets filled with the different purées around each fillet.

Serves: 6

# Lemon Tart

500 g flour

400 g caster sugar

200 g butter

pinch of salt

2 egg yolks

7 eggs

225 g caster sugar

juice and skin of 3 lemons

1750 ml whipped double cream

Form 2 pastry cases with the first 5 ingredients. Bake until slightly brown.

To prepare the lemon filling: mix the 7 eggs, sugar, lemon juice, and grated lemon skin together. Gently add the whipped cream.

Fill the pastry cases with the lemon filling and cook in the oven at gas mark 3 (340°F/170°C) for 20 minutes.

Serves: 8

**CHEF'S TIP**

Imagine that everything you cook and serve is going to be served to you in a restaurant.

# Ivy
# Restaurant

In 1911, Abel Giandellini, an acknowledged master of the culinary art, opened the small **Ivy Restaurant** in the heart of London's theatreland. His aim was to provide fine French cuisine for cultured palates.

His clientele were, from the first, selective and distinguished. Although predominantly theatrical, they also included men and women high in the counsels of the nation, artists, and men of letters.

Among the famous figures of the Twenties, the Ivy was a synonym for quality; it became an exclusive meeting place. The theatrical patronage remained predominant, and at the Ivy's tables Noël Coward and Marie Tempest could be seen regularly. They were joined by scores of other theatre and screen personalities, men and women celebrated in the arts and letters, kings and queens of sport, and newspaper editors.

At the time of the outbreak of the Second World War, the Ivy had acquired something of the position of an institution in the artistic and social life of London. Its fame had spread to the United States and Europe, and today, distin-guished men and women from abroad seldom fail to include visits to the Ivy to sample the offerings of Chef Guiseppe Pedri who came to England from the Tyrol 30 years ago and has been maître chef at the Ivy for the past ten years.

## Ivy Restaurant

**1–5 West Street
London, WC2**

**01-836-4751**

Lunch: Monday — Friday
12 to 3 p.m.
Dinner: Monday — Saturday
6 p.m. to 12.30 a.m.
Reservations

Proprietor: The Lady Grade
Chef: Guiseppe Pedri

# Avocado Trianon

3 ripe avocados

3 oz chopped smoked salmon

3 oz peeled prawns

3 tbsp fresh mayonnaise

dash of Worcestershire sauce

juice of ½ lemon

seasoning, to taste

mayonnaise, as needed to coat

3 chopped hard-boiled eggs, to garnish

chopped parsley, to garnish

12-15 prawns, to garnish

6 lettuce leaves

Cut avocados in half and remove stone. Spoon out flesh, being careful not to damage the shells. Put flesh into a basin and mash with a fork. Add smoked salmon, prawns, mayonnaise, Worcestershire sauce, lemon juice, salt, and pepper and mix thoroughly. Return mixture to shells and smooth. Spread a thin layer of mayonnaise over the top. Decorate each half with a chopped hard-boiled egg, parsley, and 2–3 prawns. Serve each stuffed avocado half on a lettuce leaf. Serves: 6

# Escalope de Veau Delysia

6 scallops of veal, sufficient for 6 portions

bread crumbs, to dust

fat, to sauté

18 cooked asparagus tips

sliced cooked mushrooms, as needed

6 spoonfuls tomato concasse (roughly chopped tomato)

jus *lie* (thin meat sauce), as needed

6 knobs nut butter, heated

Dust veal with bread crumbs and fry quickly in hot fat until crisp and light golden brown on both sides. Arrange on a large dish. Place 3 asparagus tips diagonally across each scallop. To one side, place a few sliced cooked mushrooms. On the other side, put a spoonful of tomato concasse. Put under a grill for 2 minutes to warm garnish. Pour a little *jus lie* over the vegetables and put a knob of hot nut butter on the veal.

Serves: 6

# Trifle

1 × 4 egg sponge sandwich, prepared

2 tbsp strawberry jam

apples, pears, oranges, peaches, and cherries, cut up as needed for fruit salad

½ glass sherry

1½ pt strawberry jelly

1 pt milk

1 oz custard powder

1 oz sugar

Spread strawberry jam over sponge sandwich and cut into strips. Line the bottom of a serving dish with ½ sponge. Peel and core the fruit and cut into small cubes. Place in a bowl together with their own juices. Put a layer of the fruit salad on top of the sponge, cover with the remaining sponge, and sprinkle generously with sherry. Pour strawberry jelly over and allow to set.

To prepare custard: make a roux by mixing a little cold milk, custard powder, and sugar in a jug. Heat the remaining milk until nearly boiling, then pour heated milk into the roux and stir vigorously. Return to pan and bring to a boil again, stirring constantly. Remove from heat.

Pour 1 pint custard over the sponge and allow to set. Chill in the refrigerator.

Serving suggestion: decorate with sweetened whipped cream, toasted nuts, and glacé cherries and angelica.

# Kundan Restaurant

**Kundan Restaurant** specialises in selected Indian and Pakistani dishes prepared in the traditional manner favourite to both kings and Nawabs.

The chef at Kundan is Aziz Khan. Mr. Khan learned his cooking in Pakistan where he worked in restaurants for eight years. He then came to England where he cooked in a number of top Eastern restaurants before joining the Kundan when it opened four-and-a-half years ago.

Chef Khan's use of the many spices is subtle and sophisticated to insure that no menu selection will be unkind to the stomach. Managing director Nayab Abbasi adds, "The spices are not only used for developing taste and flavour in our food, but also as blood purifiers and for producing heat in the body, for cleaning and burning out cold, etc. For instance, the use of turmeric, ginger, clove, and so on maintain health or correct body disfunctions."

The restaurant is very spacious and comfortable and is elegantly decorated in smart shades of brown and gold. Indian/Pakistani food is traditionally eaten with the fingers, but to accommodate Western needs, each table is set with silver service. To round out the atmosphere, there are candles and soft background music. A modest but excellent wine list is available, as is a cocktail lounge.

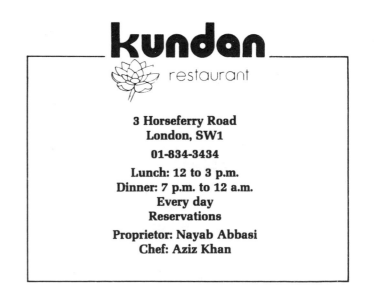

**kundan** restaurant

**3 Horseferry Road
London, SW1**

**01-834-3434**

**Lunch: 12 to 3 p.m.
Dinner: 7 p.m. to 12 a.m.
Every day
Reservations**

**Proprietor: Nayab Abbasi
Chef: Aziz Khan**

Gravetye Manor

Plumber Manor

# Tikka Kabab Lamb

1 dessertspoon Worcestershire sauce

juice of ¼ lemon

juice of ½ in fresh root ginger

juice of 1 garlic clove

½ tsp dry mustard

½ tsp white pepper

1 tsp paprika

salt, to taste

1 lb meat from a marcel of lamb (leg of lamb), cut into 1 in cubes

1 large onion

4 firm tomatoes

2 oz clarified butter

Combine liquid ingredients with the mustard, spices, and salt in a bowl, add meat, and allow to marinate for at least 8 hours (or, preferably, overnight). Just before cooking, cut onion and tomatoes into bite-size pieces and arrange on skewers by alternating a cube of lamb with a piece of onion, cube of lamb with piece of tomato, etc. Cook under a hot grill for approximately 8 minutes (2 minutes per side) and baste with a little butter during cooking.

Serves: 3

# Murgh Korma with Polao Arasta

oil, to fry

6 cloves

2 cinnamon sticks

2 cardamoms

2 large onions, sliced

2 cloves garlic, chopped finely

1 very small piece fresh root ginger, chopped finely

1 medium-sized chicken, skinned and cut in 12 pieces

1 × 4-5 oz carton natural yogurt

pinch of saffron

1 lb tomatoes, chopped

2 red chilis, cut in ¼ in pieces

salt, to taste

pinch of *jaiful* (mace) and *javatri* (nutmeg)

Polao Arasta *(recipe follows)*

Heat a little oil in a saucepan and fry cloves, cinnamon, and cardamoms. Add onions and fry until golden brown. Add garlic and ginger and fry another 5 minutes. Add chicken and fry until brown.

Put yogurt in a bowl, add saffron and beat until smooth. Add to chicken mixture along with tomatoes, chilis, and salt. Cover saucepan tightly and cook over low heat until chicken is tender. Uncover and cook another 5–10 minutes. Garnish with a little powder of *jaifal* and *javatri*.

Serving suggestion: serve with Polao Arasta.

Serves: 3

## Polao Arasta

1 large onion

8 oz butter

2 lb bones with meat

1 in fresh root ginger

4 cloves garlic

2 tsp coriander seeds

2 tsp aniseed

4 cloves

3 large cardamoms

6 whole black peppercorns

2 × 1 in sticks cinnamon

1½ tsp salt

3 pt water

1 lb Basmati rice

fried onion rings, to garnish

Brown the onion in butter until golden. Add meat bones and fry for 5 minutes, then add all remaining ingredients except rice and onion ring garnish. Bring the water to a boil and simmer gently until ¼ of the liquid has evaporated. Strain the stock.

Wash the rice thoroughly in running water until the water runs clear. Soak the rice in water for 35–40 minutes, then drain.

Reheat the strained stock, add the rice, cover, and simmer until the rice is cooked and the stock has evaporated. Serve decorated with golden fried onions.

# Langan's Brasserie

**Langan's Brasserie** is "an unholy alliance of a chef, an actor, and a drunk." It opened six and a half years ago and has become one of London's most talked about restaurants.

The partners are Peter Langan, a self-proclaimed "soak with spots of spasmodic genius," celebrated actor Michael Caine, and Richard Shepherd, one of England's best chefs. While Caine is acting and Langan drinking, Shepherd does most of the work and produces a good standard of cooking at a price that most still consider okay.

If there is a café society in London, it's here. The *frisson* of actors, journalists, and everyone-who-wants-to-be-someone is what this "happening" is about. And it is an artists' restaurant: Hockney, Francis Bacon, *et al.* seem to live here permanently. Hockney drew the menu, and many pictures crowd the restaurant's walls. What is wrong with many restaurants is that they take themselves too seriously and one ends up eating in a church; by comparison, this place is a rock opera.

The food is quite good. Shepherd's Artichaut Farci à la Nissarda; Soufflé aux Épinards, Sauce Anchois; Carré d'Agneau; and Crème Brûlée can hardly be bettered. A modest but excellent list of wines and two quality house wines are available. Seating is extensive at 175.

## Langan's Brasserie

**Stratton Street**
**Piccadilly, London, W1**

**01-493-6437**

**Lunch: Monday — Friday 12.30 to 3 p.m.**
**Dinner: Monday — Friday 7 p.m. to**
**12 a.m.**
**and Saturday 8 p.m. to 1 a.m.**
**Reservations**

**Proprietors: Peter Langan,**
**Michael Caine, Richard Shepherd**
**Chef: Richard Shepherd, M.C.G.B.**

# Artichaut Farci à la Nissarda

white wine, as needed

water, as needed

few coriander seeds

few peppercorn seeds

lemon juice, as needed

thyme, bay leaf, and salt, to taste

6 globe artichoke hearts rubbed with lemon juice

1¼ lb duxelles of mushrooms

double cream, optional

2 oz chopped shallots

3 oz diced ham

pepper, to taste

½ pt Hollandaise sauce

chives, to garnish

Make a bouillon of ¼ white wine and ¾ water. Add a few coriander and peppercorn seeds and a little lemon juice, thyme, bay leaf, and salt. Cook artichokes in bouillon until tender. (Test with point of small knife.)

Cook the duxelles until all moisture has evaporated. (If mushrooms are a little bitter, add a drop of cream.) Reduce the shallots in white wine. Add shallots, ham, salt, and pepper to the duxelles.

Dress the artichokes on a serving dish and fill with the mushroom mixture. Cover with Hollandaise sauce, sprinkle with chives, and serve hot.

Serves: 6

# Poulet Sauté Safrané

6 oz butter

oil, as needed

2 × 3½ lb chickens cut in 16 equal pieces

salt and pepper, to taste

2 large finely chopped onions

good pinch of saffron, leaves preferred, *not* ground saffron

½ bottle white wine

2 pt veal stock, slightly thickened, or use stock cubes

½ pt double cream

chopped parsley, to garnish

Heat butter and just enough oil to prevent burning in a thick-bottomed pan. Season the chicken with salt and pepper and sauté the pieces until golden brown. Remove chicken, strain fat, and wipe out pan.

Return fat to pan, add onions, and sweat without colouring them. Add saffron and white wine and reduce by ½. Add stock, return chicken, and cover and cook for 20 minutes. If necessary, add more stock.

Remove chicken and skim off any grease from top of sauce. Reduce sauce if needed to get correct flavouring. Add cream and stir until sauce returns to boil.

Dress chicken on serving dish, cover with sauce, and sprinkle with chopped parsley. Serving suggestion: serve with boiled or plain rice.

Serves: 4

# Crème Brûlée

1 litre double cream

5 egg yolks

200 g caster sugar

vanilla essence, as needed

Demerara sugar, to sprinkle

Bring ¾ double cream to a boil and remove from heat. Mix the rest of the cream, egg yolks, caster sugar, and a little vanilla essence thoroughly together. Add to the boiled double cream. Return to heat and stir constantly with a wooden spoon until just at the boiling point.

Remove pan from heat and pour into 8 × No. 1 ramekin dishes. Allow to go cold and set.

Sprinkle each mould with Demerara sugar and glaze quickly under a salamander. Return to refrigerator, allow to set, and serve.

Serves: 8

# Lichfield's

**Lichfield's** is a small and simply decorated restaurant run by its chef/patron Stephen Bull to appeal to people for whom the quality and variety of the food is the most important aspect of a restaurant. The menu is small and changes frequently, particularly with reference to the changes in the seasons. Everything used is fresh; the vegetables are cooked to order for each customer, and even the ice creams and sorbets are made on the premises.

The food is, on the whole, French with some emphasis placed on the developing fashion for the lighter and more adventurous styles known as *la nouvelle cuisine*, but traditional methods and some of the better dishes from other national cuisines are also featured occasionally.

Stephen Bull is an ex-advertising man whose long-standing and intense interest in cooking inspired him to open his own restaurant one day. Before starting Lichfield's six years ago, Chef Bull was the proprietor and chef of a restaurant in North Wales. He has a noticeable tendency to innovate, which may be due to his lack of formal training. He is self-taught and subscribes to no one set of principles that have been passed on from a mentor; therefore, all styles and approaches can be seen as potential influences upon him. He has also developed an imaginative list of predominantly French wines from which to choose.

*Lichfield's*

**Lichfield Terrace, Sheen Road
Richmond, Surrey**

**01-940-5236**

**Dinner: Tuesday — Saturday
Reservations**

**Proprietor/Chef: Stephen Bull**

# Ragout of Scallops with Dill

8 large or 12 medium scallops

2 oz butter

white of 2 medium leeks, julienne

½ large carrot, julienne

½ stick celery, julienne

¼ pt fish stock

¼ pt white wine

⅛ pt double cream

salt, to taste

1 tbsp chopped fresh dill

Wash and clean scallops, retaining only white meat and orange coral. If large, slice horizontally into 3, if medium, into 2; remove coral.

In a large heavy pan, melt ½ the butter, add prepared vegetables, cover, and cook over low heat for 5 minutes. Do not let brown. Uncover, add stock and wine, and reduce by fast boiling to about ⅛ pint. Add cream and boil for a few moments until it thickens. Season lightly with salt. In a heavy frying pan, melt remaining butter and pour in scallops and coral. Salt lightly and sprinkle with most of the dill. Cook 1 minute on each side until just becoming opaque. Do not let brown. Pour off a small amount of the liquid released into the other pan, shake to mix thoroughly.

Divide the sauce and vegetables among 4 dishes. Arrange the scallops on top of the sauce, sprinkle the remaining dill on top, and serve.

Serves: 4

# Rosettes de Boeuf Persillées

1 fist-sized bunch of parsley, finely chopped

rind of 1 lemon, grated

4 cloves garlic, finely chopped

½ tsp thyme

8 slices middle cut fillet steak, ½ in thick

butter, to sauté

⅛ pt meat glaze or ¼ pt beef or veal stock

2 oz anchovy butter

watercress, to garnish

Mix the parsley, lemon rind, garlic, and thyme together to make a *persillade*. Press both sides of each slice of beef into the mixture and cook them in hot butter for 2 minutes per side without scorching the coating. Remove beef and keep hot.

Deglaze the pan with meat glaze or stock, reduced to a thin syrup, and thicken with anchovy butter, cut into small pieces and added piece by piece. (Shake the pan to incorporate butter smoothly into the sauce.) Pour sauce over the beef slices, garnish with watercress, and serve.

Serves: 4

# Rum and Brandy Mousse

8 eggs, separated

7 oz caster sugar

3 tbsp brandy

2½ tbsp rum

5 tsp gelatine dissolved in a little water

¾ pt double cream

grated chocolate or toasted almonds, to garnish

Whisk the yolks and sugar until pale, then add brandy and rum and whisk for 30 seconds. Add gelatine. Beat the cream until thick, beat the egg whites until soft peaks form, then gently fold whipped cream, then the egg whites, into the gelatine mixture. Put mixture into glasses, chill, and serve with some grated chocolate or toasted almonds on top.

# Mes Amis

**Mes Amis** is a sunny, airy, garden-fresh, green and white "Provençal" restaurant located just behind Harrods, the famous London store. Knightsbridge businessmen, handsome Arab families, and well-dressed shoppers make a pretty picture under the dark rustic beams, arched whitewashed walls, and hanging pots of ferns and ivies. There is a beautiful arrangement of fresh vegetables, cheeses, herbs, and sausages on a table that welcomes you just inside the entrance. The wooden tables all have rush mats, candles, and more fresh flowers.

The pretty menu is sensibly divided into hot and cold hors d'oeuvres, potages, poissons entrées, grillades, légumes, and desserts. The experienced chef, Martin Cunningham, makes sure every dish is properly prepared, in a large portion, and using only ingredients of the highest quality. Chef Cunningham's Cotelettes en Croûte, for example, are absolutely perfect; the pastry is light and flaky. Fillet steaks are also excellent, and the duck is deliciously honey-roasted. Portions of vegetables are equally large and very fresh. Salads are crisp and fresh, the cheese board is impressive, the desserts are delicious, and the waiters, dressed in fresh green, are always attentive.

There is an extensive wine list in all price ranges available, and there is a cocktail lounge on the premises.

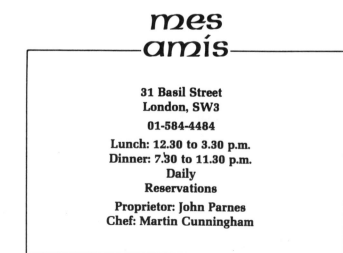

# mes amis

**31 Basil Street**
**London, SW3**

**01-584-4484**

Lunch: 12.30 to 3.30 p.m.
Dinner: 7.30 to 11.30 p.m.
**Daily**
**Reservations**

Proprietor: John Parnes
Chef: Martin Cunningham

# Cassolette Cap Ferrat

1 oz unsalted butter

1 oz shallots, diced

2 oz fresh prawns, shelled and diced

2 oz fresh scallops, shelled and diced

2 oz scampi, shelled and diced

fresh basil, to taste

1 gill French white wine

1 gill *fumet de poisson* (fish stock)

2 oz crawfish

½ oz lobster butter

½ gill double cream

seasoning, to taste

Melt butter in a sauté pan. Add shallots, prawns, scallops, scampi, and fresh basil. Pour white wine and fish stock over the ingredients and poach. After 2 minutes, add crawfish. Cook for 6–8 minutes. Remove all ingredients from pan, place in a dish, and keep warm.

To prepare sauce: reduce liquid in pan by ½, add lobster butter and double cream and season.

Return ingredients to finished sauce, correct seasoning, and serve.

Serving suggestion: decorate with fresh prawns with shells on.

Serves: 2

**CHEF'S TIP**

Don't rush your sauce — be patient, exercise care, and don't be afraid of the recipe.

# Côtelettes d'Agneau

1 lb prime best end of lamb, cut into 2 cutlets

2 oz unsalted butter

½ oz diced shallot

2 oz diced mushrooms

herbs, to taste

1 oz strudel paste

fresh watercress, to garnish

Seal the lamb cutlets in butter. Set aside to cool.

To prepare mushroom duxelles: place diced shallot, mushrooms, and herbs into a deep frying pan and cook quickly. Remove from heat.

Roll out strudel paste very thinly then place in melted butter. Put enough mushroom duxelles on each cutlet, then carefully wrap each cutlet in strudel paste. Cook in oven for 15–20 minutes.

Decorate with fresh watercress. Serving suggestion: serve with sauce vin blanc.

Serves: 2

# Vacherin Mont Blanc

1 × 1 oz meringue base

1 whole chestnut

1 oz vanilla ice cream

2 oz crème chantilly

1 oz chocolate sauce

½ oz flaked almonds

Fill the meringue base with vanilla ice cream, top with whole chestnut, and surround with crème chantilly. Coat with chocolate sauce, sprinkle with flaked almonds, and serve.

Serves: 1

# Mirabelle

**Mirabelle** is situated on Curzon Street in London's fashionable area of Mayfair. When you arrive, the doorman will look after your car and you can go straight down into the silvery-oak panelled bar for newspapers and nuts with your drink. Or you can wait on a soft banquette in an ante-room filled with mirrors and alcoves of china.

The dining room is large and airy, has brocade or tapestries on the walls, and opens onto a patio planted with flowering shrubs and plants. The tables are decorated with flower arrangements of red, yellow, and glossy green touches which blend in beautifully with the surroundings.

The two chefs, Jean Drees and Edward Robinson, have both been with Mirabelle for 26 years. Jean Drees, a Frenchman, is polite, self-assured, and obviously dedicated. Edward Robinson is very English, gently spoken with a shy, genuine smile. He is as dedicated, self-assured, and as positive in his views on food as his colleague.

They work closely together, yet apart in two separate domains. Jean Drees governs the meat,

fish, poultry and game cookery, while Edward Robinson creates trifles and dresses the desserts and pastries. They both agree that you should never overlay the inherent flavours and subtleties of good food with heavy sauces, strong flavours, or artifical brightness. Testimonies to their philosophy appear on the opposite page.

*Mirabelle*

**56 Curzon Street
Mayfair, London, W1**

**01-449-4636**

**Lunch and Dinner:
Monday — Saturdays
and Public Holidays**

**Proprietor:
De Vere Restaurants, Ltd.
Chefs: Jean Drees, Edward Robinson**

# Gratin de Crabe

2½ lb cooked crab, fresh or cooked

3 oz cooked mushrooms

½ pt double cream, and as needed

1 small glass sherry

1 coffeespoon English mustard

salt and pepper, to taste

pinch of cayenne pepper

1 egg yolk

bread crumbs, as needed

Remove every scrap of flesh from the crab by breaking the inside. Put the brown and white flesh, which is mostly from the claws, in separate bowls. Reserve the shell for serving.

Purée the mushrooms with ¼ pint cream and line the shell. Gently simmer the white flesh in a small pan with sherry and another ¼ pint double cream for about 10 minutes.

Pound the brown flesh with a wooden spoon, mix it with mustard, salt, pepper, and pinch of cayenne pepper. Warm the brown flesh without boiling it, then mix it with the yolk and a little double cream until mixture is of a smooth, soft consistency for spreading.

Lay the white flesh on the mushroom purée in the shell, then spread brown mixture on top. Cover with bread crumbs and grill until coloured.

Serves: 2

Wine: *Chablis Fourchaumes, Louis Jadot, 1977-78*

# Côtelettes d'Agneau Prince de Galles

3 oz mushrooms

3 sprigs of tarragon

salt and pepper, to taste

1-2 dessertspoons brandy

½ c double cream

½ lb veal

3 thin lamb cutlets, trimmed

butter, to sauté and as needed

thinly sliced raw potatoes, as needed

button mushrooms and artichoke hearts, to garnish

Madeira or Perigourdine sauce, prepared

Purée the mushrooms and season with tarragon, salt, pepper, and brandy. Mix in the double cream. Mince the veal and add it to the purée. Consistency should be stiff. Spread the mixture on both sides of the cutlet (crumb if desired, but it's not necessary). Sauté the cutlets in butter for 5–6 minutes per side. Sauté the potatoes in a separate pan and spread them on a dish. Lay the cooked cutlets on top. Warm the button mushrooms and artichoke hearts in butter, cover them with Madeira or Perigourdine sauce and use them to garnish the dish.

Serves: 1

Wine: *Château Lynch Bages, Pauillac*

# Coupe Glacée Mirabelle

4 oz caster sugar

water, as needed

1 tsp glucose

sponge fingers, as needed

strawberry ice cream, 2 scoops per person

cream, as needed

chopped fruit marinated in Grand Marnier, as needed

whipped cream and flaked almonds, to garnish

To prepare caramel sauce: put sugar in a pan and just cover it with water. Add glucose and bring to a boil, stirring all the time. (Glucose prevents crystallising.) Boil furiously. Watch mixture carefully and lower heat as soon as colour begins to change (can happen very quickly). Put into the sink and add cold water, a drop at a time, until you've added about 2 tablespoons. Return to stove and mix well. If you see a slight thread of spun sugar when you lift a little boiled sugar on the end of the spoon, the consistency is right. (This keeps well refrigerated.)

Put 2 tablespoons caramel sauce in bottom of a tall glass, preferably a sundae glass, and insert a sponge finger. Add a small scoop of ice cream, pipe cream around, then add marinated fruit with Grand Marnier. Place another scoop of ice cream on top and decorate with a rosette of cream and garnish with flaked almonds. Serve extra sponge fingers with it.

# Poissonnerie de l'Avenue

**Poissonnerie de l'Avenue** is owned by Peter Rosignoli, who began his career in the restaurant business in 1946 when he went to work as an apprentice in the kitchen of a restaurant in Cremona, Italy, at the age of 14. "In Italy at that time," he says, "an apprentice was paid the equivalent of two pounds a month and the work was hard, very hard. But you learned with your eyes and intuition because you wanted to progress."

And progress he did. After leaving Cremona, he worked as a waiter in grand hotels in Italy, Switzerland, and France before coming to England in 1959 to work in a famous Mayfair restaurant. He married the English receptionist of that restaurant, then the two of them bought Poissonnerie in 1962 and began the process that would turn it into one of the best known seafood restaurants in London.

Poissonnerie is a small, intimate, wood-panelled "French fish cooking" restaurant that seats 80. There is no cocktail lounge, but there is bar service at the tables. There is also a modest but excellent wine list.

The kitchen is run by Chef Roses, a native of Spain who learned classical French cooking in several top kitchens and has been at Poissonnerie since shortly after its opening. He and his associate, Chef Tomassi, cast a French touch to each seafood dish they prepare and, thereby, take what could be otherwise ordinary cuisine and make it something special.

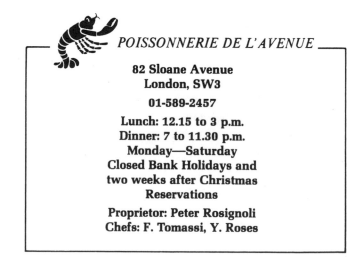

## POISSONNERIE DE L'AVENUE

**82 Sloane Avenue
London, SW3**

**01-589-2457**

**Lunch: 12.15 to 3 p.m.
Dinner: 7 to 11.30 p.m.
Monday—Saturday
Closed Bank Holidays and
two weeks after Christmas
Reservations**

**Proprietor: Peter Rosignoli
Chefs: F. Tomassi, Y. Roses**

# Coquilles St. Jacques

½ lb butter, cut in small pieces

3 tbsp finely chopped shallots

24 medium-sized scallops

1 lb chopped white mushrooms

2 glasses dry Muscadet wine

1 pt double cream

pinch of freshly ground pepper

pinch of salt

1 handful finely chopped parsley

Put a thick-bottomed saucepan on moderate heat, then add butter in small pieces and let melt. Add shallots and let cook until a golden colour. Add whole scallops and cook gently for 5 minutes. Remove scallops and reduce liquid for 5 minutes. Add mushrooms and cook another 5 minutes, then return scallops and add wine; stew for 5 more minutes. Add double cream, pepper, salt, and parsley and simmer for 5 minutes. Pour into 4 shallow dishes.

Serves: 4

# Fillets of Mackerel in White Wine

½ lb butter

2 spoonfuls cooking oil, not olive oil

1 medium-sized onion, sliced very finely

2 shallots, sliced very finely

½ glass white wine vinegar

1 glass dry Muscadet wine

4 × 1 lb mackerels

2 garlic cloves, crushed

black peppercorns, as needed

1 handful chopped parsley

salt, to taste

Melt the butter in a thick-bottomed frying pan, add oil, and fry onion and shallots until golden. Add vinegar and wine and simmer for 25 minutes.

Fillet the mackerel by cutting down the backbone so each fish falls in 2. Make sure fillets are clean. Put fish into a shallow pan and pour the sauce over it. Be sure fish is completely covered by liquid. Add crushed garlic, a few peppercorns, parsley, and salt. Test seasoning; it should be nice and sharp. Let fish simmer gently for 5 minutes. Leave to cool and serve the following day. This dish can be kept refrigerated for up to 10 days.

Serves: 4

# Petit Pots au Chocolat

2 pt milk

peel of 1 lemon

½ glass water and as needed

2 lb bitter chocolate, chips or broken in small pieces

½ lb sugar, caster preferred

12 egg yolks

½ glass Grand Marnier

Boil the milk in a heavy-bottomed pan and set aside.

In a clean pan, boil the lemon peel in water until it is almost reduced to nothing. Remove the peel. Add the chocolate and melt very gently (make sure it does not get too dry, add more water if necessary). Add sugar and boiled milk and set aside.

Gently beat the egg yolks and add Grand Marnier. Being sure chocolate is not too hot, add it to the egg mixture. Check for sweetness. Fill 10 small ramekin dishes up to ½ inch from the top with the mixture. Place them in a baking tin containing about 1 inch of water. Bake at 250°F (120°C) for 20 minutes, taking care that the baking tin does not boil dry. Drain the water and leave to cool. These will keep for up to 10 days in the refrigerator.

Serves: 10

# Le Poulbot

**Le Poulbot** opened in May 1969 and is one of the "city" restaurants owned by Michel and Albert Roux. This restaurant is only open for breakfast and lunch. It has two floors: "Le Coffee Shop" is on the ground floor and serves Continental breakfasts of croissants, baked in their own bakery, and café au lait, from eight until ten. Simple lunches, such as Navarin d'Agneau, Blanquette de Veau, and Cassoulet au Boudin Noir, are served from twelve noon to three p.m.

Downstairs, Le Poulbot has the successful and chic atmosphere of a first-class French restaurant, with plush upholstered cubicle-style seating, discreet lighting, prints on the walls, glistening silver plate, crisp linen, and waiters in classic livery.

The brief luncheon menu consists of original Roux creations and those of Chef Chris Oakley, along with his interpretations of dishes from a classical repertoire. The main courses include the Boudin Blanc Sauce Perigueux, the Filets de Sole Eleonora, and the Grenadin de Veau Vallée d'Auges. The salads are always very good, and the cheese board is up to the usual high Roux standard. A list of wines in all price ranges is also available.

Almost from the time it opened, Le Poulbot was acclaimed to be one of the most outstanding restaurants in the British Isles, and today it has a star in the Michelin guide.

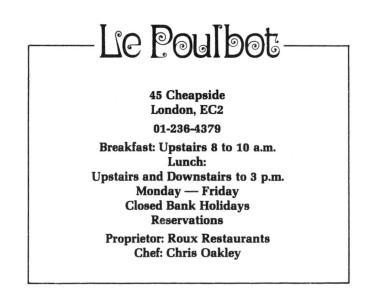

## Le Poulbot

**45 Cheapside
London, EC2**

**01-236-4379**

**Breakfast: Upstairs 8 to 10 a.m.
Lunch:
Upstairs and Downstairs to 3 p.m.
Monday — Friday
Closed Bank Holidays
Reservations**

**Proprietor: Roux Restaurants
Chef: Chris Oakley**

# Snails Poulbot

20 hazelnuts

20 g butter

4 shallots, sliced in small pieces

3 dozen snails, cleaned and dried

1 tbsp Grand Chartreuse Verte

600 g cream

1 clove garlic, sliced in small pieces

salt and pepper, to taste

knob of butter

20 g parsley, to garnish

Put the hazelnuts on a baking tray in the oven until slightly brown. Put in a tea towel and rub together to remove skin. Chop.

Melt butter in a frying pan, add shallots, and when brown, add snails and hazelnuts. Flambé with Grand Chartreuse. Add cream and garlic and simmer slowly for 5 minutes. Add salt and pepper and knob of butter.

To serve: put 6 snail dishes under a grill to warm, then in each hole place a snail with a sprig of parsley on top.

Serves: 6

**CHEF'S TIP**

**Tinned snails can be used for this dish, but their taste is not as sharp as fresh snails.**

# Poussin Françoise

50 g red/green pepper, sliced in small pieces

250 g poultry mousse, prepared from chicken breast, egg white, and cream

30 g sweet corn

6 baby chickens, boned

1500 ml chicken stock

40 g butter

30 g flour

15 g chives

pepper and salt, to taste

knob of butter

2 tbsp cream

Mix the peppers with chicken mousse and ½ sweet corn. Divide into 6 equal portions and stuff chickens carefully

with the mixture. Put string around the chickens in 3 places to hold together, but not too tightly as they expand during cooking. Cook chickens in stock for 10 minutes. Cover pan with greaseproof paper.

Make a roux with butter and flour. Slowly add 500 millilitres stock and boil. Leave to stand. Add chives and strain. Add pepper, salt, knob of butter, remaining sweet corn, and cream. Mix the sauce well.

Remove chickens from stock, put them on their backs on plates. Remove string. Pour sauce generously over the chickens, keeping some to be served separately in a sauce boat.

Serving suggestion: serve with rice pilaff or spinach with butter.

Serves: 6

# Mousse au Chocolat

4 tbsp water

125 g caster sugar

5 egg yolks

1 egg

150 g cooking chocolate, melted

100 ml double cream, beaten and refrigerated

12 macaroons

2 tbsp rum

Put water in a pan, then add sugar. When boiling, skim top with a skimmer and leave to cook until it reaches

285°F (140°C). Put into a bowl and then place the bowl in a few inches of cold water to cool the mixture.

Beat yolks and whole egg, add cooled sugar mix, and keep beating until lukewarm. Break chocolate into small pieces and melt in a bain-marie. Whisk melted chocolate, eggs, and sugar together. When smooth, add cream carefully. Half-fill 6 serving bowls with the mixture. Crumble 1 macaroon on top of each. Place remaining mousse on each, then place a whole macaroon which has been soaked in rum on top of that. Leave refrigerated for a couple of hours in the refrigerator before serving.

Serving suggestion: serve with petits fours secs.

Serves: 6

# The Ritz

The London **Ritz** must be one of the best known hotels in the world and its restaurant is equally famed — for its decor, its clientele and its food. In this, arguably the loveliest dining room in London, have dined the rich, the famous and the aristocratic since the beginning of the century. The restaurant's sumptuous elegance is legendary: the walls are panelled in polychromatic marbles of melting hues, and the great chandeliers are linked to each other by bronze garlands, "so that the room appears to be permanently en *fête*".

The kitchens of The Ritz, originally supervised by the great master Escoffier, are managed today by a young Yorkshireman, Michael Quinn. Chef Quinn served his apprenticeship with British Transport Hotels before taking up his first post at Claridge's. He was Chef de Cuisine at Gravetye Manor until his appointment in December 1981 as Maître Chef of The Ritz.

Michael Quinn has a unique philosophy about food: "It should have the qualities of life ... gentleness, lightness, fun, sincerity." His major innovation at The Ritz is the introduction of totally original and creative à la carte and set menus in English, all personally signed. His dishes, although remaining faithful to the basics of cooking, have moved away from Le Répertoire de Cuisine. Like Escoffier, Chef Quinn is a true creator.

*The Ritz*

Piccadilly, London, W1V 9DG
**01-493-8181**
**Lunch: 12.30 to 2.30 p.m. Monday — Saturday**
**12.30 to 2 p.m. Sunday**
**Dinner 6.30 to 11 p.m. Monday — Saturday**
**6.30 to 10.30 Sunday**
**Reservations**
**Managing Director: Michael R. Duffell**
**Chef: Michael Quinn, M.C.G.B.**

# Quenelles of Sweetbread
## with a tomato and vinegar sauce

1 oz pistachio nuts, finely chopped

8 oz sweetbread mousse

   a little chicken stock and white wine
for poaching

4 cooked artichoke bottoms (small no 4 size)

1 fl oz white wine

1 fl oz tarragon vinegar

3 fl oz tomato coulis

2 oz butter, softened

   fresh parsley

Mix ½ ounce of the pistachio nuts into the sweetbread mousse. Shape into 4 small quenelles using two dessert spoons. Gently poach in chicken stock and white wine.

Warm the artichoke bottoms through. Meanwhile, reduce down the white wine and tarragon vinegar, add the tomato coulis and bring to the boil, incorporating the softened butter near the end. Keep warm.

Drain the artichoke bottoms. Slice one side only, to form fans. Arrange a cooked quenelle next to the fantail of each artichoke bottom, and garnish with the fresh parsley. Add the remaining pistachio nuts to the tomato butter sauce. Pour a cordon of the sauce around each quenelle and artichoke. Serve while still hot.

Serves: 4

**CHEF'S TIP**

To make Tomato Coulis, sweat ½ ounce shallots in butter, add 1 tbsp Noilly Prat, and flesh of 8 tomatoes. Cook till tender. Add 1 teaspoon lemon juice and seasoning. Sieve finely.

---

# Roast Loin of Veal with Tarragon and Mustard Sauce

1 × 6 lb whole loin of veal, boned out and fatless, barded and wrapped to roast

1–2 veal kidneys, trimmed and skinned

4 oz shallots, finely chopped

12 tarragon leaves (extra to garnish)

   trimmings from veal, diced

   butter for frying (ans sauce)

3 tbsp tarragon vinegar

1 glass white wine

½ pt veal stock

¼ pt double cream

   tarragon mustard to taste

Roast the whole loin quickly in a hot oven, keeping it very pink. Cook the kidney by sealing it in a hot pan then cooking it, covered, on a bed of shallots and tarragon stems. Keep it pink/rosy also. When cooked, remove, and reserve shallots and tarragon.

In the roasting pan, sauté off the veal trimmings quickly until golden brown. Remove the grease, add a nut of butter and sweat down the shallots and tarragon for 5–10 minutes. Deglaze with tarragon vinegar and reduce, add white wine and reduce again. Add veal stock, cream, and tarragon mustard, reduce by ¼ and pass through a fine chinois. Add a knob of butter.

To serve: place 3 slices of veal on each plate in a fan shape. Arrange 1 slice of kidney in the centre. Pour the sauce around the meat and garnish with leaves of blanched tarragon.

Serves: 4

---

# Pears Poached in Red Wine, Honey and Armagnac

4 William pears

½ bottle red wine (Mouton Cadet Rouge)

½ bottle water

8 oz honey

2 measures Armagnac

2 sprigs of fresh thyme

1 cinnamon stick

   sprig of mint to decorate

   pastry cream mixed with cream to decorate

Peel and core the 4 pears and poach gently in the wine, water and honey mixed together. Add the Armagnac, thyme and cinnamon stick, and simmer until barely cooked. Remove pears and keep moist. Freeze ½ of the cooking liquid in a *sorbetière*. Reduce remainder by ¾ to a thin glaze (veil).

Slice each pear finely from the top (but not right through the base) around ⅓ of the pear only. Hold the pear firmly together and fill the core cavity with the iced crystals.

To serve: arrange on a plate with the slivers of pear opened out onto the plate to reveal the iced heart. Spoon the syrup onto the plate, decorate with fresh mint and pipe a pattern in the sauce with pastry cream and cream.

Serves: 4

# Tante Claire

**Tante Claire**, a small, warm and very cosy restaurant in Chelsea, was named after an aunt who enjoyed cooking and good food.

Owner/Chef Pierre Koffmann, who was born in the South West of France, attended the École Hotelière de Tarbes and spent several years working in different restaurants in France, Switzerland, and England before opening Tante Claire in 1977.

Chef Koffmann imports most of the ingredients used in his kitchen from France and, with his French kitchen team, produces imaginative cooking with unusual recipes, most of them created by himself. He says, "I enjoy cooking and mainly cook what I like and what I believe my clientele will like, not what they want," and he seems to be right because his two most popular dishes are the "Pieds de Cochon aux Morilles" and "L'Andouillette aux Fruits de Mer," both his personal favourites. Tante Claire's wine cellar, with over 100 different French wines, and the cheese board, with all cheeses being made in the traditional way in France by a Maître Fromager, are also very noteworthy.

Chef Koffmann's main project for the future is the opening of a bigger restaurant that will provide his clientele with more ambiance and his staff with more working room. But Tante Claire will always maintain the standards of cooking, quality, and personal service for which it has become justly renowned.

**68 Royal Hospital Road**
**London, SW3**

**01-352-6045**

**Lunch and Dinner: Monday — Friday**
**Reservations**

**Proprietor/Chef:**
**Pierre Koffmann, M.C.G.B.**

# Salade de Homard aux Fines Herbes

1 medium-sized lobster

2 tbsp olive oil

vinaigrette, for seasoning

1 avocado pear

1 chopped shallot

1 tsp parsley

1 tsp tarragon

1 tsp chives

1 head lettuce

225 g red salad ("raddichio")

100 g cooked French beans

1 breast of chicken

butter, to fry

1 peeled tomato

seasoning, to taste

Roast the lobster in the oven with olive oil. Put the vinaigrette with ½ avocado, shallots, parsley, tarragon, and chives in the liquidiser for a few seconds. Dress the salads in a large bowl. Cut the lobster into small pieces and put on top. Slice the breast of chicken and fry it in butter. When cooked, add to the salad and lobster. Add tomato and seasoning.

Serves: 4

# Pieds de Cochon aux Morilles

4 pigs trotters, boned

1 breast of chicken

butter, to sauté

1 small onion, chopped

20 dried morels, cleaned and soaked in water

200 g calf sweetbreads, blanched and cut in pieces

port, as needed

100 g cubed carrots

100 g cubed onions

veal stock, as needed

knob of butter

Braise the trotters in a slow oven for 3 hours while preparing the stuffing. Fry the breast of chicken in butter, then cut in cubes. In a separate pan, fry the onion in butter without colouring. Add the morels, then the sweetbreads, and leave to cook for 10 minutes. Deglaze pan with a drop of port, reduce heat, and add the cubed breast of chicken. Cook together for 3 minutes then set aside to cool.

When the trotters are cooked, remove them from the oven and put each, wide open, on a piece of tin foil and let cool. When cool, stuff with the chicken preparation, then roll them in the tin foil. Let sit for at least 2 hours.

Put cubed carrots and onions in a saucepan, put the trotters on top, and cook in the oven for 15 minutes at gas mark 7 (425°F/218°C). When cooked, deglaze with a glass of port and some veal stock. Remove the trotters, add a knob of butter to the sauce, then pour the sauce on top of the trotters and serve.

Serves: 4

# Feuilleté aux Poires

200 g puff pastry dough

1 tin preserved pears, sliced

200 g caster sugar, caramelised

fresh cream, optional

Roll the pastry for 2 minutes, cut 4 pieces into the shape of a pear, and lay them on a baking tray. Refrigerate the tray for 10 minutes, then bake for 10 minutes at gas mark 7 (425°F/218°C) and then for an additional 10 minutes at gas mark 5 (390°F/200°C). When cooked, put the sliced pears on top of the pastry and pour the hot caramel on top of it.

Serving suggestion: serve with fresh cream.

Serves: 4

# Tiger Lee Restaurant

**Tiger Lee Restaurant** is a classy, seven-year-old Cantonese restaurant located on Old Brompton Road. Many stars of stage and screen, prime ministers, politicians, heads of industry and finance have frequented the restaurant. The greatest accolade however is the constant flow of leading personalities from all walks of life in Hong Kong, and the many banquet parties for Chinese government officials.

Chef Cheong Hong met the owners whilst he was a chef working in London. Hong was born in Canton, China, and first became interested in cooking as an art form at the age of 17. After a year's apprenticeship at a local seafood restaurant, he travelled to Hong Kong where he studied at the Hong Kong Catering Institute for four years. He then worked for five years at an exclusive Hong Kong seafood restaurant and emerged as somewhat of an expert on exotic seafood preparations as well as a specialist of Ching Dynasty Banquets, which sometimes take weeks to prepare. Chef Hong then moved to England in the hopes of someday introducing his high class Oriental cuisine to the West.

Tiger Lee Restaurant opened in March 1979. The decor is simple and uncluttered, with soft lighting, champagne and celadon colours, plush armchairs, crystal glassware, silver service, and the sounds of running water emanating from the four stocked fish tanks, which are looked after by manager Stanley Lau.

**251 Old Brompton Road**
**London, SW5**

**01-370-2323**

**Dinner: 6 p.m. to 1 a.m. every night**
**Reservations**

**Proprietors: Tiger Lee Restaurants**
**Managing Director: Claudio Cassuto**
**Manager: Stanley Lau**
**Chef: Cheong Hong**

# Crispy Stuffed Eel Rolls

1 × 2 lb eel

2 oz ham, smoked preferred

3 oz bamboo shoots

1 oz ginger, sliced finely into 2 in sticks

whites of spring onions, sliced into 2 in strips, to taste

20 × 2 in slices coriander stalks or sprinkling of freshly ground white pepper

8 oz self-raising flour

12 fl oz water

2 fl oz vegetable oil, and as needed to sauté

1 small coffeespoon salt

Bone the eel by slicing through the underpart in a "V" shape and extracting bone. Flatten the eel, then use a sharp knife to slice flesh sideways into 2 inch strips without the skin (about 15–20 strips). Cut the ham into ¼ inch strips, 2 inches long. Cut the bamboo shoots the same way.

Fill the eel slices with a mixture of ham, bamboo shoots, ginger, onions, and coriander and roll tightly to seal. Make a batter by mixing the flour, water, oil, and salt together well. Heat a sauté pan with 2 inches of oil until sizzling, then reduce heat to half flame. Dip the eel rolls into batter, then drop into the pan and cook until golden. Serve whilst very hot and crispy.

Serves: 6

Wine: *Corton Charlemagne (Bonneau de Hartray) 1977, Hedges & Butler*

---

# Stuffed Fish

1 lb trout or bass

7 fl oz water

1 tbsp plain flour, and as needed to dust

½ egg white

1 flat coffeespoon salt

2 oz shelled prawns, finely chopped

finely chopped spring onions and fresh coriander leaves, to taste

vegetable oil, to fry

1 large dried black Chinese mushroom

2 tbsp oyster sauce

1 flat coffeespoon caster sugar

1 finely chopped spring onion

½ coffeespoon finely chopped fresh ginger

1½ coffeespoons cornflour

1 spoon vegetable oil

finely chopped crisp lettuce, to garnish

Scrape off scales and bone the fish by opening the stomach through the underside and removing flesh, bones, and inside gills. Incise edges of fish ¼ inch from opening in a downward direction, being careful to keep clear of skin. Cut with a sharp knife through the incision and gently pull away from skin. Remove flesh, leaving only complete head and tail and skin of body.

Scrape flesh from bones with a fork and chop flesh finely. Mix into a large bowl with 3 tablespoons water, plain flour, ½ egg white, and salt. Add prawns and beat together for 1 minute. Use your hands to blend the mixture and beat against inside of bowl for 5 minutes until it feels tender and starts to stick. Add finely chopped spring onions and coriander leaves to taste. Turn fish gently inside out and dust with flour, then return as before and fill with mix until firm and to exact fish shape. Dust outside with flour and deep fry in vegetable oil. After oil is sizzling, reduce to low heat, cover, and cook for 20 minutes until golden.

To prepare sauce: soak mushroom in hot water for 15 minutes then chop finely. Place mushroom, oyster sauce, sugar, spring onion, coriander (to taste), remaining water, ginger, and cornflour in a pan. Heat and stir until mixture rises. Add vegetable oil, stir again quickly, then remove from heat.

Slice fish into ½ inch slices, pour sauce over sliced fish, and serve piping hot on a garnish of chopped crisp lettuce.

Serves: 6

Wine: *Vouvray, still or sparkling Marc Bredif*

# Waltons of Walton Street

**Waltons of Walton Street,** now ten years old, is internationally famous for its modern interpretation of traditional English recipes. Inventive new Chef David Nicholls has extended the menu to include such delicacies as Moneybag of Salmon and Noisette of Veal with ribbons of vegetables. While Head Chef at the Old Lodge, Limpsfield, Chef Nicholls became the youngest chef ever to win an Egon Ronay star. He buys daily from the nearby markets to ensure freshness, but does not follow *la nouvelle cuisine*, which he describes as "bikini food — small portions and elaborate garnishes"!

The restaurant's high society clientele is regally enveloped in opulent elegance: the walls are covered in silk and dark mirrors, and the lamplit tables, each adorned with Georg Jensen cutlery and Royal Copenhagen china, are well spaced for privacy. The service is top class.

Waltons is also known for its extensive wine cellar that is rated internationally as one of the most outstanding available in all of Great Britain. The wines are French and German and featured are 90 château bottled clarets and more than 40 Burgundies. Choices from an extensive list of champagnes, liqueurs, and vintage cognacs are also available.

---

## WALTONS OF WALTON STREET

**121 Walton Street
London, SW3**

**01-584-0204**

**Lunch: 12.30 to 2.30 p.m. (2 p.m. Sunday)
Dinner: 7.30 to 11.30 p.m. (10.30 p.m. Sunday)
Reservations**

**Proprietor: Waltons Restaurants Ltd.
Chef: David Nicholls**

---

# Mille Feuilles de Foie Gras aux Poireaux

2 lb young leeks

bay leaf

peppercorns

½ pt white wine

2 tbsp olive oil

¼ pt white wine vinegar

1 fresh, cooked foie gras

Wash the leeks whole and cook with the bay leaf, peppercorns, white wine, oil and vinegar until tender. Leave for 24 hours.

Remove leeks and reduce liquid almost to a glace. Brush 8 ramekin moulds with the liquid and place thin slices of foie gras in the bottom of each. Continue with alternate layers of liquid and foie gras.

Leave to set for 6 hours. Tuen out and serve with hot slices of brioche.

Serves: 8
Wine: *Sancerre*

---

# Lamb Cutlet Soufflé

8 lamb cutlets

4 oz chicken mousse

pigs' caul

2 oz lambs' sweetbreads

4 oz finely chopped vegetables
(carrot, celery, shallots)

8 tbsp red wine vinegar

4 cloves garlic

half a bulb of fennel

½ pt lamb jus

Ricard

The cutlets should have just the eyes of meat remaining, with long cutlet bones. Seal them in butter flavoured with whole fennel and garlic and allow to cool. Place a spoonful of chicken mousse on the eye of lamb and wrap in pigs' caul. Cook in hot fat in the oven for 3–4 minutes.

Braise the sweetbreads with the vegetables and vinegar in the oven for 25–30 minutes.

To prepare sauce: flambé the Ricard and add lamb jus. Reduce to required consistency. Place a small bouquet of sweetbreads at head of plate, and serve the cutlets on sauce.

Serves: 4

---

# Terrine du Cassis

½ pt milk

8 oz sugar

8 eggs

11 leaves of gelatine

⅓ pt syrup of cassis

1 pt lightly whipped double cream

1 lb frozen blackcurrants

Make a crème Anglaise with the milk, sugar and eggs. While hot, add gelatine. Allow to cool, then add syrup of cassis.

Fold in whipped cream. Add frozen blackcurrants. Place in a terrine and leave to set.

Serves: 10

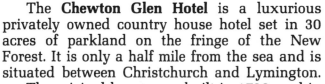

# Chewton Glen Hotel

The **Chewton Glen Hotel** is a luxurious privately owned country house hotel set in 30 acres of parkland on the fringe of the New Forest. It is only a half mile from the sea and is situated between Christchurch and Lymington.

The original house was built in 1732, and in 1837, it was bought by Colonel George Marryat. His brother, Captain Frederick Marryat RN, stayed at the house in the 1840s and gathered material for his famous novel, *The Children of the New Forest*. After a succession of owners, the house became a hotel in 1962. The Skan family bought it in 1967 and have developed and improved the hotel since then. It now has 55 beautifully appointed bedrooms and suites, as well as the Marryat Room Restaurant, renowned for its delicate French cuisine and impeccable service.

The oak-panelled restaurant has a warm, relaxed atmosphere. French windows open onto a terrace and gently sloping lawns. The room is candlelit in the evenings, and both table d'hôte and à la carte menus are offered for lunch and dinner. Chef Pierre Chevillard expertly prepares his French dishes with a bias towards *la nouvelle cuisine*. He believes in using fresh, preferably local produce, which is lightly cooked to preserve flavour. The wine list is very extensive, with more than 300 choices in a wide price range covering every region of France as well as several other major wine producing countries.

## Chewton Glen Hotel

**New Milton, Hampshire**
**04252-5341**
**Lunch: 12.30 to 2 p.m.**
**Dinner: 7.30 to 9.30 p.m.**
**Daily**
**Reservations**

**Proprieter: Martin Skan**
**Chef: Pierre Chevillard**

# Terrine de Poireaux et Artichauts

15 medium-sized leeks (12 in long
   if possible)

10 carrots

 8 artichoke bottoms

   a little flour and lemon juice

500 g salted lean green gammon, without fat
   or sinew

   juice of 5 lemons

 2 egg whites

240 ml olive oil

   salt and pepper

400 ml olive oil

150 ml truffle juice

   salt and pepper

Cook the leeks whole in salted water, also the carrots in a separate pan. Cook the artichoke bottoms in water with a little flower and lemon juice. Refresh all the vegetables under running cold water to stop the cooking, and drain well. Thinly slice the carrots and artichoke, and wrap in a cloth, with the leeks, to dry.

Cut the gammon into small dice and process in a food processor until a smooth paste is formed. Add the juice of 2 lemons, and the egg whites and continue mixing. With the machine running, add olive oil slowly, allowing it to thicken as for mayonnaise. Season with a little salt and pepper.

Line the sides and bottom of a long terrine (approximately 12 inches long) with a little of the mixture. Place 5 of the leeks side-by-side at the bottom. Mix the sliced carrot and artichoke in a bowl with ¾ of the gammon mixture — add ½ of this mixture to the terrine in a layer over the leeks. Place 5 more leeks in the terrine and cover with the remaining carrot-and-gammon mixture. Finish with a final layer of leeks and cover with the remaining original gammon mixture.

Place the terrine in a bain-marie (or another container filled with water) and cook at gas mark 6 (400°F/200°C) for 40 minutes. Allow to cool. Eat the same day if possible.

To serve: mix together the juice of 3 lemons, olive oil, truffle juice and seasoning to make a vinaigrette sauce. Pour a little over individual slices of terrine.

Serves: 15

Wine: *Chablis Premier Cru Fourchaume, 1982*

# Filet d'Agneau Malleroy

 1 large celeriac root (about 2.30 g
   before cleaning)

   a little lemon juice

100 ml double cream

   salt and papper

 2 best ends of lamb

60 g unsalted butter

10 g anchovy fillets

100 ml dry white wine

400 ml veal stock

Peel celeriac and place immediately in a bowl of water with some lemon juice until required. Cut celeriac into pieces, place in boiling salted water and cook thoroughly. Drain, liquidise, add the cream and seasoning and mix together. Put the mixture into a small bowl and keep warm.

Roast the lamb at gas mark 6 (400°F/200°C) for 20–25 minutes. Whilst this is cooking, liquidise the butter and anchovy fillets together. When the lamb is cooked, leave to cool, and remove. Pour the fat from the baking tray and deglaze with white wine and veal stock. Reduce by ½ and whisk in the anchovy butter a little at a time.

Cut the fat and bone from the lamb. Slice lamb into 2 portions per each best end (8 slices per pertion). Arrange the slices of lamb on plates in the shape of a fan and place 1 tablespoon of celeriac purée in the middle. Coat lamb with the sauce. Serve with green vegetables (broccoli, mangetouts and French beans) on a separate plate.

Serves: 4

Wine: *Château Gruaud Larose 1976*

# Gravetye Manor

**Gravetye Manor** is an Elizabethan manor house set in the famous gardens created by William Robinson and surrounded by a thousand acres of forest. The interior has log fires and antique furniture as well as the modern comforts of central heating and private bathrooms, all presided over by Peter Herbert, whose father and grandfather were both hoteliers. Mr Herbert trained in Austria and France and, in the course of his training, became interested primarily in small, first-class hotels and restaurants.

Gravetye Manor, indeed, boasts one of the best restaurants in Great Britain. It is now twenty-five years old and features classic French and English dishes prepared by Chef Allan Garth. Chef Garth came to Gravetye Manor nine years ago as second chef and took over the kitchen in 1981. He has continued to maintain the reputation gained by the two previous chefs of the last seventeen years, ably assisted by the manager Helmut Kircher who has been at Gravetye for the past decade.

There is an outstanding wine list that presents more than 350 choices from Europe's classic wine regions. The service in the restaurant is unhurried, and the atmosphere of Gravetye Manor is one of relaxation, space and comfort.

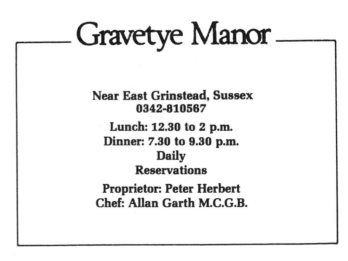

# Gravetye Manor

**Near East Grinstead, Sussex**
**0342-810567**

**Lunch: 12.30 to 2 p.m.**
**Dinner: 7.30 to 9.30 p.m.**
**Daily**
**Reservations**

**Proprietor: Peter Herbert**
**Chef: Allan Garth M.C.G.B.**

# Saddle of Rabbit

## stuffed with chicken and pistachio

4 saddles of rabbit

150 g chicken breast

25 g pistachio nuts, peeled

1 egg white

salt and pepper

250 ml double cream

150 g pigs' caul

750 ml rabbit stock (made from the bones)

3 shallots, chopped

3 button mushrooms, sliced

30 ml Noilly Prat

400 ml cream

12 basil leaves

Remove the fillet from the saddles. Discard all sinews and use the bones for the stock. Cut fillets in half lengthwise, and beat out a little.

To prepare the mousse: liquidise or mince the chicken and pistachio nuts twice. Place in a bowl over ice. Beat in the egg white and the cream slowly. Season.

Place 4 halves of rabbit on a table to form an oblong and pipe the mousse on to them. Place the other halves on top, season, and wrap in the caul. Sauté in butter and place in a moderate oven at gas mark 3 (325 °F/160 °C) for about 15 minutes. Remove from oven and rest for 5 minutes.

To prepare sauce: put the stock, shallots, mushrooms, and Noilly Prat into a pan and reduce to ½. Add the cream and basil, and reduce a little more until the right consistency is reached. Season to taste.

To serve: carve rabbit at an angle and place on a bed of fresh noodles, accompanied by the basil sauce.

Serves: 4

# Braised Salmon with Pike Mousse

250 g pike, skinned and boned

salt and pepper

1 whole egg

300 ml double cream

4 × 125 g pieces salmon fillet

600 ml fish stock

100 ml white wine

2 shallots, chopped

25 g white mushrooms, sliced

3 tomatoes, chopped

200 ml double cream

salt and pepper

chopped chives to serve

To prepare mousse: put the pike flesh through the mincer twice. Season, add the egg and press mixture through a fine sieve. Place in a bowl over ice, and slowly add the double cream with a wooden spoon.

Spread the mousse over the fillets of salmon and smooth with a palette knife. Place in a buttered ovenproof dish with 500 ml stock and braise in a hot oven gas mark 7 (425 °F/220 °C) for 15 minutes. Glaze under the grill.

To prepare sauce: place the remainig fish stock and wine in a pan with the shallots, mushrooms and tomatoes. Reduce by ½. Add the cream and reduce a little more. Season.

To serve: place the braised salmon on the sauce and sprinkle with chopped chives.

Serves: 4

# Chocolate Mousse with Coffee Sauce

125 g bitter chocolate

50 g milk chocolate

1 whole egg, 7 egg yolks

300 g cream (half double and half single)

20 ml crème de cacao

10 ml brandy

coffee essence

3 tbsp sugar

20 ml coffee liqueur

3 tbsp whipped cream

Melt the chocolate in a bowl standing in warm water. Whisk the whole egg with 1 egg yolk over a pan of hot water until it becomes a thick sabayon. Lightly whip the 300 grams cream, crème de cacao, and brandy together. Fold melted chocolate into the eggs, making sure they are about the same temperature. Lastly, fold in the cream. Pour the mousse into a bowl and refrigerate for about 4 hours.

To prepare sauce: whisk the remaining 6 yolks, essence, sugar, and coffee liqueur in a bowl over hot water until thick and the yolks are cooked. Mix in the 3 tablespoons whipped cream. Chill.

To serve: when set, make the mousse into cigar-chaped quenelles and place on the chilled coffee sauce.

Serves: 4

# Lythe Hill Hotel, Auberge de France

The **Lythe Hill Hotel** is a beautifully timbered, 14th century farmhouse that is now a supremely comfortable country hotel with a glowing reputation for good food.

In its elegant restaurant, **Auberge de France,** you can enjoy the finest dishes and wines of France. Here the soft lighting reflects on copper pans and silver candelabras. The oak beamed and panelled dining room, with picture windows overlooking the gardens and one of the finest views in Surrey, is a truly romantic setting. There is also an intimate bar overlooking the hotel's own terrace and lake.

Chef Bernard Guillot, who is originally from Lyon and has been at Lythe Hill for five years, expertly prepares not only the classic dishes, but also his own specialities. It is French cooking at its best. There is an extensive à la carte menu, and some of the dishes are cooked right at the table.

The wine list includes a good choice of imported as well as English wines, and the excellent house wine is bottled in France exclusively for the Auberge de France.

Philip Ford, managing director of the Lythe Hill Hotel, can be justly proud of the warm atmosphere and superb cuisine of this lovely French restaurant.

**Petworth Road**
**Haslemere, Surrey**
**0428-51251**
**Open mid-February to Christmas**
**Lunch: Wednesday — Sunday**
**12.30 to 2.30 p.m.**
**Dinner: Tuesday — Sunday**
**7.30 to 11 p.m.**
**Reservations**
**Proprietor:**
**Haslemere Hotels, Ltd.**
**Chef: Bernard Guillot**

# Grenadin de Veau Jeanette

butter, to sauté

8 medallions of veal, 100 g each

seasoned flour, to dust

1 glass white wine

2 tsp tomato purée

½ tsp chopped tarragon

300 ml Hollandaise sauce

4 fresh artichoke bottoms, warmed

500 g duxelles of mushrooms, heated

2 tbsp chopped fresh parsley

Melt butter in a sauté pan. Dip the medallions in seasoned flour and colour in the butter for 6–8 minutes, depending on the thickness of the medallions. Remove medallions from pan and keep warm. Drain fat from pan and deglaze pan with white wine. Reduce by ⅔ until slightly thick. Stir in the tomato purée and tarragon, then gently blend in the Hollandaise sauce.

Fill the warm artichoke bottoms with the hot duxelles of mushrooms. Dress neatly in a dish with the veal, then coat the medallions with the sauce. Finish with chopped parsley and serve immediately.

Serves: 4

Wine: *Château Calon Ségur,*
*St. Estèphe Medoc, 1970*

---

# Supreme of Chicken Souvaroff

50 g butter

4 tbsp flour

4 × 200 g supremes of chicken

200 ml veal stock

150 ml double cream

100 ml port

100 g goose liver mousse

1 tbsp brandy

4 thin slices of truffle

Melt the butter in a sauté pan. Flour the supremes and colour in the butter for 3 minutes per side. Drain off the fat, add veal stock, cream, and port reduced by ½ to the sauce. Remove from heat and blend in the goose liver mousse with a fork. Add brandy to the sauce and coat each supreme with sauce and decorate each with a slice of truffle.

Serves: 4

Wine: *Fixin la Maziere,*
*Domaine Marion, 1974*

**CHEF'S TIP**

**Goose liver mousse mixed with half its original weight of butter blends better with any sauce.**

---

# Tarte Lyonnaise

200 g flour

100 g butter

25 ml water

pinch of salt

100 g fresh bread crumbs

250 ml milk

100 g sugar

30 ml kirsch

50 g ground almonds

4 egg yolks

2 egg whites, beaten very stiffly

One hour in advance, prepare shortcrust pastry with the first 4 ingredients. Roll the pastry in a flan case. Soak the bread crumbs in milk, then put bread crumbs and all other ingredients into the flan case. Bake for 30 minutes at gas mark 6 (400°F/205°C).

Serves: 4

# Manleys Restaurant

**Manleys Restaurant** is located in the small West Sussex area of Storrington, nestled at the foot of the South Downs. The house was built during the reign of Queen Anne. The dining room, candlelit in the evenings, looks out onto a small courtyard, which is gently floodlit on summer evenings. In the winter, the bar and lounge, with their genuine old beams, are made cosy and warm by a huge log fire. The atmosphere is most welcoming and comfortable.

The menu is mostly classic French with a few Austrian and Swiss dishes reflecting owner/chef Karl Löderer's nationality and training. His specialities include Venison Maison, Crêpe Pêcheur, and his own Pêche Manley, among others.

Everything is cooked to order with the finest and best quality ingredients available. The menu is comprehensive and changes several times a year. On Sunday, there is a table d'hôte luncheon that has proved extremely popular. That menu changes every four or five weeks and always boasts unusual and interesting dishes.

The small, dedicated staff works well as a team and is run by manager Tom Deegan and Mrs. Löderer.

In addition to the excellent cuisine, this eight-year-old restaurant also features an above-average wine list that is worth your attention. There are also two vintage house wines from which to choose.

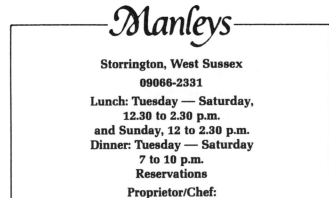

**Manleys**

**Storrington, West Sussex**
**09066-2331**

Lunch: Tuesday — Saturday,
12.30 to 2.30 p.m.
and Sunday, 12 to 2.30 p.m.
Dinner: Tuesday — Saturday
7 to 10 p.m.
**Reservations**

Proprietor/Chef:
Karl Löderer, M.C.G.B.

# Crêpe Pêcheur

1 knob of butter
1 tbsp onions, sliced
1 small green pepper
1 small red pepper
2 tbsp double cream
1 lb mixed brown and white flesh crabmeat
2 medium-sized shallots
1 clove crushed garlic
1 dessertspoon Dijon mustard
salt and pepper, to taste

flour, eggs, and bread crumbs, as needed
oil, to fry
4 thin pancakes, prepared

To make pancake filling: heat the butter then add onions, peppers, and cream. Bring to a boil, then add crabmeat, shallots, garlic, mustard, salt, and pepper.

Fill the pancakes and fold each into a triangular shape. Dip in flour, eggs, and bread crumbs. Deep fry for 5 minutes on medium heat.

Serving suggestion: garnish with lettuce and a lemon wedge and serve with cocktail sauce.

Serves: 4

Wine: *Sancerre*

# Médaillons de Chevreuil Baden-Baden

1 wine glass red wine
1 bay leaf
1 tsp crushed peppercorns
1 tbsp shallots
8 lb prime Scottish saddle of venison
ground pepper and salt, to taste
pinch of sweet ground paprika
oil, to sauté
knob of butter
2 tbsp double cream
wild cherries and chopped parsley, to garnish

Mix the red wine, bay leaf, peppercorns, and shallots together to make a marinade. Bone the venison, leaving the fillet. Trim well and marinate in the marinade for 4 days, refrigerated.

Cut 3 medallions per person, ½ inch thick. Beat out and season well with pepper, salt, and paprika. Fry quickly for 30 seconds on each side (*do not overcook*) and place in a heated dish.

Thicken the marinade with a knob of butter and the cream; reduce gently to make a sauce. Pour the sauce over the venison and garnish with wild cherries and parsley.

Serving suggestion: serve with potato croquettes.

Serves: 6

Wine: *Châteauneuf du Pape*

# Salzburger Nockerin

5 egg whites
4 oz granulated sugar
2 egg yolks
1 dessertspoon flour
drop of vanilla essence
zest of 2 medium-sized lemons
zest of 1 large orange
1 oz butter
1 tbsp double cream

1 tbsp honey
1 measure rum, or to taste

Whip egg whites stiffly then add sugar gently. When sugar is dissolved, add egg yolks, flour, vanilla essence, and lemon and orange zest. Mix together evenly. Form 3 large mounds (*nockerln*) with the mixture.

Melt butter, double cream, and honey together in an ovenproof dish until warm, then add nockerln. Bake for 10 minutes at gas mark 6 (400°F/205°C).

Warm the rum in a ladle and set aflame. Pour rum over the cooked nockerln and serve immediately.

Serves: 3

Wine: *Muscadet de Beaumes de Venise, chilled slightly*

# The Marquee

**The Marquee** is a pretty restaurant situated by the River Lea in the centre of historic Hertford. Designed by its owner Norman Swallow, the restaurant is stylishly decorated in warm fabrics and features a beautiful 18th century birdcage chandelier. Off the main first floor dining area, which overlooks the river, is a small comfortable sitting area where one may relax over coffee and liqueurs. The sunny ground floor dining room with french doors opening on to the outdoor terrace by the river is an ideal spot for lunch.

Chef de Cuisine Ernst Stark has produced an interesting and unusual menu offering a selection of English and international dishes. Chef Stark trained in his native Germany before working at Carrier's. He was then invited to be the first chef at Waltons of Walton Street, where he achieved international acclaim.

There is a comprehensive and well-balanced wine list featuring over 150 wines at competitive prices.

## THE MARQUEE

1 Bircherley Green, Hertford

0992-58999

Lunch: 12.30 to 2 p.m.
Dinner: 7.30 to 10 p.m.
Daily
Reservations

Proprietors: Roger Wren,
Norman Victor Swallow
Chef: Ernst Stark

# Iced Stilton Soup

2 medium potatoes

1 large onion

2 leeks

  butter for frying

1 pt chicken stock

1 pt single cream

  salt and pepper

½ lb Stilton or other blue cheese, finely grated

2 cooking apples

bunch of chives, chopped

bunch of parsley, chopped

Peel and chop the vegetables and fry lightly in butter in a thick-bottomed pan. Add stock and simmer for 20 minutes. Blend or sieve. Add cream, seasoning and grated cheese. Leave to stand to absorb flavour, then chill.

Just before serving, finely dice the apples and add with chopped chives and parsley. Serve with fingers of hot brown toast and lemon butter.

Serves: 4

---

# Pork Fillet with Prunes

1 large pork fillet

  seasoned flour for coating

4 oz butter

10 stoned prunes

1 tbsp finely chopped onion

1 glass non-vintage port

½ pt double cream

  salt and pepper

  chopped parsley to garnish

Trim fat from pork, cut into 8 pieces and beat flat. Coat with seasoned flour, seal on both sides for 1 minute in heated butter, and fry lightly. Garnish with prunes, then place in a warmed dish and keep warm.

To prepare sauce: remove excess butter from pan, add onion and port and reduce. Add cream. Season to taste. When sauce thickens, remove from heat, add a knob of butter and pour over meat.

Serve garnished with chopped parsley.

Serves: 4

**CHEF'S TIP**

Beat out pork fillets against the grain of the meat, using small metal bat or wooden mallet. This prevents any meat from becoming tough and sinewy.

---

# Christmas Pudding

2 oz currants

4 oz raisins

3 oz sultanas

2 oz mixed peel

4 oz suet

1 oz ground almonds

4 oz brown sugar

4 oz bread crumbs

2 oz flour

  pinch of salt

¼ oz ground ginger

¼ oz mixed spice

3 oz apples, grated

2 oz black treacle

zest and juice of ½ lemon

zest and juice of ½ orange

2 eggs

1 pt milk

½ wine glass stout

½ wine glass beer

1 measure rum

1 measure port

1 measure brandy

Mix all the dry ingredients together. Add liquid and mix well. Leave in a cool place for 3–4 days. Place into greased basin, cover with greaseproof paper and a cloth tied down firmly. Steam for 6–7 hours. Serve with brandy butter.

Serves: 4–6

# Oakley Court Hotel

**Oakley Court,** built in 1858 for Sir Ronald Saye, is now a hotel of distinction, standing in a 35 acre estate, with gardens sloping gently down to the banks of the Thames. Inside, the luxury is refined and understated, with impeccable service, in keeping with the traditional English-country-house style of restful lounges, library and billiard room. Every bedroom is superbly appointed to high standards of comfort, and there is full waiter service from bar to lounges and library. Only 3 miles from Windsor, Oakley Court is ideally located for London, Heathrow and the historic Royal Counties.

Its elegant Oak Leaf Restaurant, which seats 120, is renowned for the modern French and traditional English cuisine of one of England's finest chefs, Murdo MacSween. His early training was at BTH Hotels, and he became head chef of both the Elms Hotel, Worcester and Waltons, London. Chef MacSween likes to keep presentation simple, though attractive, and he specialises in terrines, soufflés, fish, and pastry — try his pâté of scallops and sole served with a light tomato sauce, and refresh your palate with a complementary passion fruit sorbet.

The Oakley Court wine list is above average and wide ranging, with plenty of choice in the medium price range, and a Côte de Provence house wine.

---

## Oakley Court Hotel

**Windsor Road, Water Oakley
Windsor, Berkshire**

**Maidenhead 0628-74141**

**Lunch 12.30 to 2 p.m.
Dinner: 7.30 to 10 p.m.
Daily
Reservations**

**Proprietor: Celebrated Country Hotel Group
Chef: Murdo MacSween M.C.G.B.**

The Sundial Restaurant

The Castle Hotel

# Smoked Salmon and Avocado Soufflé

1 pt milk

1 oz butter

3 oz flour

2 whole eggs

6 egg yolks

3 oz cheese

seasoning

4 egg whites

2 oz smoked salmon

2 oz avocado

6 green peppercorns

Boil ¾ of the milk with the butter. Mix remainder of milk with flour and whole eggs to a paste. Add to the boiled milk and cook until smooth (panada). Add egg yolks, cheese and seasoning at end.

Butter and chill 4 small soufflé dishes. Whisk egg whites. Mix 4 ounces of panada mixture with smoked salmon, avocado and green peppercorns. Fold in egg whites and season.

Take soufflé dishes from refrigerator and fill with mixture. Glaze the top under the grill, then cook in moderate oven gas mark 3 (325°F/170°C) for 10 minutes.

Serves: 4

---

# Fillet of Veal Stuffed with Garlic Cheese
### served with a butter sauce

4 × 6 oz noisettes of veal

4 oz garlic cheese

6 oz unsalted butter

1 tsp chopped shallots

1 oz white wine vinegar

2 oz dry white wine

2 tbsp double cream

few chives, finely chopped

Slit each noisette of veal to form a pocket and stuff with garlic cheese. Cut butter into small cubes to soften.

Put shallots, vinegar and wine in a pan and reduce by ½. Add double cream and boil. Remove from heat, whisk in the butter and add chives. Keep warm.

Sauté veal, place on serving dish and serve with butter sauce poured over.

Serves: 4
Wine: *Meursault*

---

# Burnt Cream

1½ pt double cream

6 egg yolks

2 oz sugar

vanilla essence

grated rind of 1 lemon

fine brown sugar to glaze

Boil the double cream. Mix together egg yolks, sugar, vanilla essence and lemon rind. Mix together the boiled cream and egg mixture. Return to the pan and cook until thick. Pour into individual dishes and allow to set. Sprinkle with fine brown sugar, glaze under the grill and serve.

Serves: 4

# Plumber Manor

**Plumber Manor** has been a country home of the Prideaux-Brune family since the early 17th century and is now being run as a "Restaurant with Bedrooms" under the personal supervision of Richard and Alison Prideaux-Brune.

The Manor makes a perfect halfway setting between London and Cornwall and is within easy reach of Bath, Salisbury, Sherborne, Bournemouth, and the historic splendours of Longleat, Stourhead, and Wilton. The coast is less than 30 miles away, and several golf courses, fishing on the Stour, and riding are all close at hand.

There are six very comfortable bedrooms, all with private bathrooms, that are accessible from a charming gallery hung with portraits of the family.

The restaurant at Plumber Manor, part of which is in the elegant old drawing room, seats 70 and provides an exceptional standard of cuisine and wines. The cuisine is Anglo/French and is administered by Chef Brian Prideaux-Brune, Richard's brother. Brian trained extensively in London and has created many of the items appearing on the menu. The wine list offers a comprehensive choice of French and German vintages, most at reasonable prices.

The restaurant, which opened in 1973, is actually made up of three separate dining rooms that have been designed to afford guests with a maximum amount of comfort. The colour scheme of blue with light blue linen on large tables and the paintings hanging on the walls add to an already pleasant eating atmosphere.

---

## PLUMBER MANOR

**Sturminster Newton
Dorset**

**0258-72507**

**Dinner: Tuesday — Sunday
Reservations**

**Proprietor: Richard Prideaux-Brune
Chef: Brian Prideaux-Brune**

---

# Paupiettes of Smoked Salmon with Avocado Fromage

2 ripe medium avocados, peeled, stoned, and chopped roughly

juice of 1 lemon

¼ lb cream cheese, Philadelphia preferred

generous dash Worcestershire sauce

1 tsp finely grated onion

salt and pepper, to taste

½ pt double cream

24 slices smoked salmon, each 3 by 4 in

sprigs of watercress, to garnish

lemon wedges, to garnish

To prepare avocado fromage: purée the chopped avocado with lemon juice until smooth. Add the cream cheese gradually and blend until smooth. Transfer to a large bowl, then add a generous dash of Worcestershire sauce, the grated onion, and a good seasoning of salt and pepper. Whisk the cream until thick, then fold in. Check and adjust seasoning if needed. Cover the bowl with cling foil and chill for 15–20 minutes.

Put a dollop of the avocado fromage in the centre of each slice of smoked salmon and roll up carefully. Place 3 paupiettes on each place, garnish each with a sprig of watercress and wedge of lemon and serve.

Serves: 8

# Chicken Indienne

8 good-sized chicken breasts, boned

4 small bananas, finely sliced

24 white grapes, halved and pitted

4 tbsp crushed hazelnuts

2 oz butter

12 fl oz basic curry sauce

8 fl oz double cream

Remove the fillet (the underside flap) from the chicken breasts, then pound (not too vigorously) each until flat. Flatten each fillet. Stuff each breast with ½ banana, 6 grape halves, and ⅛ hazelnuts. Place fillet on top and fold the ends over to make a rectangular parcel.

Place the breasts, rounded side up, close together in a shallow roasting tin in which the butter has been melted. Bake in a preheated oven at gas mark 5 (375°F/190°C) for 20–25 minutes, basting frequently, until cooked through and golden brown.

Make up the curry sauce or use prepared sauce and whisk in the cream. Transfer chicken to a shallow flameproof dish and pour the sauce over. Put over gentle heat until bubbling and slightly thickened. Remove from heat and serve.

Serves: 8

# Athollbrose Plumber Manor Style

¾ pt whipping cream

clear honey, to taste

whisky, to taste

2 tbsp flaked almonds

Whip the whipping cream until thick. Gently fold in the clear honey and whisky to taste. Add the flaked almonds. Put into glass bowls and chill. Serve cold.

Serves: 4

# Restaurant Seventy Four

**Restaurant Seventy Four** was opened in December 1983 in one of Canterbury's most important historic buildings, Wincheap House, which dates from around 1560. The original 16th century front door now forms the entrance to the lounge, and there are two magnificent fireplaces, one of which was uncovered during the renovation. Chef Patron Ian McAndrew and his wife Jane take justifiable pride in the building and the relaxed enjoyable atmosphere they have created. The excellent food is matched by attentive service, helped by a great care never to overbook.

Chef McAndrew trained under Anton Mossiman at the Dorchester before joining Eastwell Manor where he was Head Chef for 3½ years. He is very much influenced by *la nouvelle cuisine*, attending the markets regularly to select his own produce, and his specialities are any fish dishes and hot and cold terrines. The menu changes every week. There is also a cocktail lounge, and the wine list has been carefully selected to offer quality wines at outstanding value — with several house wines.

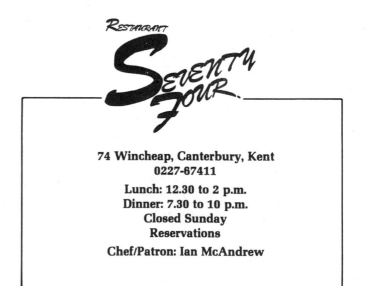

**74 Wincheap, Canterbury, Kent**
**0227-67411**

**Lunch: 12.30 to 2 p.m.**
**Dinner: 7.30 to 10 p.m.**
**Closed Sunday**
**Reservations**

**Chef/Patron: Ian McAndrew**

# Oysters and Spinach Mousse

### in a light puff pastry case

3–4 oysters

6 fl oz fish stock

2 fl oz white wine

1 oz leeks, cut in julienne

1 oz celery, cut in julienne

1 oz carrot, cut in julienne

2 oz butter, in small pieces

¼ oz green peppercorns

salt and pepper

1 individual puff pastry case

2 oz spinach purée

½ fl oz whipping cream

Shell and wash the oysters thoroughly, then poach them for a few seconds in the fish stock and white wine. Remove them, add the julienne of vegetables and poach until cooked but still crisp. Remove vegetables.

Reduce the liquor to ⅛ and whisk in the butter. Return the oysters and the julienne of vegetables to the sauce and add the green peppercorns. Correct the seasoning and keep warm.

Warm the pastry case. Heat the spinach purée with the cream and pour into the pastry case. Place the oysters on the spinach, pour the sauce over and arrange the vegetables attractively on top.

Serves: 1

Wine: *Chablis*

# Fillet of English Lamb

1 best end of lamb

salt and pepper

½ oz butter

2 artichoke bottoms

2 fl oz white wine

3 fl oz lamb stock

tarragon stalks, and 6–8 blanched leaves to garnish

6 fl oz whipping cream

Season the meat and sauté in ½ the butter, leaving it pink. When cooked, remove from pan and tip off excess fat.

Remove the chokes from the artichoke bottoms, slice into about 4 slices, season and brown lightly in the pan on both sides with the remaining butter. Remove from pan.

Add the white wine to the pan and reduce. Add the lamb stock and tarragon stalks, reduce by at least ½. Add the cream and reduce until thickened. Correct seasoning and strain.

To serve: pour the sauce onto the plates, arrange artichoke slices down the centre, then arrange slices of lamb (6 each) on top of the artichoke. Garnish with tarragon leaves on the lamb.

Serves: 2

Remove all the bone and fat from the best end, leaving only the eye of the meat which should be about 6 inches long.

Wine: *Chassagne Montrachet*

# Brown Bread Ice Cream

2 egg yolks

4 oz caster sugar

½ pt milk

¼ pt double cream

¼ vanilla pod

1 oz brown sugar

2 slices brown bread

½ measure Madeira

2 oz sugar

¼ oz glucose

Whisk the egg yolks and caster sugar until white. Bring the milk and cream to the boil with the vanilla pod, and pour onto the egg mixture, whisking all the time. Return to the pan and stir continuously over a low heat until thickened (do not overheat or the mixture will curdle). Allow to cool and strain into an ice cream machine or freeze in an ice cream tray, whisking from time to time.

Sprinkle the brown sugar over the bread, place in a hot oven until sugar has caramelised and bread has toasted. Allow to cool. Break into crumbs in a liquidiser. When the egg mixture is almost set, mix in the brown bread and Madeira. Refrigerate.

To make caramel sauce: boil 2 ounces of sugar with glucose in enough water to cover until caramelised. Cool slightly then add cold water until thin enough to pour. Serve poured over the ice cream.

Serves: 4

# The Sundial Restaurant

**The Sundial Restaurant** is a 17th century cottage that has been converted into a comfortable French-style auberge restaurant. It is owned and run by Guiseppe and Laurette Bertoli, who 17 years ago began to provide customers with inventive dishes together with polite but informal service.

Fresh ingredients, in general, are delivered daily, and Chef Bertoli personally selects the provisions according to the season. Specialities are created with imagination, according to the occasion, and to individual taste. This is why all the orders are taken by Chef Bertoli; this enables him to discuss the menu and to recommend the specialities available to his customers. Laurette Bertoli is the perfect hostess, and she also advises customers in their choice of wines from the extensive and original list.

The restaurant is set in a typical Sussex village, where one can witness beautiful, unspoilt views, in the midst of a very natural garden where customers can stroll at their leisure. In the front and to the side of the restaurant, two terraces provide a picturesque location for an apéritif and an unhurried lunch on a warm summer's day. In the evening, the garden and terraces are lit by old-style lamps that emit an inviting glow on this unique setting. A recently built wing has given the Sundial a new bar lounge, banqueting room and kitchen.

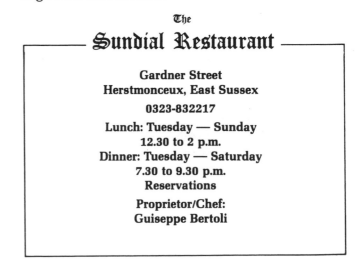

The
## Sundial Restaurant

**Gardner Street
Herstmonceux, East Sussex**

**0323-832217**

**Lunch: Tuesday — Sunday
12.30 to 2 p.m.
Dinner: Tuesday — Saturday
7.30 to 9.30 p.m.
Reservations**

**Proprietor/Chef:
Guiseppe Bertoli**

# Fricassée d'Écrevisse au Velouté Rose

6 × 6 oz live crayfish
1 pt strong fish fumet
2 tbsp butter
2 shallots, sliced
1 clove garlic, chopped
   salt and pepper
2–3 tbsp tomato purée
1 glass Noilly Prat or dry champagne
½ pt double cream
   potato purée to garnish
   small crescents of puff pastry to garnish

Boil the live crayfish in the fish fumet for 7 minutes. Allow to cool, remove meat from shells and cut into medallions. Strain the fumet and reduce.

Sauté the crayfish medallions for 2 minutes in the butter, with the shallots, garlic, seasoning and tomato purée. Remove crayfish and place in a serving dish. Pour the Noilly Prat or champagne and the fumet into the pan with the shallot etc. Reduce and add the cream, to produce a creamy, slightly pink sauce.

Pour the sauce over the crayfish, decorate the dish with potato purée, and place under a hot grill until slightly brown. Garnish with small crescents of puff pastry.

Serves: 6

Wine: *Sancerre*

---

# Les Rosettes de Chevreuil aux Cerises Noires

½ saddle young venison
1 glass Riesling
1 glass vodka (extra for flambé)
2–3 carrots, diced
2 shallots, chopped
   thyme
   bay leaves
   celery leaves
   fennel seeds
   salt and pepper
   olive oil and butter for frying
¼ pt fresh cream
2 tbsp black cherries
   new potatoes, celery, baby carrots, and watercress, to garnish

Remove the venison fillet and cut into steaks (rosettes) of 4 centimetres each. Make a strong stock with the remaining bones and trimmings. Marinate the rosettes overnight in the Riesling, vodka, carrots, thyme, bay leaves, onion, celery leaves, fennel seeds, salt, and pepper.

Heat a frying pan, add the olive oil and butter, cook the rosettes rather rare, and flambé with extra vodka. Remove them and place on a hot serving dish. Add the game stock to the frying pan and reduce slowly. Add the cream and black cherries.

To serve: decorate the dish with new potatoes, celery, and baby carrots, pour the well-reduced stock over the venison rosettes and garnish with watercress.

Serves: 4

Wine: *Pommard or Chambertin*

---

# Les Crêpes aux Framboises

2 oz butter
2 oz sugar
4 measures Grand Marnier
   juice of 1 fresh orange
   juice of 1 fresh lemon
12 thin crêpes
½ lb fresh raspberries

Caramelise the butter and the sugar in a frying pan and add the liqueur, orange, and lemon juice to make a clear sauce. Soak the crêpes in the sauce and simmer very gently for 5 minutes.

Remove the crêpes and place in a serving dish. Reduce the sauce slowly until thick. Fill the crêpes with the raspberries and pour the sauce over them.

Serves: 4

Wine: *Muscat de Beaumes de Venise*

# Le Talbooth Restaurant

**Le Talbooth Restaurant,** owned by Gerald Milsom, is a 16th century house perched on the banks of the River Stour, and it has a private view of Dedham Vale. With its timber frame and overhanging willows, the building looks like part of the archetypal Constable painting, and in fact he did paint the scene. The painting now hangs in the National Gallery of Scotland.

The structure became a fully-fledged restaurant 6 years ago. It began as a tea shop, but gradually Mr. Milsom has built it up, renovating and rebuilding, to make it the restaurant it is today. Le Talbooth now has a riverside dining room and bar, a new dining room (which blends in beautifully with the existing building), and two upstairs rooms available for private lunches and parties.

The young chef, Sam Chalmers, runs the kitchen with expert efficiency, which is probably due to his calm temperament and ability to inspire confidence and respect. He and his sous-chefs are creating a new, lighter style of cooking. They have built up a repertoire reflecting this change in emphasis, and new dishes are constantly being tested and perfected.

The heavily beamed restaurant is luxuriously furnished, and this complements the fine English and French cooking of Chef Chalmers. The wine list is extensive.

**Gun Hill**
**Dedham, Colchester**
**Essex**

**0206-323150**

**Lunch: 12.30 to 2 p.m.**
**Dinner: 7.30 to 9 p.m.**
**Daily**
**Reservations**

**Proprietor: Gerald Milsom**
**Chef: Sam Chalmers, M.C.G.B.**

## Salade de Coquilles St. Jaques

1 shallot, chopped

2 dessertspoons white wine

   lemon juice to taste

1 tbsp water

½ lb butter

1 dessertspoon double cream

16 scallops, cut in half

   mixed salad

Boil the shallot in the white wine, lemon juice and water. Reduce by ⅔. Remove from heat and incorporate the butter a little at a time, stirring continuously. Add the cream.

Poach the scallops lightly for 30 seconds. As soon as they are cooked, drain well, mix with the salad and toss lightly in the butter sauce. Serve immediately.

Serves: 4–6

Wine: *1981 Pinot Blanc de Blancs, Hugel*

---

## Fillet of Trout with Spring Vegetables

8 oz vegetables, cut into thin strips (carrots, celery, leeks, fennel)

4 oz butter

   salt and pepper

12 fillets of trout

⅛ pt white wine

¼ pt fish stock

1 tsp fresh lemon juice

1 tsp very finely chopped shallots

¼ pt double cream

   a little cayenne pepper

Cook the vegetables for 2 minutes in a little butter, salt and pepper. Spread a little of this mixture onto 6 of the fillets, then place the other fillets on top. Check seasoning again. Wrap in tinfoil and bake in the oven at gas mark 7 (425°F/220°C) for 5 minutes.

To prepare sauce: put the white wine, fish stock, lemon juice and shallots in a pan and reduce by ½. Add the cream. Roduce again by ½ to a coating consistency. Check seasoning. Add a little cayenne pepper. Pass through a very fine sieve and pour over the fish.

Serve immediately.

Serves: 4–6

Wine: *1980 Fumé Blanc, Mondavi*

---

## A Selection of Fruits au Gratin

4 egg yolks

2 oz sugar

2 tbsp Grand Marnier

   a selection of fresh fruits soaked in Grand Marnier

   flaked almonds

Cook the egg yolks, sugar and Grand Marnier over a bain-marie until light and fluffy, and pour the mixture over the assorted fruit. Sprinkle with flaked almonds. Glaze under a salamander. Serve with an almond biscuit.

Serves: 4–6

Wine: *1976 Eitelsbacher Karthäuserhofberger, Kronenberg, Auslese, Werner Tyrell*

# The Waterside Inn

**The Waterside Inn** at Bray is the latest acquisition of Michel and Albert Roux. It is set in delightful surroundings, on the banks of the River Thames, near Windsor. The restaurant looks out onto the river through the weeping willows, which are floodlit at night.

The interior is decorated in pastel pinks and greens, giving a bright and sunny atmosphere. Everything in the restaurant is special, from the little choux canapés served with apéritifs to petits fours with coffee, as well as the impeccable service and the excellent cooking.

The meals at Waterside are all prepared by the esteemed, award-winning Chef Michel Roux. Most of the dishes on the menu are Roux creations. They include a masterly fish mousse and rich, flavoursome shellfish bisque, among the starters, all admirably designed to whet the appetite before such beautifully sauced and garnished main courses as veal kidneys in sweet and sour sauce, lamb cutlets with sorrel sauce, or venison in a well reduced cream sauce with morels. The sweets are just as delightful, whether a simple sorbet or a delicately balanced confection such as sable aux poires.

Only three months after opening, The Waterside Inn was acclaimed by the gastronomic press. It is now one of four restaurants in Britain to rate two stars in the Michelin Guide.

## The Waterside Inn

**Ferry Road**
**Bray, Berkshire**

**0628-20691**

**Lunch: Tuesday — Sunday**
**12 to 2 p.m.**
**Dinner: Tuesday — Saturday**
**7.30 to 10 p.m.**
**Closed Sunday November to Easter**
**and 4 weeks from 27 December**
**Reservations**

**Proprietor: Roux Restaurants**
**Chef: M.A. Roux, M.C.G.B.**

# Cervelas de Brochet Vallée de l'Adour

300 g pike meat

1½ egg whites

1 litre double cream

salt and white pepper, to taste

100 g Parisian mushrooms, sliced

205 g butter

10 g green peppercorns

120 g sausage skin (pig intestines)

300 g white part of leek, sliced thinly

200 g bread crumbs

Mix pike meat with egg white in a mixer. Mix a couple of times and strain. Put mixture in a bowl and place on ice. With spatula, mix in ½ the double cream, gradually add salt and pepper, then place in refrigerator. Sauté mushrooms for 1 minute in 5 grams butter in a frying pan. Keep in a cool place. Mix pike mousse, green peppercorns, and mushrooms together.

Place sausage skin in water then hang. Knot 1 end. Stuff the skin with mousse, then knot other end with piece of string. Pierce skin all over with a needle to prevent bursting. Divide sausage into sections by tying with string, but not too tightly or sausage could split while cooking. Put hot salted water in a large pan. When water reaches 150°F (80°C), put in sausage for 15 minutes. Remove carefully and place carefully in iced water.

Melt 100 grams butter in frying pan on low heat. Add remaining double cream, let simmer. Add salt and leeks. Cook until crispy, then remove and keep warm.

With a sharp knife, remove skin of sausage but don't destroy shape. Roll in bread crumbs, place on baking tray, pour 100 grams melted butter on top. Leave in oven for 7 minutes at 345°F (190°C). When half-cooked, turn.

Put leeks on plate, place sausages carefully on top, and serve immediately.

Serves: 10

# Veal Chops Boucanière

50 g flour

1 egg

125 ml milk

salt and pepper, to taste

100 g butter

60 g sweet corn

3 bananas

pinch of icing sugar

4 × 200 g veal chops

20 g fresh ginger, very finely grated

3 tbsp raspberry vinegar

200 ml veal stock

25 g powdered coconut

Make a batter by mixing flour, egg, and milk in a bowl. Add salt and let rest in a cool place 1 hour. Melt ½ teaspoon butter in a frying pan, add ¼ pancake mixture and ¼ sweet corn. When half-cooked, turn and cook other side.

Make 3 more pancakes. Set aside on a plate.

Peel and slice bananas into 1 centimetre thick pieces. Place on butter-coated baking tray. Sprinkle with icing sugar and cook in hot oven 2–3 minutes.

Melt 2½ grams butter in frying pan. Cook veal chops 2–3 minutes on each side. Centre of chops should be slightly pink. Keep in a warm place.

Remove fat from pan. Add ginger and leave for 1 minute. Add vinegar and reduce. Add veal stock and reduce by ½ to syrup consistency. Mix together with remaining butter, chopped in pieces, salt, and pepper. Strain and keep sauce warm.

Place 1 corn pancake on each plate, sprinkle with coconut, and place chop on top. Put the 4 plates in the oven for 2 minutes at 340°F (170°C). Arrange the banana around the edge of each plate, pour sauce over veal, and serve.

Serving suggestions: serve with gratin dauphinois or savoyard, or purée de panais.

Serves: 4

# The White Horse Inn at Chilgrove

**The White Horse Inn at Chilgrove** was built in 1765 by a group of Chichester businessmen as a stopping place for travellers journeying to Chichester from Petersfield and Midhurst. Additions were made to the building 25 years ago to incorporate eating facilities. After passing through the ownership of several brewery companies in national takeovers, the Inn was bought in 1979 from Grand Met by the present owners, Barry and Dorothea Phillips.

As tenants during the previous ten years, they had concentrated on the food in the restaurant, but as owners, they have embarked on a programme of modernising the kitchens, the toilets, the restaurant, etc. — all without destroying the original character of the lovely old building.

The White Horse Inn features an excellent wine list, a small team of waiting staff (all of whom have been with the Inn for several years), and the talents of a most capable chef, Adrian Congdon. Chef Congdon previously worked on the *Queen Elizabeth* and in other establishments before joining The White Horse Inn 11 years ago. His menu consists mainly of plainly cooked local fish, game, and vegetables, and his customers now supply, as well as consume, a considerable proportion of the fresh ingredients he uses daily.

One of the Phillipses' passions is wine, and it is reflected in their excellent list of French, German, English, and California wines available for your enjoyment. There are also several fine house wines to choose from.

## THE WHITE HORSE AT CHILGROVE

**Chilgrove near Chichester**
**Sussex**

**East Marden 024359-219**

**Lunch: 12 to 2 p.m.**
**Dinner: 7 to 9.30 p.m.**
**Tuesday — Saturday**
**Reservations**

**Proprietors:**
**Barry & Dorothea Phillips**
**Chef: Adrian Congdon**

# Prawns Cheval Blanc

1 pt freshly made mayonnaise

2 lb unpeeled Selsey prawns, or
1 lb ready-peeled prawns

4 oz finely chopped onion

6 oz celery in small dice

6 oz tomatoes, blanched, peeled,
seeded, and finely chopped

1 heaped tbsp tomato purée

3 fl oz whipped double cream

6-8 lettuce leaves

3-4 lemons, halved

6-8 sprigs parsley

3-4 tomatoes, halved and starred

To the freshly made mayonnaise, add prawns, onion, celery, chopped tomatoes, tomato purée, and whipped double cream and stir gently to mix. Allow to stand for 2 hours in the refrigerator to thicken. Serve in wooden bowls on a large lettuce leaf and garnished with ½ lemon, sprig of parsley, and ½ starred tomato.

Serves: 6–8

Wine: *chilled German Nahe Cabinet or dry white Loire wine*

# Escalope Bourguignonne

2 cloves garlic, finely chopped

4 oz butter, softened

4 oz chopped parsley

24 snails, finely diced

6 escalopes of veal cut from the rump,
about 6-7 oz each

2 egg whites

2 oz seasoned flour

½ lb freshly made white bread crumbs

4 oz clarified butter

3 lemons, halved

Mix the crushed garlic, soft butter, ½ the parsley, and snails together. Beat the veal between 2 polythene sheets until thin, taking care not to tear the meat. Spread some snail mixture on the veal, leaving an inch around the outside clear. Brush this outside edge with egg white. Fold each escalope in ½, dust with seasoned flour, brush with remaining egg white, and coat with bread crumbs.

Fry veal in clarified butter until golden (about 3 minutes on each side) and sprinkle with the remaining parsley. Garnish each with ½ lemon and serve.

Serves: 6

Wine: *chilled Beaujolais or young Côtes du Rhone*

# Pineapple Tam-o-Shanter

1 × 7 oz tin of condensed milk

1 fresh pineapple, firm and not too ripe

10 fl oz double cream

1 tbsp kirsch

1 oz sugar

glacé cherries, to decorate

Place tin of condensed milk, unpunctured, in a pan of boiling water, covering completely with water. Boil for 5 hours, adding water as needed to keep covered. Allow to cool.

Peel and slice the pineapple into rings, removing the centre core with a sharp knife.

Open both ends of the tin and push out the dark brown contents. Slice with a sharp serrated knife by first dipping knife in boiling water to prevent sticking. Lay a slice of condensed milk on each slice of pineapple.

Whip the double cream with kirsch and sugar until thick. Pipe whipped liqueur cream around each pineapple slice to decorate, top with glacé cherries and serve.

Serves: 6

# The Wife of Bath

**The Wife of Bath** restaurant was opened in 1963 by Michael Waterfield. The building is small and plainly decorated and furnished, but with character and charm.

Brian Boots joined the restaurant soon after as a waiter, and in 1965, Robert Johnson came in as a part-time waiter in the evenings. Towards the end of 1971, Mr. Waterfield invited the two others to join him as partners; Boots would run the restaurant and Johnson would join Waterfield in the kitchen. By 1975, Mr. Waterfield had slowly begun to withdraw, and in 1978, he became a sleeping partner, leaving Boots and Johnson to run the restaurant.

Their staff in the bar, restaurant, and kitchen is composed mainly of local people, and most have been with the restaurant since the beginning. This is something that the regular customers much appreciate; the owners have created a family atmosphere in which the people are always familiar.

The menu, featuring mainly French cuisine, is small, yet imaginative. It changes weekly in order to present selected seasonal dishes using fresh game, salmon, and vegetables. The restaurant also offers homemade pâtés, terrines, sorbets, and ices. Of particular note is the use of freshly picked flowers in the preparation of some of the dishes. There is a modest wine list and several house wines to choose from as well.

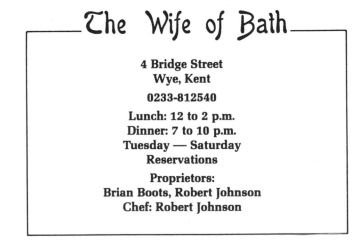

## The Wife of Bath

**4 Bridge Street
Wye, Kent**

**0233-812540**

**Lunch: 12 to 2 p.m.
Dinner: 7 to 10 p.m.
Tuesday — Saturday
Reservations**

**Proprietors:
Brian Boots, Robert Johnson
Chef: Robert Johnson**

# Fleurs de Courgettes Farcies

1 lb fresh or frozen spinach

¼ lb soft cream cheese

½ nutmeg, grated

juice of ½ lemon

salt and pepper, to taste

1 bunch spring onions, finely chopped

butter, as needed

12 open courgette flowers, freshly picked

¼ oz fresh yeast

warm water, as needed

½ tsp mixed salt and pepper

2 tbsp olive oil

¼ lb plain flour

lager, as needed

lemon wedges, to garnish

Chop the spinach lightly and add to cream cheese, nutmeg, lemon juice, and salt and pepper to taste. Sweat onions in butter until soft and add to mixture. Fill flowers with mixture, gently close petals around flowers and refrigerate.

To prepare batter: melt yeast in a little warm water. Add salt, pepper, and oil. Make a well in the flour, add mixture and stir. Thin to coating consistency by adding lager. Leave for at least 1 hour. Batter should then be of a consistency to coat a finger dipped in it. If too thick, add more lager. Dip courgette flowers in batter and deep fry at 320°F (160°C) until golden brown. Serve with lemon wedges.

# Escalopes de Dinde aux Trois Épices

6 spring onions

1½ oz butter

1½ oz flour

1½ pt dry white wine

¾ oz cumin seeds, powdered

¾ oz cardamom seeds, powdered

1½ oz coriander seeds, powdered

½ pt chicken stock

1 garlic clove, crushed

salt and pepper, to taste

12 slices fresh turkey breast

seasoned flour, to dust

butter, to sauté

½ pt double cream

Sweat spring onions in butter until soft, then add flour and mix. Add wine, spices, stock, and seasonings. Cook thoroughly.

Dust turkey with seasoned flour and gently cook in a little butter until brown; turn over, then add onion, spice, and wine mixture. Allow to cook a few minutes, then add cream. Allow sauce to brown slightly and thicken. Serve at once. Serving suggestion: serve with new potatoes and vegetables or salad.

Serves: 6

# Elderflower Sorbet

¾ pt fresh lemon juice

zest of 1 lemon

7 oz sugar

1¼ pt cold water

6 large elderflower heads

2 egg whites

Add lemon juice, lemon zest, and sugar to the water. Submerge elderflower heads in liquid and bring heat slowly up to just below boiling. Leave to cool, then strain off flowers. Either churn in an ice cream maker or freeze, constantly stirring until frozen. Whip egg whites and fold into sorbet just before serving.

Serves: 6

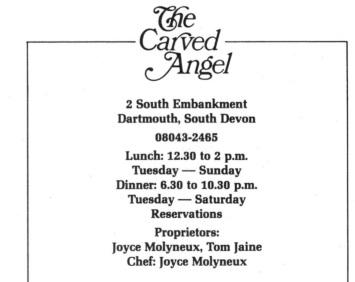

# 3
**WEST COUNTRY AND WALES**

# The Carved Angel

**The Carved Angel** was started in 1974 by the same partnership that opened its sister restaurant, Riverside in Helford, the same year. The links between the two houses are more in the mind and in approach to cookery than in administration; while George Perry-Smith and Heather Crosbie run Riverside, Joyce Molyneux cooks and Tom Jaine runs the front of the house at The Carved Angel.

Joyce Molyneux, together with George Perry-Smith and Heather Crosbie, was a partner in The Hole in the Wall in Bath, which Mr. Perry-Smith founded in the 1950s. She cooked there, having previously been at the Mulberry Tree in Stratford-upon-Avon and Birmingham College of Domestic Science. Tom Jaine is related to George Perry-Smith and was brought up at The Hole in the Wall. After university, he worked in archives and historical manuscripts for some years before joining The Carved Angel restaurant partnership in 1974.

The Carved Angel benefits from its proximity to the sea. The fish is fresh and often brought in by the fishermen or sportsmen who have spent the day in Start Bay, four miles down the coast. Lobster, crayfish, crab, scallops, prawns, mussels, winkles, cockles, and clams are readily available. Thus, although it did not set out to be a seafood restaurant, there is often a preponderance of fish dishes on the menu. The remainder of the menu offers a wide variety of European dishes. A good wine list and two house wines are also available.

---

### The Carved Angel

**2 South Embankment
Dartmouth, South Devon**

**08043-2465**

**Lunch: 12.30 to 2 p.m.
Tuesday — Sunday
Dinner: 6.30 to 10.30 p.m.
Tuesday — Saturday
Reservations**

**Proprietors:
Joyce Molyneux, Tom Jaine
Chef: Joyce Molyneux**

---

The Bell Inn

Fairlieburne House Hotel

# Ceviche of Dover Sole

1   very fresh Dover sole

    lemon or lime juice, as needed

    olive oil, as needed

    chopped parsley, to taste

    salt, to taste

1   lb ripe tomatoes

½   green pepper, diced

1   tbsp grated onion

2   cloves garlic, diced

1-6  chilis, depending on strength, diced

    chopped fennel, to taste

Fillet the sole and cut it into thin strips. Place strips in a bowl and squeeze enough lemon or lime juice onto them to cover. Stir to insure juice has reached all surfaces of the fish. Leave strips in marinade for about 4 hours. Flesh is "cooked" when it has changed colour and is slightly firmer than when raw. Drain marinade, then dress strips with olive oil, chopped parsley, and salt.

To prepare sauce: peel and dice the tomatoes, then mix them with green pepper, onion, garlic, and chilis. Add 2 tablespoons olive oil and check seasoning. Add the chopped fennel and more chopped parsley.

**CHEF'S TIP**

Any very fresh, flesh of firm fish, such as turbot, conger, salmon, or monk may be prepared this way.

---

# Dartmouth Pie

2   lb trimmed leg of mutton

    salt, to taste

2   tsp black peppercorns

1   tsp blade mace

1   tsp whole allspice

2   in cinnamon stick

2   tsp coriander

1   lb sliced onions

1   tbsp flour

½   pt beef stock

5   oz dried apricots

5   oz dried prunes

4   oz raisins

    grated rind and juice of 1 orange, Seville preferred

    prepare pie crust dough

Cut the meat in small squares, season with salt, and brown it with its drippings. Whiz the spices in a coffee grinder, then add ground spices to the meat and fry again. Add onions, flour, and stock, and simmer to mix. Put the fruit into a casserole without soaking it. Add the contents of the frying pan and bring to a boil. Add the grated rind and juice of the orange. Check seasoning, then cover and cook in a cool oven, gas mark ¼ or ½ (230°–275°F/ 110°–135°C) for about 1½ hours until the meat is tender.

It is best if the pie filling is pre-cooked a day in advance to let it mature and the spices blend and soften. It can then be put in your favourite pie dish, covered with your favourite pie crust, and baked in a hot oven.

---

# Cranberry Sorbet

    rind and juice of 1 lemon

    rind and juice of 1 orange

8   oz cranberries

1   pt water

6   oz caster sugar

1   egg white

Put rind and juice of the lemon and orange in a pot with the cranberries and water and simmer until cranberries are tender. Put through a fine sieve and add sugar. Stir until sugar is dissolved. Put mixture to freeze in a *sorbetière* or in the freezer.

When frozen solidly, thaw until just workable. Put into a mixing bowl and with a beater beat it vigorously with the egg white to incorporate air into the mixture. Return to the freezer.

Serving suggestion: serve with a simple orange salad.

# The Castle Hotel

Once part of Taunton Castle, **The Castle Hotel** is steeped in atmosphere and historic interest. Some of the 40 bedrooms are inside the Norman gatehouse itself, yet all are supremely elegant and comfortable, with a different style in each. Proprietor Christopher Chapman is a fourth generation hotelier with experience in Europe's top hotels. He and his family have been running The Castle for over 30 years, and pride themselves on giving their guests a warm welcome and personal attention. Centrally based for exploring the West Country, they provide helpful information for touring and sightseeing.

The Castle's distinguished restaurant has an Egon Ronay star, and a rising young Head Chef, Christopher Oakes, who was named one of the "Top Ten Star Chefs of Tomorrow" by the 1984 AA Guide. Before joining The Castle in 1980, Christopher Oakes worked at Le Talbooth, Gleneagles and the Post Hotel in Davos, Switzerland.

Chef Oakes presents a blend of *la nouvelle cuisine*, to which he adds a basis of English tradition, and his own creative combinations. His particular interest is fish, where freshness and skill are paramount. Menus change regularly to take advantage of high-quality local produce.

The wine list is very extensive, rated by Egon Ronay as "outstanding".

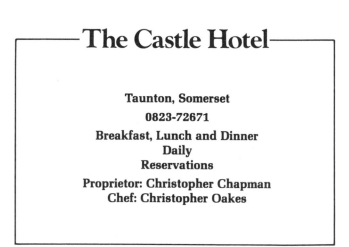

### The Castle Hotel

Taunton, Somerset

0823-72671

Breakfast, Lunch and Dinner
Daily
Reservations

Proprietor: Christopher Chapman
Chef: Christopher Oakes

# Smoked Haddock and Leek Soup

## Chef Oakes' variation on "Cock-a Leekie"

2 **boiling fowl (old hen birds)**

4 **leeks**

6 **egg whites**

2 **fillets of smoked haddock**

2 **prunes**

**salt and pepper**

To prepare the chicken stock: cut each fowl into 4 and wash under cold water. Place in a large saucepan with 3 leeks and cover with water. Bring to the boil and simmer for 3 hours to reduce. Add water as necessary to keep the chicken covered. Strain stock and leave to cool. Return to heat and whisk in egg whites (to clear the stock). When boiling point is reached, leave to simmer until reduced to an amber colour. Strain through a muslin cloth.

Skin and bone the haddock fillets and cut into fine dice. Trim and wash remaining leek. Cut leek and prunes into julienne (matchsticks).

To serve: boil stock with haddock and leeks for 1 minute. At the last moment, add the prunes and salt and pepper to taste.

Serves: 6

---

# Sea Bass with Chive and Lemon Dressing

1 **lemon**

3–4 **fl oz white wine vinegar**

10 **fl oz olive oil**

**large pinch of sugar**

**bunch chives**

**salt and pepper**

1 × **12 oz whole sea bass**

2 **oz butter**

1 **glass white wine**

To make the dressing: remove lemon zest and cut into very fine julienne. Remove and discard pith. Extract the juice and place into a small bowl with the julienne. Add the vinegar and whisk in the oil a little at a time. Add salt, pepper and sugar to taste. Chop the chives very finely and add to the dressing.

NB This dressing will keep for 4–5 days *without* chives — with them it must be used quickly or the bright green of the chives will be lost.

Gut and wash fish, remove the head, and cut both fillets from the main bone. Remove skin, dark fatty flesh, and bones from each fillet. Place fillets in deep buttered tray. Add white wine and seasoning. Cover with tinfoil and bake at gas mark 2 (300°F/150°C) for 5 minutes. Transfer each fillet to a dinner plate. Spoon over the dressing and serve at once.

Serves: 2 (dressing serves 6)

---

# White Chocolate and Banana Mousse

¾ **lb white chocolate**

6 **egg yolks**

4 **oz caster sugar**

1¼ **oz gelatine**

1½ **pt milk**

½ **pt double cream, slightly whipped (plus extra for sauce)**

4–5 **bananas**

**banana and orange segments to decorate**

3 **oz walnuts**

Place chocolate into a bowl over a pan of boiling water and stir occasionally until it melts. Place 4 egg yolks and sugar into a large bowl and whisk together until nearly white. Dissolve gelatine in enough cold water to cover.

Meanwhile, boil 1 pint milk, then pour slowly onto the eggs and sugar, whisking fast. Put the mixture into a clean pan over a very gentle heat and stir continually until thickened — it should coat the back of a wooden spoon. Do not allow to boil. Take off the heat. Add the melted chocolate and gelatine. Pass through a fine sieve. Place in a clean bowl in a tray of iced water. Stir occasionally.

When the mixture starts to set on the bottom of the bowl and feels chilled, gently fold in the whipped cream. Line a rectangular mould with cling film and pour in half of the mixture. Refrigerate until set.

Peel bananas, slice lengthways and place along the sides of the set mixture. Pour in the rest of the mixture and return to refrigerator to set.

To make the sauce: liquidise walnuts (in a strong liquidiser) with enough water to make a paste. Push paste through a sieve to remove the smaller pieces. Beat together the remaining 2 egg yolks and sugar until white. Boil the remaining ½ pint milk and pour *slowly* onto egg and sugar. Pour into a clean pan, return to the heat and stir until it coats the back of a wooden spoon. Allow to cool and add a small amount of cream to reach the correct consistency. Combine with walnut paste.

To serve: place a little sauce on a plate. Take the mousse from the mould, remove the cling film and cut a slice about ¾ inch thick (a hot knife is recommended). Arrange the slice on the plate and decorate with orange and banana.

Serves: 6–8

# Count House Restaurant

The **Count House Restaurant** is situated close to Lands End in the old tin mining village of Botallack. Perched high on the cliffs looking out over the Atlantic Ocean, lashed by the winter's gales, it affords superb views westward to the Isles of Scilly.

The restaurant was created out of an old tin mine workshop; its rough stone walls and high vaulted roof add to the relaxed feeling of space that diners enjoy. Tables of different styles and sizes are set well apart, adding to the informal atmosphere. Roaring log fires in the magnificent old fireplace together with subdued lighting and candles on each table give a cosy feeling on wild winter evenings.

The restaurant is now thirteen years old; it was purchased by its present owners, Ian Long and his wife, Ann, nine years ago. Both have trained extensively with London breweries; Mr. Long has been in the trade for more than 20 years, five of which were in management, and Mrs. Long, who is the chef, worked with many highly qualified chefs.

Their dinner menu, featuring carefully chosen examples of English/European cuisine, is changed daily. A traditional family luncheon is served on Sundays.

A small, selective wine list is also offered. This is revised two or three times a year, and one can usually find some interesting "bin ends" available.

---

**THE COUNT HOUSE RESTAURANT**

Botallack, St. Just
Penzance, Cornwall

0736-788588

Lunch on Sunday
Dinner: Wednesday — Saturday
Reservations

Proprietor: Ian G. Long
Chef: Ann Long

# Melon with Lime Jelly

½ lb caster sugar

½ pt water

1 oz gelatine, soaked in a little water

grated peel and juice of 3 limes

2 small Ogen or Charentais melons

black cherries for decoration

Dissolve the sugar in the water, in a saucepan, and bring to the boil. Pour onto the dissolved gelatine, whisk and return to the pan. Add the juice and peel of the limes, boil for 1 minute and strain into a jug. Leave to cool.

Cut the melons in half and scoop a hole in the centre, removing the pips. Pour in the cooled jelly. Leave to set. Any leftover jelly should be put in a basin to set.

To serve: chop the spare jelly finely, and place on top of the melons. Decorate with the black cherries.

Serves: 4

Wine: *Harvey's Amoroso Light Oloroso Sherry, bottled 1964*

---

# Chicken Breasts with Crabmeat

4 chicken breasts, boned and skinned

salt and pepper

4 oz white crabmeat

4 oz brown crabmeat

2 sprigs of mint, chopped

1 tsp curry powder

1 egg yolk

flour and beaten egg as required

4 oz brown bread crumbs

2 oz butter

lemon butter (juice of 1 lemon mixed with 4 oz melted butter)

Flatten the chicken breasts and season with salt and pepper. Mix the crabmeat with the mint, curry powder and egg yolk. Divide the mixture between the chicken breasts and roll up carefully, making sure the crab is folded in. Coat with the flour, beaten egg, and then bread crumbs. Refrigerate for about 1 hour.

Melt the butter slowly, and sauté the breasts for about 10 minutes until golden brown. The butter should not be too hot. Whilst cooking the chicken make up the lemon butter.

To serve: pour the hot lemon butter onto plates, slice the chicken and arrange on top.

Recommended vegetables: sliced green beans and buttered new potatoes.

Serves: 4

Wine: *Pouilly Blanc Fumé*

---

# Curd Cake

4 oz butter

4 oz caster sugar

1 lb cream cheese

4 hard-boiled egg yolks

1½ oz ground almonds

3 oz raisins, marinated in 2 tsp rum

½ pt double cream, lightly whipped

½ oz gelatine, dissolved in 3 tsp strong black coffee

Cream butter and caster sugar until white. Add cream cheese, stir until smooth, and set aside to cool. Chop egg yolks in a blender, then combine with almonds. Stir in raisins and rum. Fold in cream, then cooled gelatine mixture. Pour into a lightly greased mould and leave to set.

To serve: turn out and decorate.

Serves: 4—6

Wine: *Château Filhot*

# The Drangway Restaurant

**The Drangway Restaurant**, opened nearly six years ago by Colin Pressdee, is situated in the oldest part of Swansea. Its decor combines old and new, as does the cuisine. The modern ground floor restaurant is bottle green and bentwood, with soft shades of brown and cream, blended nicely together with a whitewashed cellar which is little changed from how it has been for more than a hundred years.

The food served is based on pure simple freshness of ingredients, cooked in the appropriate manner, whether *nouvelle* or *ancienne*. Post-Christmas pheasants are braised, but they are finished in the touch of the lighter style of the new cooking, whereas the freshest sea bass or brill or turbot is treated with all the delicacy that it deserves.

The menu offered changes with the seasons and the availability of the produce, as well as with the ever open ideas of the proprietor and chefs. The newest recipes, such as Terrine of Woodcock with Port and Blackcurrant Sauce and Hot Oyster and Avocado Salad, are supported by well-proven favourites such as Fillet of Beef "en chevreuil," Norfolk Duck au Poivre Vert, and Turbot au Beurre Blanc.

A fine selection of wines complements the menu. They range from a superb Muscadet Sèvre et Maine Sur Lie and a Vinification Personelle Rhône to Corton Charlemagne and Clos de la Roche 1971 at the top end of the range.

---

**┌─ DRANGWAY RESTAURANT ─┐**

**66 Wind Street**
**Swansea, West Glamorgan**

**0792-461397**

**Lunch: 12 to 2.15 p.m.**
**Dinner: 7.30 to 10 p.m.**
**Tuesday — Saturday**
**Reservations**

**Proprietor/Chef:**
**Colin Pressdee**

# Braised Pheasant with Leeks and Juniper

2 large cock pheasants, plucked, drawn, and hung for 5-7 days

oil, as needed

1 medium onion, finely chopped

1 carrot, finely chopped

2 sticks celery, finely chopped

3 large leeks, diced

salt and pepper, to taste

500 ml red Rhône wine

500 ml good veal or lamb stock

bouquet garni: fresh parsley, thyme, bay

10 juniper berries

20 ml oil

40 ml wine vinegar

1 whole medium leek (white and green parts), cut julienne

50 ml good L.B.R. port

20 pink peppercorns (*Baies rose*)

Trim pheasants of excess fat in body cavity. Heat a little oil in a cast-iron pan and seal pheasants thoroughly, turning carefully, until entire outside is light golden brown. Remove from pan and keep warm.

Add mirepoix (onion, carrot, celery) to the same pan and cook for 2 minutes, then add leeks and cook another 2 minutes over brisk heat. Season with salt and pepper. Add red wine and reduce to ½, then add stock, bouquet garni, and juniper berries. Return pheasants to cooking pan, check seasoning, cover and cook in a slow oven, gas mark 3 (340°F/170°C) for 1 hour until tender and legs separate easily from the body of the birds. Remove birds from oven, cut each into 4, and keep warm. Pour off all fat from pan. Remove bouquet garni. Purée sauce then press through a sieve to make a smooth sauce.

In a clean saucepan, combine oil and wine vinegar, heat, and add julienne of leeks. Stir for about 1 minute over brisk heat until leeks are just cooked (green parts will remain very crunchy). Drain off and arrange julienne around and over pheasant pieces.

Add port and pink peppercorns to the sauce, heat through and simmer for 1 minute. Pour over pheasants and serve immediately.

Serves: 6–8

*Wine: Burgundy — Aloxe Corton, Chassagne Montrachet, Morgeot, or Beaune Clos des Mouches*

---

# Soufflé Glacé aux Marrons au Coulis de Fraises

6 egg yolks

550 g sugar

200 ml water, and as needed

200 g egg whites

250 g tinned chestnuts in syrup

20 ml dark rum

500 ml cream

250 g fresh strawberries

100 ml strawberry syrup

20 ml eau de vie kirsch, optional

Whip egg yolks until light and stiff. Cook 150 grams sugar with a little water until just before caramelisation. Stir into whipped yolks. Repeat with the egg whites: whip until stiff, add 200 grams sugar cooked with water. (This must be done in 2 stages or sugar mix may set hard.)

Purée the *marrons* (chestnuts) with their syrup and the rum until smooth. Whip the cream until *au ribbon* stage (thick but flowing). Fold ½ the cream into the chestnut purée. Reserve remaining cream.

Fold egg yolk mix into egg white mix, then fold all into the remaining cream. Fold in the purée of chestnuts. The soufflé should be of even consistency but do not overstir. Pour mix into either one 2 litre mould or into several individual moulds and place in freezer until set. (About 4 hours for small moulds, 24 hours for large mould.)

To prepare strawberry purée: boil remaining sugar and water, add fresh strawberries and strawberry syrup, and cook, covered for 2–3 minutes. Purée the fruit and liquid in a liquidiser, press through a sieve to remove seeds, and allow to cool. Stir in eau de vie kirsch if desired.

To serve: turn out the soufflé glacé onto a plate. Decorate with pieces of *marron glacé*, surround with strawberry purée, and serve immediately.

# Gidleigh Park

**Gidleigh Park** is a remote country house located in Chagford, Devon, about 200 miles from London. It is owned and operated by a charming American couple, Paul and Kay Henderson, who in 1978 purchased the then rundown property and refurbished it to its current beauty.

The Tudor-style structure sits in a magnificent setting next to the North Teign River in 30 acres of gardens and woods. Dartmoor, with its majestic open scenery and prehistoric ruins, is a little more than a mile away. The interior of the house is attractively furnished with antiques. Public rooms are all oak-panelled, and fresh flowers and open log fires appear every day.

Kay Henderson has created her own version of *la nouvelle cuisine*, presenting first-class food with the minimum elaboration. In 1980 she was joined by her talented young Head Chef, John Webber, previously at The Dorchester, and one of the founder members of the Country Chefs Seven. Since then, the hotel and restaurant have won great acclaim and every distinction that the independent guides grant: Michelin rosette and red turrets, Egon Ronay star, AA rosette and three red stars. In 1983, Gidleigh Park became the Good Food Guide's first ever "Country House Hotel of the Year," and is one of only two British hotels to receive that guide's highest rating.

Paul Henderson has accumulated one of the best cellars in England, offering over 350 wines, with almost certainly the best selection of American wines in Europe.

## *Gidleigh Park*

**Chagford, Devon**

**06473-2367**

**Breakfast, Lunch, and Dinner
Daily
Reservations**

**Proprietors: Paul and Kay Henderson
Chef: John Webber**

# Steamed Fillets of John Dory

### with samphire on a lemon butter sauce

6 oz fresh marsh samphire

4 fillets of John Dory, trimmed and skinned

salt and cayenne pepper

juice of 1 lemon

6 oz unsalted butter, cut into small pieces

Wash the samphire and remove any dark or soft parts. Season the fish very lightly (the samphire is salty) and sprinkle with ½ the lemon juice. Butter a large sheet of tinfoil, place a thin bed of samphire on it and lay the fish on top. Fold the tinfoil over but do not seal too tightly. Steam for 5–6 minutes.

To prepare sauce: place remaining lemon juice in a stainless-steel or copper pan on a very low heat and whisk in the butter. Take care not to overheat. Check seasoning.

To serve: pour the sauce onto the plates, carefully lift the fish with samphire underneath and place on the sauce. Serve immediately.

Serves: 4

**CHEF'S TIP**

Marsh samphire contains a hard core at the base of the stem. When picking, snap off the base to ensure the core is removed.

---

# Sautéed Best End of Lamb

### on a bed of leek purée with a shallot and rosemary sauce

2 best ends of English lamb

5 cloves garlic, crushed

1 lb untrimmed leeks

4 oz unsalted butter

2 tbsp chicken stock

salt and pepper

3 oz shallots, chopped

6 fl oz dry vermouth

15 fl oz good veal stock (jus lie)

½ oz fresh rosemary, leaves separated

Bone the best ends. Remove the "eye" of the meat and trim off all fat and sinew. Rub in 2 of the cloves of garlic. Trim the leeks (leaving on 2 inches of green), wash twice, slice finely and wash again in deep water. Drain for 1 minute.

Melt the butter in a large flat thick-bottomed pan. Add leeks and the chicken stock, season lightly and cook steadily until most of the liquid has reduced and the leeks are soft. (Do not overcook or the leeks will discolour.) Purée the leeks in a food processor and check seasoning.

Place the shallots, remaining garlic and vermouth in a pan and reduce by ¾. Add the veal stock and reduce by ⅓. Add the rosemary leaves, cook for 5 minutes, check the seasoning and keep warm.

Sauté the seasoned lamb lightly, keeping it underdone. Make a bed of leek purée in the centre of each plate and pour sauce around. Slice the lamb thinly and place on top of the purée, in the shape of a flower. Serve immediately.

Serves: 4

---

# Kiwi Cups

8 medium-large kiwi fruits (just ripe)

2 oz pastry cream (stiff)

2 oz sweetened whipped cream

kirsch to taste

3 fl oz raspberry purée

4 tsp brown sugar

Cut off the hard end of the kiwi fruits, taking care not to waste too much. Use a potato scoop to hollow out the fruit. Dice the flesh. Mix the pastry cream and the whipped cream together, add a little kirsch to taste.

Place the kiwi shells into egg cups, and place 1 teaspoon of raspberry purée in each. Half-fill with the diced fruit and top with the cream mixture (to the top). Sprinkle with brown sugar and colour with a red-hot poker to form a crisp top.

Serve in the egg cups, with biscuits.

Serves: 4

**CHEF'S TIP**

The fruit may be prepared and filled in advance, but should be coloured just before serving.

# The Hole in the Wall Restaurant

**The Hole in the Wall Restaurant** is set in the basement area of two Georgian terraced houses (circa 1790), right in the centre of Bath. It derives its name from the entrances at road level into the old coal holes under the high pavement. Originally, it was a war-time café run by a Mrs. Wintle, who is fondly remembered to this day by servicemen who were stationed in Bath. George Perry-Smith took over the establishment in 1951 and immediately set about making the restaurant one of the most celebrated and best-loved in the country. The current owners, Tim and Sue Cumming, began their association with The Hole in the mid-1960s when they worked for George Perry-Smith. Later, they opened their own restaurant in Salisbury, called Crane's, and after seven years, they returned to Bath to purchase The Hole.

The building lends itself very well to the business of a restaurant. There are cocktail lounges on the ground (or upper) floor, modernly but tastefully furnished. The dining room below, the real Hole, is more informal and relaxed. It has old carriage lamps, whitewashed alcoves, an open fireplace (with burning logs in the winter),

and in the centre, a magnificent cold buffet spread. It now has 6 letting rooms.

The à la carte menu is short and changes every fortnight or sooner to accommodate the seasons and the availability of a varied supply of fresh fish and vegetable produce. The food is predominantly French provincial with a scattering of specialities created by Tim.

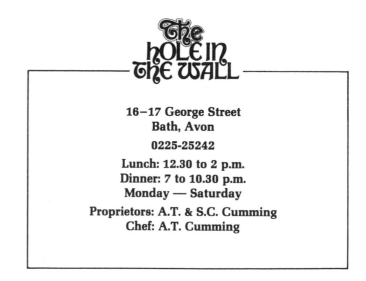

**16–17 George Street
Bath, Avon**

**0225-25242**

**Lunch: 12.30 to 2 p.m.
Dinner: 7 to 10.30 p.m.
Monday — Saturday**

**Proprietors: A.T. & S.C. Cumming
Chef: A.T. Cumming**

# Tartelettes aux Crabes

9 oz flour

7 oz butter

   salted cold water, as needed

4 oz finely sliced button mushrooms

3 fl oz tawny port

3 fl oz double cream

   salt and pepper, to taste

7 fl oz milk, heated

7 fl oz light chicken or fish stock, heated

1 tsp French mustard

   butter, to grease

8 tbsp crabmeat

4 tbsp grated Gruyère or Jarlsburg cheese

Make a buttery shortcrust pastry by mixing 8 ounces flour, 5 ounces butter, and salted cold water together. Set aside to rest in refrigerator.

Soften mushrooms in ½ the remaining butter, add port, and reduce to almost nothing. Stir in cream, boil briefly, season, and let cool.

To prepare Béchamel: melt remaining butter and flour together and cook without browning. Add heated milk and stock, bit by bit, until glossy between each addition. Season with mustard, salt, and pepper.

Roll out pastry fairly thin into 4 rounds and tuck into 4 greased 4½ inch fluted flan rings with removable bottoms. Line with paper or foil, weigh with beans or rice, and blind bake in a hot oven for 10–15 minutes. Trim excess pastry from rim, but leave shell in rings. Spread a tablespoon of mushroom port mixture in the bottom of each, then divide the crabmeat among each. Salt and pepper lightly, then mask with 2–3 tablespoons of the Béchamel. Sprinkle equal amounts of cheese on each. Bake 10–15 minutes in a hot oven. Disgorge from flan rings onto hot plates.

Serves: 4

Wine: *Quincy, 1979*

---

# Stuffed Duck Breasts

2 × 4½ lb ducks

1 duck liver

4 green peppercorns

1 tbsp brandy

   salt and pepper, to taste

1 oz butter

2 oz finely chopped celery

2 oz finely chopped onion

6 oz spinach, blanched and chopped

1 tsp chopped fresh tarragon

1 egg, partly beaten

   butter, as needed

   watercress, to garnish

Fillet the ducks. Remove legs and wings. Trim excess fat and sinew from the 2 rounds of breast with their 2 fillets.

Mash the duck liver with the green peppercorns, brandy, salt and pepper. Spread on the duck fillets.

To prepare the stuffing: melt the butter, add celery, and cook for 2 minutes. Add onion and cook another 2 minutes. Remove from heat, add spinach, tarragon, salt and pepper, and the egg. Mix well, then leave to cool.

Divide the stuffing between ducks. Pin with cocktail sticks or sew up to make a "pasty" shape. With a sharp knife, lightly crisscross the breasts. Brown gently in a trace of butter on all sides to let the fat. Pour surplus off if necessary. Roast in a fairly hot oven for 15–20 minutes. Meat should still be pink. Remove thread or sticks. Carve slices across the fillets, garnish with watercress.

Serving suggestion: serve with Béarnaise sauce and broccoli and gratin dauphinois on a side dish.

Serves: 4

Wine: *claret, Château Cheval Blanc, 1966 or 1970*

---

# Kumquat Sorbet

½ lb kumquats, halved

7 fl oz water

2 oz caster sugar

   juice of ½ lemon

   juice of ½ orange

2 egg whites, half whipped

In a covered pot, stew the kumquats in the water and sugar for about 15 minutes. Strain through a sieve, mashing the fruit with the back of a ladle (should yield ½ pint liquid). Add the lemon and orange juice; let cool. When cool, mix in the egg whites, churn in an ice/sorbet machine, and freeze.

Serves: 4

Wine: *Muscat de Beaumes de Venise*

# Homewood Park Hotel and Restaurant

**Homewood Park Hotel and Restaurant** is situated in ten acres of garden and parkland just minutes away from the centre of Bath. The old house, built around 1780, is decorated in fresh light wallpapers and fabrics and period furnishings. Each of the eight lovely bedrooms has a private bath, colour television, and telephone.

Homewood Park was purchased and refurbished in 1980 by Stephen and Penny Ross, both of whom were associated with other establishments prior to this event. It was their intent from the beginning that Homewood Park would represent, equally, the finest in accommodation and dining. To that end, every effort was made to establish a quality restaurant as well as fine lodgings.

The dining room successfully conveys a private home atmosphere. It is decorated to blend in with the rest of the house. The menu features French provincial cuisine created ably by Chef Antony Pitt, whose experience includes study at a catering college and successful tenures with several well-known restaurants in the area. Some of the items listed on the menu are his own rec-ipes; one is Terrine de Ris de Veau, and it is the house speciality.

The wine list features 70 choices from each of the leading wine producing countries, and there are five fine house wines to select from, as well.

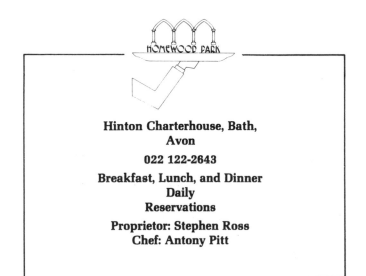

**Hinton Charterhouse, Bath, Avon**

**022 122-2643**

**Breakfast, Lunch, and Dinner Daily Reservations**

**Proprietor: Stephen Ross Chef: Antony Pitt**

# Filet de Truite au Poivre Rose

3 × **6 - 8 oz pink trout**

**rind and juice of 1 orange**

1 **lemon**

3 **tbsp olive oil**

1 **small finely diced onion**

2 **oz caster sugar**

3 **tbsp pink peppercorns**

Fillet the trout, leaving skin on each fillet. Lay fillets in a tray deep enough to hold liquids.

Mix the remaining ingredients together to make a marinade and then pour over trout. Leave in a cool place for 24 hours, spooning marinade over fillets 2 or 3 times. (After 48 hours trout will begin to lose its texture. Do not prepare dish too long in advance.)

Serving suggestion: serve with some of the marinade spooned over the fillets and with a crisp salad of perhaps fennel or frisee lettuce.

Serves: 4–6

---

# Noisette d'Agneau au Beurre à l'Estragon

1 × **4 lb loin of lamb on bone**

**butter, as needed**

4 **oz softened butter**

**handful chopped fresh tarragon**

**rind and juice of 2 lemons**

2 **oz bread crumbs**

**salt and pepper, to taste**

Bone the loin of lamb and tie into a tight sausage shape with string every 2 inches. Cut into *noisettes* by dividing the loin between every

string. Season, dot with butter, and roast in a hot oven for 10 minutes.

To prepare tarragon butter: beat the remaining ingredients together until combined, then shape into a cylinder.

When lamb is cooked, remove from oven and pour off excess fats. Place a slice of tarragon butter on each noisette, then return to oven for 5 minutes before serving.

Serving suggestion: decorate with fresh tarragon leaves and serve with a hot salad of broad beans with bacon and garlic.

Serves: 4–6

---

# Almond Tart with Raspberry Purée

8 **oz sweet shortcrust**

4 **whole eggs**

12 **oz caster sugar**

8 **oz ground almonds**

2 **oz flaked almonds**

1 **lb raspberries**

6 **oz sugar**

Line an 8 inch flan ring with shortcrust. Beat eggs with caster sugar to ribbon stage. Blend with ground almonds, then fill the flan case

with the mixture. Sprinkle the top of the tart with flaked almonds. Bake in the oven at gas mark 5 (375°F/190°C) for 30 minutes until set.

Boil the raspberries with sugar and no water. Liquidise and sieve to remove pips.

Serve the cool tart with purée of raspberries.

**CHEF'S TIP**

Check oven temperature carefully. The tart must be cooked evenly right through. If top is browning, cover with foil until centre is firm to the touch.

# The Horn of Plenty Restaurant

**The Horn of Plenty Restaurant** was started in 1967 by two professional musicians, Patrick and Sonia Stevenson, in a small country house with a view over the valley of the Tamar to distant Bodmin Moor. It has recently become a "restaurant with rooms."

Initially, they featured splendid fresh salmon of superlative quality, which was so readily to hand, and country dishes remembered from their travels or culled from cookery books from all over Europe. The set dinners, genuinely regional in character with appropriately chosen wines, soon caught on, and together with their very special salmon dishes (particularly the Quenelles de Mousseline de Saumon à la Crème), the restaurant soon gained an enviable reputation.

Quite early on, the Stevensons' magic with sauces became apparent — not only new ones of their own invention, but slight alterations of well-known classics that were subtly changed to suit particular dishes. The Stevensons now regularly teach weekend courses on sauce preparation.

Over the years, a vine planted in the terrace just outside the front has grown and covered the area, making a pleasant, leaf-enclosed rendez-vous for luncheon or drinks before dinner in reasonable weather.

The Horn of Plenty is an excellent example of a small family business, run by a couple with no prior restaurant operating experience, successfully attaining high standards in both the kitchen and in the service.

## The Horn of Plenty

**Gulworthy**
**Tavistock, Devon**

**0822-832528**

**Lunch: Saturday — Wednesday**
**12 to 2 p.m.**
**Dinner: Friday — Wednesday**
**7 to 9.30 p.m.**
**Reservations**

**Proprietor: Patrick Stevenson**
**Chef: Sonia Stevenson, M.C.G.B.**

## Quenelles de Mousseline de Salmon

1 lb raw salmon flesh

6 egg whites, approximately

salt and pepper, to taste

1 pt double cream

Liquidise the salmon with the egg whites until the mixture turns smoothly in the goblet. Add more whites if necessary. Add salt and pepper. Work the purée through a sieve to remove any bones or filaments. Beat in the cream until the mixture holds its shape again. Check seasoning. Chill.

Roll and mould the quenelles by pulling the mixture across the bowl with a hot wet spoon. Dip in simmering salted water, tap off the spoon, and poach for 8 minutes. Drain.

Serving suggestion: serve with sauce Vin Blanc.

Serves: 4

## Salmon Cutlets with Sorrel Sauce

salmon cutlets, enough per person

1 handful culinary sorrel leaves

4 egg yolks

2 tbsp water

1½ lb hot, unsalted butter

2 oz unsalted butter

salt and lemon juice, to taste

Poach the cutlets lightly in salted water until still slightly pink near the bone. Lift, drain, and remove skin and centre bone. Keep warm.

To prepare sorrel sauce: simmer sorrel leaves for 15 seconds until they turn colour, then place in a liquidiser with egg yolks and water. Cover and switch on. With a ladle, slowly spoon the hot butter into the liquidiser, including some of the butter milk which will have sunk to the bottom of the pan in which the butter was heated. Regulate the thickness of the sauce with the clarified butter from the top of the pan, thinning, if necessary, with the butter milk at the bottom. Season with salt and lemon juice.

Serve the poached salmon cutlets with the sorrel sauce.

## Chocolate Meringue Gâteau

9 egg whites

12 oz caster sugar

6 tsp instant coffee

1 tbsp hot water

6 oz bitter chocolate

9 oz icing sugar

18 oz softened unsalted butter

Beat or whisk 6 whites and caster sugar to make a very firm meringue mixture. Divide into 4 equal, thin rectangular shapes and bake gently overnight at the lowest possible temperature until crisp. (Meringue will keep in an airtight container for several days.)

Dissolve coffee in water and put in a bowl over boiling water. Break chocolate into the bowl. (Don't let bottom of bowl touch the water or chocolate will harden.) Stir occasionally while preparing rest of dish, but as soon as completely mixed, remove from heat and let cool, but don't let harden.

Beat butter thoroughly with a mixer or wooden spoon until creamy. Put icing sugar and remaining whites in another bowl over a pan of water. Bring water to a boil. Beat or whisk whites and sugar over boiling water until thick and glossy and leaves a trail on the surface. Beat mixture into the butter with the soft but cooled chocolate. Continue to beat until creamy and fluffy. Trim all baked meringue sheets to same size. Layer sheets and chocolate meringue mixture and coat top and sides with chocolate meringue. (Do in foil if dessert will be transferred to a serving dish.) Smooth sides and top with a warm knife and scrape with a knife. Serve chilled and sliced.

Serves: 10

# Hunstrete House

**Hunstrete House** is an old Georgian country manor house, dating back to the early 18th century, that is surrounded by 90 acres of its own gardens and pastures. It was converted into a small luxury hotel in 1968 by Thea and John Dupays.

The house features 20 bedrooms (each with its own bathroom, telephone, and colour television), elegant reception rooms with log burning fireplaces, conference and private dining rooms, a heated swimming pool, a tennis court, and an excellent French restaurant.

The restaurant, which features French provincial cuisine, is headed by Chef Martin Rowbotham who has trained extensively under Robert Harrison and Alain Dubois.

Much of the fresh produce Chef Rowbotham uses in his preparations, both vegetables and fruits, is grown right on the estate grounds and he places great emphasis on food being delicate, crisp and light.

Chicken Breasts stuffed with Basil and Chicken Mousse is one of his favourite dishes and is considered the house speciality.

The restaurant also offers a modest but adequate wine list, a fine house wine, bar service, and a cocktail lounge.

---

## *Hunstrete House*

**Chefwood near Bristol
Avon**

**07618-578**

Breakfast: 8 to 9.30 a.m.
Lunch: 12 to 2.30 p.m.
Dinner: 7.30 to 9.30 p.m.
**Daily
Reservations**

Proprietors: Thea and John Dupays
Chef: Martin Rowbotham

---

# Spinach Pots

1 lb cooked fresh spinach, drained

¾ pt double cream, and as needed

2 oz chopped ham

2 oz white bread crumbs

grated nutmeg, to taste

salt and pepper, to taste

3 tomatoes, skinned and halved

4 eggs, separated

Purée the spinach with ½ the cream. In a mixing bowl, add the puréed spinach, ham, bread crumbs, remaining cream, nutmeg, and seasoning. Place the halved tomatoes into the bottoms of 6 deep ramekins, pressing down gently to cover the bottoms. Add egg yolks to the spinach mixture (if slightly stiff, add more cream). Whip egg whites until firm, fold into the spinach mixture, then spoon a generous amount into each ramekin. Place the pots into a deep baking tray, cook in bain-marie covered with tin foil at gas mark 5 (390°F/200°C) for 40–45 minutes or until spinach is firm to the touch.

When spinach pots are cool, turn onto entrée dishes and serve. Serving suggestion: serve with fresh tomato sauce.

Serves: 6

*Wine: Sylvaner Riesling*

---

# Chicken with Lemon and Garlic

1 chicken

grated peel and juice of 1 lemon

½ glass dry white wine

2 cloves garlic, crushed

flour, to dust

salt and pepper, to taste

2 oz butter

½ c olive oil

pitted black olives, to garnish

Bone the chicken and cut the meat into bite-sized pieces; place in a bowl. Sprinkle the grated peel, lemon juice, wine, and garlic over the chicken. Stir the marinade from time to time for at least 2 hours.

Squeeze the pieces of chicken dry, dust them lightly with flour and season. Heat the butter and oil in a frying pan and sauté the chicken pieces until they are golden brown.

Serving suggestion: serve either on a bed of chopped chicory with a light French dressing or with a light tomato sauce. Garnish with pitted black olives.

Serves: 4

*Wine: a young claret or a Beaujolais*

---

# Pear and Frangipane Tart

½ lb plain flour

6 oz unsalted butter

1 oz sugar

2 eggs

2 oz caster sugar

½ oz flour

2 oz ground almonds

1 drop almond essence

1 tbsp kirsch

1 tbsp blackcurrant jam

2 large, firm pears, peeled and cored

apricot glaze, as needed

To prepare sweet pastry: sift the plain flour onto a work surface, make a well in the centre, and put in ⅔ the butter, cut into small pieces, and the sugar. Knead together well. Add 1 egg and mix. Gradually work in the flour until it becomes a firm dough. Roll out and line an 8 inch flan ring. Chill, then blind bake for about 15 minutes at gas mark 5 (390°F/200°C) until pastry is cooked but not brown.

To prepare frangipane: cream the remaining butter and caster sugar together until soft; add the egg, work in quickly, then add flour, ground almonds, almond essence, and kirsch.

Line the bottom of the cooked flan pastry with a thin layer of jam, then the frangipane, filling ½ the flan case. Put a rough layer of 1 pear over the frangipane, then place a second layer of thinly sliced pear on top. Bake at same oven temperature for 20 minutes or until the frangipane is firm and a golden colour. Leave on the flan ring whilst cooking to avoid pastry turning too brown. When cool, brush lightly with apricot glaze and lift onto serving plate.

Serves: 6

# The Priory Hotel

**The Priory Hotel**, owned by Mr. John Donnithorne, was converted from a private house to a hotel in 1969. This Georgian structure, built in 1835, is constructed of Bath stone in a Gothic style. It stands in two acres of garden. Although only one mile from the Abbey and the centre of Bath, it has more the atmosphere of a country house than of a city hotel.

Mr. Donnithorne, whose hotel and restaurant career began in 1949, took over The Priory five and a half years ago.

The hotel's 15 bedrooms are all individually decorated and furnished with antiques. The restaurant, whose reputation has grown rapidly since its opening in 1970, draws a clientele from a wide area. There are two separate rooms: one an imposing Gothic room with Georgian furniture and period paintings; the other is a terrace room overlooking a courtyard with an ornamented pond and fountain.

The menu features a wide variety of Continental dishes with an emphasis on traditional French cuisine. Several offerings are unique creations by experienced Chef Michael Collom, who was with the Gravetye Manor in Sussex for five years before coming to The Priory.

There is a small bar and two spacious reception rooms, one of which leads to a large terrace where guests can relax with a drink in the summer. An extensive list of French and other imported wines, most moderately priced, is available.

## THE PRIORY HOTEL

**Weston Road**
**Bath, Avon**

**0225-331922**

**Breakfast: 8 to 9.30 a.m.**
**Lunch: 12.30 to 2 p.m.**
**Dinner: 7.30 to 9.30 p.m.**
**Daily**
**Reservations**

**Proprietor: John Donnithorne**
**Chef: Michael Collom**

# Suprême de Pintade Rôti au Torte de Légumes

3 guinea fowl

salt and pepper, to taste

1 egg white

½ pt double cream

½ tbsp brandy

1 lb puff pastry dough

½ lb French green beans, blanched

½ lb thinly sliced rounds of carrot, cooked

eggwash, as needed

stock made from bones from guinea fowl

2 oz morel mushrooms, chopped

½ pt double cream

1 tbsp Madeira wine

1 oz butter

To prepare the mousseline: remove the legs from the guinea fowl and then the meat from the legs. Discarding skin and sinew, pass this meat through a fine mincer, then through a fine sieve. Place in a bowl on crushed ice, add a little salt, and work with a wooden spoon. Add the egg white, then slowly mix in cream and brandy. Adjust the seasoning, cover, and keep cool.

To prepare the torte of vegetables: line a 6 inch flan ring with the puff pastry. Spread a layer of mousseline ¼ inch in depth on the bottom of the flan. Place a layer of blanched green beans on top, followed by the sliced cooked carrot. Repeat this until the flan is full. Roll out the remaining pastry, egg wash the sides of the flan, cover the flan and decorate the top with leaves made from the pastry.

To prepare the sauce: reduce the stock to ½ pint. Add chopped mushrooms and simmer gently for 10 minutes. Add double cream and Madeira and reduce by ⅓. Correct the seasoning. Cover with a buttered paper and put aside.

Gently roast the double breasts of guinea fowl for 15–20 minutes at gas mark 6 (400°F/205°C), basting with butter frequently. At the same time, bake the torte of vegetables and mousseline at the top of the oven for 25 minutes until golden brown.

To serve: separate the breasts of guinea fowl, place on a large round silver flat, cover with a buttered paper, and keep warm. Take the torte from the oven, remove the flan ring, and cut into 6 equal portions. Arrange in the middle of the silver flat, placing the guinea fowl around the outside. Place a small bouquet of watercress in the centre and serve sauce separately in a sauce boat.

Serves: 6

# Pommes Chatelaines

1 pt dry cider

6 oz sugar

6 evenly sliced Bramley apples, peeled and cored

1 vanilla pod

water, as needed

4 oz sultanas

4 oz butter

4 oz caster sugar

2 eggs

1 oz flour

4 oz ground almonds

3 egg yolks

1 dessertspoon Calvados

¼ pt double cream, half whipped

Boil the cider and 4 ounces sugar together for 5 minutes. Place the apples in the resulting cider syrup and poach gently for 5 minutes. Remove the apples and place on a well-buttered baking sheet at least 4 inches apart. Let cool.

Boil the remaining 2 ounces sugar, vanilla pod, and water together for a few minutes, and then soak the sultanas in it. Fill the middle of the apples with the soaked sultanas.

To prepare frangipane: cream the butter and caster sugar together until light and white. Add the 2 whole eggs slowly, beating all the time. Add the flour and ground almonds and mix well. Fill a piping bag with a large plain piping tube with frangipane and pipe just enough to cover the top of each cooled apple.

To prepare sabayon sauce: whip the syrup in which the apples were poached with the egg yolks over a gentle heat. When thick and creamy, add the Calvados. Cool, then add the half-whipped double cream.

Place the apples with the raw frangipane on top in a hot oven, gas mark 8 (450°F/250°C). The frangipane will slip down around the apples and collect at the bottom. When golden brown, remove from oven. Using a large, round plain cutter, cut around the base of each apple, lift carefully onto a hot plate, and serve. Serve sabayon sauce separately in a sauce boat.

Serves: 6

# Riverside

**Riverside** is located in Helford, a picturesque village built on either side of a tidal creek off the Helford River estuary. This is the soft, sheltered corner of Cornwall, a complete contrast to the wild moors inland. There is plenty of walking and sailing, a pub, a post office, but no "bright lights." Old Celtic Cornwall, modern artists and craftsmen, lovely gardens, and fine houses, are within easy driving distance.

The proprietor/chef of Riverside is G. Perry-Smith, who began his cooking career during the Second World War "when," he says, "simplicity and good housekeeping were essential." In 1951, he opened The Hole in the Wall in Bath and stayed there until 1972. In 1974, he purchased Riverside, which features overnight accommodation and a marvellous restaurant.

The restaurant is decorated like a cottage with settings and furnishings that complement the international food, which is French provincial in approach. Rather than just providing an attractive milieu in which to eat mediocre food, Chef Perry-Smith places his emphasis on preparing tasty dishes that are simple, clean, and colourful in presentation.

Riverside also features an extensive list of wines from which to choose, and there is also a fine house wine available.

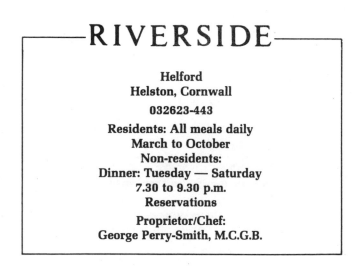

## RIVERSIDE

Helford
Helston, Cornwall

032623-443

**Residents: All meals daily**
**March to October**
**Non-residents:**
Dinner: Tuesday — Saturday
7.30 to 9.30 p.m.
**Reservations**

Proprietor/Chef:
George Perry-Smith, M.C.G.B.

# Sole with Green Herbs and Sorrel

1 lb Dover sole

seasoning, to taste

flour, to dust

butter, to sauté and as needed

2 oz chopped fresh herbs:
thyme, parsley, lemon balm, etc.

2 oz finely chopped sorrel

2 fl oz fish stock, optional

Fillet the Dover sole, season, and flour it. Fry the fillet in butter on one side. Turn, sprinkle with chopped herb mixture and sorrel. Add a little more butter, add fish stock, if desired, and cook 1 minute longer.

Serves: 2

Wine: *Auxey Duresses, 1976*

---

# Rabbit with White Wine and Mustard

2 × 3 lb rabbits

seasoning, to taste

flour, to dust

3-4 oz butter

½ lb fat bacon, diced

24 small onions

2-3 oz flour

½ pt dry white wine

¾ pt stock

thyme, parsley, and garlic, to taste

1 bay leaf

grated rind and juice of 1 large lemon

1 egg yolk

¼ pt cream

mustard, to taste

Joint the rabbits, then season and flour them. Fry rabbits in butter until golden, then put them in a casserole. In the same frying pan, fry the diced bacon and onions. Add flour to make a roux. Add wine, stock, thyme, parsley, garlic, bay leaf, and rind and juice of the lemon. Check seasoning, pour over the rabbits, cover, and cook gently in a cool oven (300°F/150°C) until tender. (Time will depend on size of rabbits.) Finish with a liaison of egg yolk, cream, and mustard.

Serving suggestion: serve with boiled potatoes and a salad of finely sliced fennel and Chinese leaves. Serves: 6–7

Wine: *Morgon, 1978*

---

# Peaches with Lemon and Brandy

3 thinly sliced lemons

2 pt water

1 lb sugar

12 large ripe but firm peaches

12 tsp brandy

Cook the lemons in water and sugar for about 15 minutes to make a syrup. Blanch and skin the peaches. Poach the peaches in the syrup until tender. Lift out the peaches as they become tender. Continue to cook the syrup until it is reduced by about half or until the lemon slices look transparent. Run a teaspoonful of brandy on each peach, and pour the reduced syrup over them, including the sliced lemon.

Serves: 6–12

Wine: *Quarts de Chaume, 1976*

# Thornbury Castle

With a history dating back to William Rufus, and associations with Henry VIII, Anne Boleyn and Mary Tudor, merely to visit **Thornbury Castle** would be enough for many people.

To those who have dined here, however, the name Kenneth Bell conjures up thoughts and recollections of memorable meals. To eat such meals in these historic surroundings, with vast fireplaces, ancient panelling, and old paintings, is an experience to be treasured for many years.

The menu, described as European, was originally based on Chef Bell's desire to run the sort of country restaurant that one might find in France, a place where one could get a good but unpretentious meal. Now, 15 years later, this remains his aim, and the dishes he cooks today are still classical and bourgeois French.

In 1982 Chef Bell opened his first ten bedrooms, which proved so successful that he is to open another two in 1984, and more in 1985. The kitchen staff is to be enlarged to deal with the increased demand, and changes in the menu are planned.

One way in which Thornbury Castle is probably unique are the grape vines that grow up to the castle walls. The wine yielded is very drinkable and is available at a modest price. In addition, there is a very fine wine cellar.

## Thornbury Castle

**Thornbury, Bristol**
**0454-412647**
**Lunch and Dinner daily**
**Reservations**
**Proprietor/Chef:**
**Kenneth Bell, M.C.G.B.**

# Fillet of Angler Fish

2 lb angler or monk fish

2 oz clarified butter

1½ oz ginger, preserved in syrup

1 oz carrot, cut into julienne

1 oz celery, cut into julienne

1 oz leeks, cut into julienne

salt and pepper

5 fl oz dry Martini (more if required)

½ pt cream (more if required)

small quantity dill or parsley, chopped

Trim the fish of all skin to give 1½ pounds of neat flesh, and cut this into bite-sized cubes.

Melt the butter into a large frying pan, when very hot add the fish, and turn it over in the butter. Add 1 ounce of the sliced ginger, the julienne of vegetables, salt and pepper, and Martini, and cook very fast for 5 minutes. Pour in the cream. Simmer for 5 minutes, check the seasoning, and add more ginger if flavour not strong enough. If not enough sauce add more Martini or cream; if too much sauce, remove fish and reduce sauce to syrupy consistency.

Serve sprinkled with dill or parsley, and accompanied by pastry crescents.

Serves: 4

Wine: *Sancerre or Muscadet*

---

# Medallions of Veal with Montilla

1½ lb fillet of veal (tenderloin)

salt and pepper

2 oz clarified butter

8 oz button mushrooms

5 fl oz medium to sweet Montilla

5 fl oz canned beef consommé (more if required)

⅛ pt cream

small quantity of fresh tarragon, chervil, or parsley, chopped

Trim the veal fillet, cut into rounds, and flatten into medallions. Season with salt and pepper and dust with flour. Wash the mushrooms.

Melt the butter in a large heavy frying pan (or two pans). When very hot, add a few of the medallions, colour well on both sides and lift out. Repeat with remaining medallions. Cook the mushrooms in the same pan, replace the veal, add the Montilla and ½ the consommé, and simmer for 5 minutes.

Lift our mushrooms and veal and put into serving dish. Pour the cream into pan (and more consommé if required), and add chopped tarragon, chervil, or parsley. Reduce sauce over high heat and check seasoning.

Pour sauce over the veal and mushrooms, and serve with tagliatelli or spatzli.

Serves: 4

Wine: *Jean Leon, Cabernet Sauvignon, from Penedes*

---

# Thornbury Treacle Tart

½ apple

zest and juice of ½ lemon

3 eggs

2½ oz white bread crumbs

½ pt golden syrup

¼ pt cream

short pastry to line an 8 in flan tin

Peel and core the apple, cut into very small dice or grate. Mix all ingredients (except pastry) in a bowl.

Line flan tin with the pastry and leave to rest for 30 minutes. Fill with the syrup mix and cook in the middle of a medium hot oven, gas mark 5 (375°F/190°C), until the middle of the flan is set. Serve warm.

Serves: 6

Wine: *Barsac, or Moscato d'Oro from Robert Mondavi*

# The Walnut Tree Inn

**The Walnut Tree Inn** is situated three miles from Abergavenny on the B4521. It is a long, low Welsh building painted white and kept in character with the rural surroundings. The decor inside is mostly simple with the exception of the antique gilded pub tables and orange ladderback chairs in the Bistro Bars. The old flagstones are retained in the small bar. The dining room is similar. Flowers are always in abundance throughout the Inn.

The Inn, which is 300 years old, was originally a posting house. Then, over the years, it became a centre for cyclists, then a local pub for the surrounding rural community. Seventeen years ago, it was purchased by Ann and Franco Taruschio and it became a restaurant.

Franco Taruschio is the chef. He attended hotel school in his native Italy, then went on to work in Switzerland and France before coming to the U.K. His menu is basically French and Italian, and its items are designed to suit all tastes —from robust food to *nouvelle cuisine*—and does not forget the simple fish dishes much appreciated by those on a diet. In fact, Chef Taruschio enjoys cooking with fish most of all. His house speciality is Brodetto, a marvellous fish casserole from the Marche region of Italy.

The customers, generally speaking, are regulars who come in week after week. Even travellers from abroad come regularly. Having a regular clientele tends to create a very relaxed atmosphere that is always present at The Walnut Tree Inn.

## THE WALNUT TREE INN

**Llandewi, Skirrid**
**Abergavenny, Gwent**
**0873-2797**

**Lunch: 12.30 to 2.30 p.m.**
**Dinner: 7.30 to 10.30 p.m.**
**Monday — Saturday**
**Reservations**

**Proprietor/Chef: Franco Taruschio**

# Bavarois de Saumon Fumé

1½ lb smoked salmon

1 c *crème fraiche* (fresh cream)

½ tsp cayenne pepper

juice of ½ lemon

8 tsp red salmon roe

2 lb finely chopped onion

olive oil, to sauté

2 lb tomatoes, quartered

salt and pepper, to taste

1 tsp red wine vinegar

snipped chives, to garnish

Rinse 10 ramekins with cold water; do not dry. Line with smoked salmon and trim any excessive overhanging salmon. Blend remaining salmon and trimmings in food processor with *crème fraiche*, cayenne, and lemon juice until smooth. Fold in salmon roe. Divide the mixture among the ramekins; gently fold over edges of salmon. Cover with a piece of grease-proof paper, then a sheet of tin foil. Refrigerate until ready to serve.

To prepare tomato sauce: fry onions in a little olive oil until golden. Add quartered tomatoes and stir fry until puréed. Season with salt and pepper and red wine vinegar. Sieve the purée.

To serve: tip cold bavarois out of ramekins, pour tomato sauce on top, and garnish with snipped chives.

Serves: 10

# Mignons de Veau à l'Orange et Poivres Verts

4 tbsp butter

2 tbsp granulated sugar

juice and rind of 2 oranges

salt and pepper, to taste

12 × ½ in slices fillet of veal

1 tbsp olive oil

Grand Marnier, to flame

2 tsp green peppercorns

2 tbsp Grand Marnier

¼ pt good rich veal stock

orange segments and watercress, to garnish

To prepare orange sauce: melt ½ the butter in a saucepan, add sugar, and stir continuously until the sugar and butter is golden and syrupy in texture. Prepare a handful of julienne strips from the orange rind and add them and the orange juice to the caramel mixture. Cook, stirring continuously until sauce thickens. Season.

Season the veal, sauté gently in oil and ½ the remaining butter until brown on both sides but pink in the middle. Flame veal with Grand Marnier. Transfer to a serving dish and keep warm.

Crush the green peppercorns with Grand Marnier and add to juices in the pan. Simmer a few seconds, then add veal stock and reduce by ⅔. Stir in orange sauce. Simmer for 2–3 minutes. Stir in remaining butter and correct seasoning.

To serve: arrange mignons on a serving dish. Top each one with 2–3 orange segments and spoon sauce over.          Serves: 4

# Honey and Brandy Ice Cream

6 eggs, separated

½ pt clear honey

5 fl oz brandy

½ pt whipped double cream

½ lb icing sugar

Beat egg yolks and whites separately until thick, then mix together. Mix the remaining ingredients together and fold into the egg mixture. Freeze for 6 hours.

Yields: ½ gallon

# The Bell Inn

**The Bell Inn** is owned and operated by Michael Harris, his wife, Patsy, and his mother, Mrs. Daphne Harris. The establishment dates back to 1650 when it was an old coaching inn, providing rest and refreshment for weary travellers.

The Inn offers primarily French-style cuisine with some traditional English dishes prepared by head chef Jack Dick, a Bavarian who received his training in many great European hotels. He and his sous-chef, Manuel, also train young chefs from all over the world. Cooking is a vocation and an art in Chef Dick's kitchen.

Michael Harris, himself, trained at the Lausanne Hotel School and has a passion for good wine, so not surprisingly he is in charge of the cellar. He buys and bottles a wide range of wines under his father's name, Gerard Harris. These include some interesting and lesser known wines from Beaujolais, Loire, and the petits chateaux of Bordeaux.

The interior of the restaurant is decorated in elegant green with candles, silver, and cut glass.

A cobblestone courtyard leads out to the Old Brewery opposite The Bell which was converted some years ago to provide additional hotel accommodations. The original stables and malt houses now form an attractive group of cottages round the cobbled yard.

---

## THE BELL INN

**Aston Clinton, Buckinghamshire**
**0296-630252**

Lunch: 12.30 to 1.45 p.m.
Dinner: 7.30 to 9.45 p.m.
Residents only Mondays and Sunday evenings
Reservations

Proprietor: Michael Harris
Chef: Jack Dick

---

# Frogs' Legs and Juniper Salad

4 pairs of frogs' legs
2 tbsp single cream
½ tbsp lime juice
   seasoning
1 small lettuce
4 leaves radiccio lettuce
2 sprigs lamb's lettuce
1 small curly endive
1 head of chicory
½ tbsp Dijon mustard
½ tbsp celery seed
½ tbsp wine vinegar
2 tbsp medium sherry
⅛ pt olive oil
2 tomatoes, blanched and skinned
1 tbsp plain flour
2 oz salted butter

1 tbsp each of chopped chives, parsley, and chervil
2 tbsp juniper berries marinated for 10 minutes in 1 tbsp medium sherry

Remove meat from frogs' legs and marinate in the cream, lime juice, and seasoning. Remove stalks from lettuce and radiccio. Wash well, along with lamb's lettuce, endive, and chicory. Dry on a cloth.

To make the dressing: whisk together mustard, celery seed, wine vinegar, and sherry. Gradually incorporate olive oil, and seasoning to taste.

Dip lettuce leaves and chicory in the dressing, shake well and arrange neatly on plates. Cut tomatoes in half, remove seeds, slice finely and place on lettuce leaves around outside of plate.

Drain frogs' legs and dust with flour. Heat butter in frying pan and add frogs' legs. Cook until golden brown, turning often. Drain and place on lettuce leaves.

To serve: sprinkle on chives, parsley, and chervil. Drain juniper berries and arrange on the salad.

Serves: 4

Wine: *Sancerre clos de la Poussie*

---

# Roast Lobster

2 live lobsters
2 tbsp corn oil
3 shallots, peeled and finely diced
2 oz salted butter, for frying
1 c medium-dry white wine
4 oz butter (½ salted, ½ unsalted), cut into small pieces, mixed and refrigerated
6 oz leaf spinach
1 pt salted water (using sea salt)
1 tbsp basil, chopped

Kill lobsters by taking a heavy knife and banging sharply where the shell of the head meets the body. Bash the claws. Heat a cast-iron-handled frying pan. Add the oil and place lobsters in pan. Turn lobsters over in the oil. Bake at gas mark 6 (400°F/200°C) for 20 minutes, turning occasionally. Whilst lobsters are cooking, prepare sauce and spinach.

To prepare sauce: heat a small sauteuse, add 1 ounce of butter for frying and half of the diced shallots. Sweat off the shallots until transparent. Add the wine and reduce until there is 1 tablespoon left in sauteuse. Whisk in the pieces of refrigerated butter a little at a time. Pass through a fine chinois and check for seasoning.

Wash the spinach well, and boil the salted water. Blanch spinach in the water and immediately refresh under cold water. Chop coarsely. Heat the remaining 1 ounce of butter for frying in a sauteuse. Add the remaining shallots and cook until soft. Add chopped spinach, season and heat through.

When lobsters are cooked remove from the oven. Place them on a board and cut down their backs. Clean the front shells, remove the meat from the tails and discard the tail shells.

To serve: place hot spinach on plates with front shells. Arrange the tails behind the shells. Remove the meat from the claws and place it in the shells. Pour sauce over the top and sprinkle with basil. Serve immediately.

Serves: 2

Wine: *Chablis Premier Cru 1981*

# Restaurant Croque-en-Bouche

Six years ago, Marion and Robin Jones opened **Restaurant Croque-en-Bouche**, a small, comfortable restaurant in a Victorian house, set in the lee of the Malverns with a bar overlooking the Severn valley. The Joneses offer meals prepared French provincial style. The table d'hôte menus change each week, and each dish is prepared using only the best fresh produce available.

Dinner is five courses: A tureen of soup, such as Soupe de Poisson or Soupe au Pistou, precedes a choice of starters, mainly fish. (Gravad Lax is a speciality, served with local asparagus when in season.) This is followed by a choice of main dish (the list usually highlights the local lamb and game), served with potatoes and a salad with walnut oil dressing. There is much use of fresh herbs grown in their garden. A selection of French cheeses (including four goat cheeses) and various desserts complete the meal. Sunday lunch is three courses with hors d'oeuvres as the first course.

This restaurant serves only 22 people at a sitting and is presided over by the Joneses alone.

Marion Jones is the chef; her expertise has won her numerous culinary awards. The half-dozen tables are looked after, without help, by Robin Jones. You can, therefore, count on special personal service.

---

### RESTAURANT CROQUE-EN-BOUCHE

**221 Wells Road
Malvern Wells, Worcester**

**Malvern 06845-65612**

**Lunch: Sunday
Dinner: Wednesday — Saturday
Reservations**

**Proprietors: Mr. & Mrs. R.G. Jones
Chef: Marion Jones**

---

# Homard Gratiné au Porto (Lobster with Port)

2 × ½ lb cooked lobsters or equal amount crabmeat

    freshly ground black pepper and salt, to taste

3 tbsp double cream

½ lb button mushrooms, sliced

1 oz butter, heated

2 tbsp port

½ pt Béchamel sauce

    grated Gruyère cheese, as needed

Remove lobster flesh and coral. Slice, season with pepper and salt, and moisten with ⅓ the cream. Toss mushrooms quickly in hot butter in a pan, add port, and reduce by ½ over high heat. Remove from heat and, when cool, add remainder of cream and season. Divide mushroom mixture into 6 ovenproof dishes, add lobster, top with Béchamel sauce, and sprinkle cheese on top. Bake for about 12 minutes in a hot oven until browned.

Serves: 6

---

# Pheasant "Truffée" with Tarragon

4 oz butter, softened

4 rashers smoked bacon cut into small lardons

1 tbsp chopped fresh tarragon

1 tbsp finely chopped shallot

1 garlic clove, finely chopped

    salt and freshly ground black pepper, to taste

2 pheasants

1 tbsp flour

1 tbsp sherry vinegar

2 tbsp white wine

¼ pt chicken stock

¼ pt double cream

Mix the first 7 ingredients to make the stuffing. Spread the mixture inside the birds, between the skin and body, using a small spatula. Roast birds on a rack in a roasting pan near the top of an oven at gas mark 6 (400°F/205°C). Baste frequently with the flavoured butter which runs into the pan. When cooked, remove birds from oven and keep to one side covered.

Pour off all but 1 tablespoon butter. Dust flour into pan. Cook over heat gently. Add vinegar, wine, and stock. Cook for a few minutes, scraping bits from bottom of pan. Strain into a saucepan, whisk in cream, reduce to a good sauce consistency, and season.

Carve pheasants into pieces and arrange on a serving dish. Cover with the sauce.

Serves: 4–6

---

# Reine de Saba (Chocolate Almond Cake)

4 oz softened, unsalted butter

4 oz plus 1 tbsp caster sugar

3 eggs, separated

    pinch of salt

7 oz plain chocolate

4 tbsp coffee

2 oz ground almonds

¼ tbsp almond extract

2 oz plain flour

1 oz unsalted butter

4 tbsp sieved apricot jam, heated

Cream the softened butter and 4 ounces sugar until pale yellow and light. Beat in egg yolks. Beat egg whites with a pinch of salt to form soft peaks. Add remaining caster sugar. Beat until stiff. Melt 4 ounces chocolate with ½ the coffee until smooth. With a spatula, stir chocolate into butter and sugar mixture, then add almonds and extract. Fold in gently ¼ egg whites and ¼ flour. Repeat in stages until rest is folded in. Turn into an oiled and floured 8 inch cake tin, spreading mixture up to the rim. Bake in the middle of an oven at gas mark 4 (360°F/180°C) for about 25 minutes. Cake is done when puffed and needle inserted 2½ inches from the edge comes out clean. Centre should remain soft and slightly undercooked. Let cake cool in tin for 10 minutes. Reverse onto a rack and allow to cool thoroughly.

To prepare icing: melt remaining chocolate and coffee together until smooth. Whisk in the remaining butter. Allow to cool to spreading consistency. Brush cake with hot apricot jam, then allow to cool. Ice the cake using a spatula.

# Dormy House

**Dormy House** sits on a hilltop vantage point, overlooking beautiful Cotswold countryside and the village of Broadway — and surrounded by a golf course. The mellow stone walls, exposed beams and open fires have changed little since the building was a 17th century farmhouse, but every home comfort and modern amenity is provided, carefully blended with the hotel's special character. Some bedrooms have french windows opening onto small walled gardens where guests can sit among the flowers; and the service throughout the hotel is welcoming and attentive. There are private dining rooms, a spectacular ballroom and a fully equipped conference centre.

The restaurant is in several of the original farmhouse rooms, which gives an intimate and private air to every table. There is a balanced menu, which changes every month and always has one Scandinavian and one *nouvelle cuisine* dish. Chef Roger Chant came to Dormy House two years ago from the Carlton Hotel, Bournemouth after working under Christian Delteil at the Chewton Glen Hotel.

A well stocked cellar offers a carefully selected range of quality wines, including a French house wine which is bottled under the Dormy House label. The convivial bars also serve real ale.

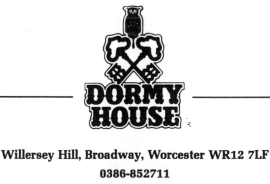

**Willersey Hill, Broadway, Worcester WR12 7LF**

**0386-852711**

**Breakfast: 7.30 to 10 a.m.**
**Lunch: 12.30 to 2 p.m.**
**Dinner: 7.30 to 10.30 p.m.**
**Reservations**

**Proprietor: Group 4 Conference Services Ltd.**
**General Manager: Harvey Pascoe**
**Chef: Roger Chant**

# Fillets of Sole Suchet

4 fillets of Dover sole

2 oz carrots, cut into julienne

2 oz leeks, cut into julienne

2 oz celery, cut into julienne

    salt and pepper

½ c dry white wine or Noilly Prat

1 c fish stock

1 c double cream

    lemon juice to taste

    cayenne pepper to taste

Wash the fish and place in a buttered tray. Blanch the julienne of vegetables, drain and sprinkle over the fish. Season, add the wine and fish stock. Cover with greased greaseproof paper and poach in a moderate oven at gas mark 3 (325 ° F/170 ° C) for 10 minutes. Remove the fish, drain well and place neatly on plates with garnish. Keep warm.

Strain the cooking liquor and reduce by ½. Add the double cream and reduce to an emulsion. Correct the seasoning and finish with a little lemon and cayenne pepper. Coat the fish carefully with the sauce and serve immediately.

Serves: 4

Wine: *Pouilly Fumé les Loges, 1982, J.L. Saget*

---

# Medallion of Venison
## in Cointreau and green apples

4 venison steaks

2 medium-sized carrots, chopped

3 small shallots, sliced

¼ tsp crushed peppercorns

2 cloves of garlic, finely chopped

    parsley, thyme, and a bay leaf

    salt and freshly ground pepper

    red wine as needed

½ c vinegar

4 tbsp olive oil

¼ lb lean bacon

½ Spanish onion, finely chopped

2 tbsp butter

2 small green apples, cored, and thinly sliced (extra to garnish)

4 tbsp Cointreau

1 c double cream

1 c stock

    watercress to garnish

Place venison in a basin. Add carrots, shallots, crushed peppercorns, 1 clove of garlic, parsley, thyme, and bay leaf. Season with salt and cover with red wine, vinegar, and 2 tablespoons olive oil. Leave for up to 24 hours in a cool place.

Sauté the bacon, onion, and remaining garlic in the butter and remaining oil. Add the apples and Cointreau. Cook for 5 minutes. Remove and sieve the apples, and skim the fat from sauté pan. Add the cream and stock to the pan and reduce by ½. Strain and add sieved apple. Adjust seasoning and keep sauce warm.

Sauté the venison steaks in a hot pan, to your guests' liking. Serve garnished with freshly sliced green apples and a sprig of watercress.

Serves: 4

Wine: *Château Ducru Beaucaillou, 1966, 2ème Cru St. Julien*

---

# Strawberry Sorbet

5 tbsp sugar

¼ pt water

11 oz cored strawberries (plus 4 to garnish)

    juice of 1 lemon

4 mint leaves to garnish

Dissolve the sugar in the water in a saucepan and boil to a syrup. Remove from heat and allow to cool.

Purée the cored fruit in a liquidiser (and strain for a really smooth sorbet). Stir the purée and lemon juice into the cooled syrup. Pour into an ice-cream maker and run until the mixture thickens, or freeze in an ice-cream tray, whisking from time to time.

Serve in champagne glasses, each garnished with a whole strawberry and a mint leaf.

Serves: 4

Wine: *Château Rieussec, 1976, Sauternes*

# Restaurant Elizabeth

Antonio Lopez, owner and chef of the famed **Restaurant Elizabeth** opposite Christ Church College, is a man big in stature and in heart. That he has been offering gourmet dishes for more than 20 years to a clientele that is not only academic but knowledgeable about food and wine speaks volumes about the standards he maintains.

The Elizabeth is a small, panelled restaurant with beamed ceilings and subdued lighting. Señor Lopez's white-jacketed staff, most of whom are Spanish, are attentive and add that little something special to the service that is sometimes missing even in grander establishments.

The kitchen is headed by Chef Salvador Rodriguez, who was a friend of the Lopez family since childhood and trained under their tutelage. His menu presents Continental cuisine that is both traditional and experimental. The Ttoro Soup, which is a kind of bouillabaisse finished with aioli, croutons, Parmesan cheese, and parsley, is a dish typical of the Basque country from whence both he and Señor Lopez originate. It is delicious and well worth trying.

The wines are excellent and, whilst not inexpensive, show an understanding and enthusiasm not often found. But, as the proprietor says, "The colleges in Oxford have some of the best cellars in England, so my standards have to be high."

## Restaurant Elizabeth

**84 St. Aldates
Oxford, Oxfordshire**

**0865-42230**

Lunch: Sunday 12.30 to 2.30 p.m.
Dinner: Monday — Friday 6.30 to 11 p.m.
and Sunday 7 to 10.30 p.m.
**Reservations**

**Proprietor: Antonio Lopez
Chef: Salvador Rodriguez**

# Tioro Soup

2 pt water

1 lb fillets of white fish, bones reserved

olive oil, as needed

1 large leek, sliced

1 large carrot, chopped

1 green pepper, sliced

3 tomatoes, peeled and chopped

pinch of saffron

salt and pepper, to taste

3 tbsp brandy

croutons fried in butter, to garnish

4 tbsp aioli mayonnaise

4 tbsp Parmesan cheese

parsley, to garnish

Make a fish stock by boiling water with fish bones. Strain after 30 minutes. Put a coffee cupful of oil in another pan and sweat the leek, carrot, and pepper for 10 minutes. Add tomatoes and cook another 5 minutes. Add to stock and simmer for 30 minutes.

In a separate pan, sauté the fish in 3 tablespoons oil very rapidly for no more than 1 minute, add brandy and flame. Strain the thick stock and add the fish pieces. Do not cook further. Season to taste.

To serve: add croutons, aioli, and Parmesan, then sprinkle with chopped parsley.

Serves: 4

# Rice in Paella

3 tbsp olive oil

½ lb chicken

1 lb mussels

½ lb scampi

1 clove garlic, finely chopped

3 tomatoes, peeled

1 small green pepper

1 small red pepper

8 oz rice

1½ pt chicken stock

pinch of saffron

salt and pepper, to taste

Heat the olive oil in a paella pan; once oil is hot, brown the chicken and then take it out. Add mussels and scampi and heat until mussels open. Remove scampi and mussels, return chicken to pan, then add garlic, tomatoes, and peppers. Cook gently until chicken is tender. Add rice and stir; add chicken stock. Check that it's well mixed, then add saffron and leave on heat for 15 minutes.

Return scampi and mussels to the pot and leave on heat another 5 minutes. Remove pan from heat and leave to rest for 5 minutes. Do not stir until on table for serving. Season with salt and pepper.

Serves: 6

# Oeufs à la Neige (Snow Eggs)

4 eggs, separated

2 oz sugar

1 pt milk

½ pt double cream

1 small stick cinnamon

2 cloves

4 drops vanilla essence

peel of ½ lemon

½ tsp ground cinnamon

Beat egg whites until frothy. Add ½ the sugar and continue beating until whites become stiff. Put milk, cream, cinnamon stick, cloves, vanilla, and lemon peel in a large pan and bring to a boil. Once milk is boiling, shape the whites into egg shapes (collops) with 2 dessertspoons and gently cook in the milk (they cook very quickly). Put collops on a large plate.

Once all egg whites are cooked, beat egg yolks with remaining sugar, then pour in boiling milk, stirring all the time. If the desired consistency is not reached, return the creamy mixture to the pan and heat very slowly, continually stirring, until it is reached. Do not allow to boil or it will curdle. Pour mixture over the collops and allow to cool. Sprinkle with ground cinnamon prior to serving.

Serves: 4

# The Elms Hotel

**The Elms Hotel** & **Restaurant** is housed in a Queen Anne country house built in 1710 and is situated in 15 acres of parkland and formal gardens amidst the beautiful rolling Worcestershire countryside. There are croquet and putting lawns and tennis courts for guests to enjoy, as well as lounges and bedrooms that are furnished with antiques and have welcoming open log fires that burn all the year round.

The Regency-styled **Brooke Room Restaurant** has a 1981 addition — a delightful room continuing the furniture and decor of the old. Its main feature is a long series of arched windows that afford a fine view of a floodlit raised garden. The restaurant is renowned for the very high standard of Continental and British cooking set by Chef Nigel Lambert, who is a devoted exponent of *la nouvelle cuisine*.

Guests are offered a small à la carte menu together with a table d'hôte menu for lunch. In the evening, a most interesting menu is offered, the price of the main course determining the cost of a four-course meal. The dinner menu is altered at regular intervals, and in addition, every day there are at least two different hors d'oeuvres and entrées to choose from. Of particular note is the sweets trolley; throughout the winter months, a different hot English pudding is served every day. There is also an excellent wine cellar that boasts a particularly fine selection of clarets.

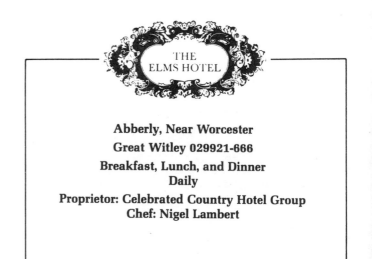

**THE ELMS HOTEL**

**Abberly, Near Worcester**
**Great Witley 029921-666**
**Breakfast, Lunch, and Dinner**
**Daily**
**Proprietor: Celebrated Country Hotel Group**
**Chef: Nigel Lambert**

## Terrine de Saumon et Turbot au Safran

125 g salmon

½ tsp salt

2 turns of a pepper mill

1 egg

125 g turbot

½ tsp salt

2 turns of a pepper mill

1 egg

500 scant ml cream

melted butter, as needed

blanched spinach leaves, as needed

100 ml dry white wine

1 heaped tbsp chopped shallots

50 ml fish stock

250 scant ml whipping cream

pinch of saffron mixed with a little white wine

½ tbsp lemon juice

salt and pepper, to taste

parsley, to garnish

To prepare the mousse: blend salmon, seasoned with salt and pepper, in a liquidiser for 3-4 minutes. When fish is a smooth purée, add whole egg and blend another minute. Put container in refrigerator for 30 minutes to firm mixture. Repeat the same steps for the turbot. Return salmon mixture to the liquidiser, add ½ the cream, and blend for several seconds. Do the same for the turbot mixture. Preheat the oven to gas mark 7 (425°F/220°C). Brush interior of terrine with melted butter and line with blanched spinach leaves. Fill bottom half with salmon mousse, put turbot mousse on top, cover with spinach leaves, and cover with the buttered lid. Cook in a bain-marie for 30 minutes.

To prepare saffron sauce: bring wine and shallots to simmering point in a small saucepan and reduce, uncovered, until 3-4 tablespoons remain. Add fish stock and whipping cream and boil until reduced to ⅔ of original volume. Strain sauce onto the saffron, add lemon juice, and season. Keep warm in a bain-marie.

When terrine is cooked, turn out onto a cutting board, divide into 6 portions, and put onto 6 hot plates. Pour saffron sauce generously around each slice, garnish with parsley, and serve.

Serves: 6

Wine: *Chablis*

## Côtelettes d'Agneau Farcie en Croûte

6 large lamb cutlets

salt and pepper, to taste

25 g butter

2 tomatoes, peeled, seeded, and finely chopped

150 g finely chopped mushrooms

100 g finely chopped ham

1 tbsp chopped parsley

400 g frozen puff pastry

1 egg yolk

2 tbsp water

Season cutlets with salt and pepper, brush with melted butter, and grill on both sides until half-cooked.

To prepare stuffing: put tomatoes into a basin with mushrooms, ham, parsley, and seasoning. Melt remaining butter, add to mixture, and blend well.

Roll out pastry and cut 6 rectangles large enough to cover cutlets completely. Put a spoonful of stuffing on each piece of pastry and place a cutlet on top. Top with another spoonful of stuffing. Brush the edges with egg yolk and water. Fold pastry over and seal edges so each cutlet is completely enclosed. Brush all over with egg wash and bake in a hot oven, gas mark 7 (425°F/220°C) for about 15-20 minutes.

Serves: 6

## Lemon Curd Tart

4 lemons, zest and juice

250 g butter

250 g sugar

3 eggs

125 g sugar

125 g butter

200 g egg

100 g bread crumbs

zest and juice of 2 lemons

1 sweet pastry case

To make the curd: whisk the first 4 ingredients together in a bowl over boiling water until thick. To make the filling: beat the sugar and butter together until white. Add eggs, bread crumbs, and lemon zest and juice. To assemble: smooth a thin layer of curd over the base of the flan. Fill to the top with lemon filling. Bake at gas mark 6 (400°F/205°C) for about 30 minutes.

Serves: 6

# The Fox and Goose Inn

**The Fox and Goose Inn** was built in the year Henry VIII came to the throne — 1509. Church authorities in the 16th century allowed church-goers to eat and drink in the naves of churches. Abuses of the privilege eventually resulted in inns being built by church authorities — The Fox and Goose was one of these.

The "Church House" or Guildhall, now The Fox and Goose, is still owned by the church. A noble building of mellow brickwork, its north front is in the churchyard. On the front the carved date 1616 indicates when the house was enlarged. Oak timber in the original North East part of the Inn is decorated with two carved figures, one of an Abbot and the other of St. Margaret.

The dining room is simple and cottage, with beams and a log fire, and the food is served informally. The ingredients are beautifully fresh. Local game is a speciality, and the pike for the famous quenelles is caught by Mr. P. Clarke. The dishes are imaginative and excellently cooked by Mrs. Clarke and her son Adrian.

An extensive international list of wines is available featuring predominantly French vintners.

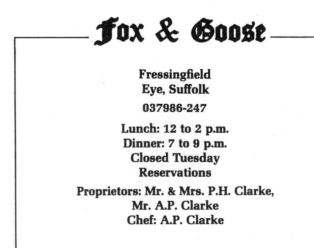

## Fox & Goose

**Fressingfield
Eye, Suffolk**

**037986-247**

**Lunch: 12 to 2 p.m.
Dinner: 7 to 9 p.m.
Closed Tuesday
Reservations**

Proprietors: Mr. & Mrs. P.H. Clarke,
Mr. A.P. Clarke
Chef: A.P. Clarke

# Fresh Lobster Salad

3 × 1½–2 lb live hen lobsters

14 pt salted water

1 medium-sized iceburg lettuce, sliced

6 medium-sized tomatoes, sliced

½ medium-sized cucumber, sliced

½ medium-sized onion, thinly sliced

1 medium-sized clove garlic, crushed

2 oz walnuts

1½ oz raisins, soaked in warm water and thoroughly cleaned

3 tbsp olive oil (first pressing)

1 tbsp wine vinegar

salt and pepper

The lobsters must be alive, so order them well in advance. Boil the water in a large pot. When boiling rapidly, drop in lobsters one after the other, and cook for 18 minutes (overcooking would be disastrous). Remove with slotted spoon and allow to cool for about 1 hour. Cut each lobster in ½ and remove the grit sack, directly behind its eyes. Clean all grit from the tail. Crack the claws with small mallet or rolling pin, remove all meat. Place a claw on each ½ of lobster.

Serving method 1: toss remaining ingredients well together, place in a bowl, and serve lobster on a large plate. Allow guests to help themselves.

Serving method 2: present the lobster on a large plate covered with the lettuce, and decorated with the tomatoes, cucumber and onion. Allow guests to dress their own salad.

Serving method 3: mix and dress salad, and serve the lobster on top — if you know guests well.

Serves: 6

Wine: *Corton-Charlemagne, Puligny-Montrachet or Chablis*

**CHEF'S TIP**

Serve with warm par-boiled eggs with garlic mayonnaise.

---

# Roast Haunch of Venison

1 × 4 lb haunch of venison

½ pt red wine

1 sprig tarragon

1 sprig rosemary

1 sprig thyme

1 sprig savory

pinch each salt and pepper

1–1½ pt vegetable oil

2 tbsp cognac

1–1½ pt beef and chicken stock

1 tbsp redcurrant jelly

3 bunches watercress

Marinate venison in a tub with red wine, herbs, and seasoning, and sufficient oil to cover, for at least 24 hours at room temperature. Immerse completely and turn occasionally. Remove from marinade and cover in foil. Cook in preheated oven at gas mark 7 (425°F/220°C) for 25 minutes. Remove foil and cook for a further 50 minutes. Remove from baking tray. Flambé the juices with the cognac and add stock and redcurrant jelly.

Carve the venison as thinly as possible and place on a large plate surrounded by watercress. Serve with redcurrant jelly and the gravy.

Recommended vegetables: carrot or celeriac purée, mangetouts, or French beans and pommes dauphinois au gratin.

Serves: 6

Wine: *Corton, Vougeot, St. Emilion, or Graves*

---

# Fresh Pineapple, Kiwi and Orange Salad

1 large pineapple, peeled, cored and segmented

3 kiwi fruit, thinly sliced

6 large oranges, peeled and segmented

3 tbsp kirsch

juice of 1 lemon

½ pt water

¼ lb caster sugar

Mix together the fruit, kirsch, and lemon juice in a large bowl. Boil the water and sugar and reduce by ¼ to make a syrup. Allow to cool and pour over the fruit.

Serves: 6–8

**CHEF'S TIP**

Make the syrup in advance, but cut up fruit at last possible moment.

# The Greenway

The Greenway country house hotel, 2½ miles from Cheltenham, was built 400 years ago as a manor house for a wealthy wool merchant. It takes its name from the historic drovers' road which runs beside the hotel up into the hills; and is ideally placed for exploring the charming Cotswold villages and nearby places of interest (e.g. Blenheim and Slimbridge). Tony and Maryan Elliott offer a warm and tranquil atmosphere, roaring log fires in winter, views through mullioned windows across gardens and parkland, beautiful antiques in the 14 bedrooms — plus every modern comfort that well-trained service can provide.

In the panelled candlelit dining room, every dish is one of Chef William Bennett's own creations, which makes his small menu highly individual. He particularly enjoys making sauces — witness his crisp local duckling with blackcurrant sauce, or a scallop mousse starter with Noilly Prat sauce. The food is always fresh and neatly presented, not over garnished, and accompanied by lightly cooked vegetables. Chef Bennett trained at Ipswich College and came to The Greenway after distinguished service at The Bridge Inn, Walshford and Hintlesham Hall.

Drinks are waiter served from the cocktail bar, and the extensive international wine list runs to 150 bins, with a house wine from the Loire.

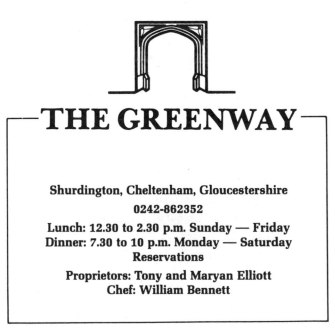

## THE GREENWAY

Shurdington, Cheltenham, Gloucestershire
0242-862352

Lunch: 12.30 to 2.30 p.m. Sunday — Friday
Dinner: 7.30 to 10 p.m. Monday — Saturday
Reservations

Proprietors: Tony and Maryan Elliott
Chef: William Bennett

# Chicken and Sweetbread Terrine

12 oz veal sweetbreads

12 pistachio nuts

1 tsp truffles

1 lb boned chicken

2 egg whites

¾ pt double cream

4 oz lardo or pork belly fat

2 tbsp brandy

2 tbsp Madeira

salt and pepper

mayonnause, mustard flavoured, to garnish

watercress to garnish

Lightly poach sweetbreads until cooked. Peel away all skin and remove all gristle and fatty pieces. Blanch pistachio nuts, then peel and halve them. Finely chop truffles.

Using a liquidiser, finely mince the chicken, adding egg whites and cream, until the mixture is thick and smooth, but not over-whipped. Allow to rest in refrigerator for 30 minutes.

Line a terrine mould with thinly cut slices of the lardo. Remove chicken mixture from refrigerator, add to it the pistachio nuts, truffles, brandy, Madeira and seasoning to taste (a slight over-salting is recommended). Half-fill terrine mould with the mixture, make suitable indentations along the surface of the mixture and place sweetbreads neatly throughout the mould. Cover sweetbreads and fill the mould with the remainder of the chicken mixture and fold over slices of lardo, thoroughly covering the top of the mould. Cover with cling film and lid and bake in a bain-marie at gas mark 1 (275 °F/ 140 °C) for about 1 hour.

To test whether the mixture is thoroughly cooked, push a needle into the centre — it should be hot. Allow to cool, and refrigerate for 24 hours before use. Serve in slices, garnished with mayonnaise and a few watercress leaves.

Serves: 4–6

# Salmis of Pheasant 'Forestière'

2 hen pheasants

1 pt double cream

1 oz dried cèpes or morels or 2 oz Chinese mushrooms

2 oz butter

2 oz plain flour

juice of 2 lemons

1 glass good red wine

salt and pepper

Roast pheasants at gas mark 5 (375 °F/190 °C) for about 30 minutes, until pink. Remove breasts and legs, and place in an ovenproof dish. Make stock with the remainder of the bones, and reduce to about ½. Add cream and sliced

mushrooms (if dried cèpes or morels are used, these should be soaked in warm water until tender, and this water should be added to the stock). Simmer this mixture for about 20 minutes.

Mix small quantities of butter and flour together into walnut-sized pieces and whisk into the sauce until they are thoroughly absorbed and sauce is thickened. Add lemon juice, red wine, and seasoning to taste.

Warm pheasant joints thoroughly in oven, add sauce, heat thoroughly (but do not boil) and serve at once.

Recommended vegetables: olivette potatoes and purée of winter vegetables (parsnips, swedes, carrots and Brussels sprouts).

Serves: 4

Wine: *Beaune Clos des Mouches, Sélection des Chevaliers du Tastevin 1977*

# Almond Soufflé

6 eggs, carefully separated

4 oz caster sugar

½ c white wine

½ pt double cream

2–3 leaves gelatine or ½ tsp powdered gelatine

2 drops almond essence

4 macaroons or Amaretti biscuits, crushed

Place egg yolks in stainless-steel bowl, add sugar and white wine and beat continuously over boiling water until

thick and creamy, with mixture forming ribbons on top.

Melt gelatine completely in a little boiling water, add to egg mixture and put aside to cool. When nearly cool, whip cream until light and add to egg mixture. Add essence. Whisk egg whites until stiff and fold into mixture.

Place in soufflé moulds on top of crushed macaroons or Amaretti biscuits. Chill for at least 2 hours before serving.

**CHEF'S TIP**

Soufflé moulds should have outer wrapping of greaseproof paper, standing 1 inch higher than rim. Remove before serving.

# Hambleton Hall

**Hambleton Hall** has a spectacular setting on a virtual island in the middle of beautiful Rutland Water, near Oakham. It is ideal for fishing, sailing, riding, and golf; for visiting historic Stamford, Burghley House, Lincoln, Belton, Rockingham, and Belvoir Castle; or simply for relaxing in romantic surroundings. Tim and Stefa Hart opened this comfortable and elegant 15 bedroom hotel in 1980, assisted by a young English staff and determined to make guests feel welcome. Only four years later, they are the Good Food Guide Country Hotel of the Year 1984.

Head Chef Nicholas Gill is responsible for devising the menu and creating dishes which have won Hambleton Hall many awards and brought it so quickly into the front rank of British restaurants. He has trained at Westminster Hotel School, and has worked (among others) at the Savoy Hotel, Waltons of London and Maxims of Paris. Chef Gill is a founder member of the Country Chefs Seven, the association of 7 distinguished young English chefs.

Complementing the menu, the wine list concentrates on bottles that are delicious to drink, avoiding fashionable labels with indifferent contents.

**Hambleton, Oakham
Rutland**

**0572-56991**

**Lunch and Dinner daily**

**Proprietors: Tim and Stefa Hart
Chef: Nicholas Gill**

# Rosette of Avocado and Lobster

1 carrot, 1 leek, 1 onion, 3 shallots, 1
  clove garlic, 2 sticks celery

2 live lobsters, 1 dessertspoon olive oil

1 dessertspoon tomato purée, 1 tbsp flour

1 glass Armagnac

2 glasses dry white wine

1 pt good fish stock

10 fresh tomatoes, peeled and chopped

   parsley stalks, fresh tarragon, 2 bay
   leaves, 1 tsp paprika

4 oz fresh mayonnaise (unseasoned)

4 oz fromage blanc

2 large, ripe avocados, juice of 2 limes

10 green peppercorns, salt, Dijon mustard,
   bunch of fresh chervil (extra to garnish)

4 beefsteak tomatoes

½ pt double cream (high fat content)

To prepare the cold lobster sauce: cut the first six ingredients into fine dice (i.e. brunoise). Heat a heavy casserole on top of the stove, add the oil, then the live lobsters and continue cooking over a fierce heat until turned completely bright red. Add the brunoise of vegetables and continue to fry for a few seconds, now add the tomato purée and the flour and cook for 2 minutes more. Flame with the Armagnac, add the wine, reduce for 1 minute and pour in the fish stock. Add the peeled and chopped tomatoes and the herbs and spices, cover the pan, bring to the boil and simmer for about 20 minutes. Remove the lobsters, take out the fish flesh and keep to one side, covered with a clean damp cloth. Pulverise remaining heads and carcasses in a pestle and mortar and add to the simmering sauce. Cover and cook gently for 2–3 hours until you are satisfied with its strength. Pass the sauce through a coarse sieve into a clean saucepan, squeezing the solids with the back of a ladle to extract all juices. Reduce sauce gently, skimming off all scum, until syrupy. Pass through a fine sieve into a clean basin and allow to cool. When cold, thicken to a good coating consistency by whisking in the mayonnaise and 3 ounces fromage blanc. Check the colour, consistency, and seasoning.

To prepare the avocado mousse: purée the avocados in a food processor with the lime juice, salt, peppercorns, mustard, and chervil and refrigerate.

To prepare the rosette: peel the beefsteak tomatoes, halve them and remove all seeds and interior flesh with a Parisienne cutter. Place shells on a clean tray, season with salt and pepper and refrigerate. Slice the lobster tails into thin medallions. Spoon the avocado mousse into the tomatoes and decorate with fresh chervil. Place 3 or 4 medallions of lobster, around the top, and crown the rosette with a lobster's tentacle. Refrigerate.

To serve: mix remaining fromage blanc with cream. Coat 8 large serving plates with the lobster sauce, pipe the fromage blanc mixture on each and, using a knife, draw a web pattern. Place the rosette carefully in the centre of this spider's web, and serve.                    Serves: 8

# Sliced Fillet of Lamb with Fresh Herbs

1 double loin of young English lamb

  olive oil, salt and pepper
  tarragon, chervil, mint, thyme, parsley,
  watercress and spinach

2 pt strong lamb stock

5 shallots, finely chopped

1 glass dry vermouth

1 pt double cream (high fat content)

2 lb French turnips and 2 carrots

2 lb potatoes (Dutch binje)

½ lb young mangetout

  dozen fresh asparagus tips

Prepare the lamb a day in advance. Strip it of all bone, fat, and sinew, producing two long fillets. Marinate the fillets overnight in olive oil and finely chopped fresh tarragon chervil, mint, thyme and parsley. Reserve the bones.

To prepare the herb sauce: blanch bunches of fresh tarragon, chervil, mint, thyme, parsley (reserving a few leaves), watercress, and spinach by plunging into rapidly boiling water, then almost immediately into cold water. Drain, purée, put into a clean bowl and refrigerate. Reduce the lamb stock, with the lightly roasted and finely chopped lamb bones, to a syrupy residue. Remove the bones. In a clean saucepan, sweat the shallots with the vermouth and the lamb glaze, until almost evaporated. Add the cream and simmer gently for 5–10 minutes until slightly thickened. Sieve and keep warm.

To prepare the vegetable garnish: using a small Parisienne cutter, cut balls out of the carrot, turnip, and the potato. Top and tail the mangetout and bundle the asparagus. Cook carrot and turnip glacé, fry the potato, blanch the asparagus and mangetout.

Heat a little olive oil in a heavy-duty pan on top of the stove, add the drained and seasoned fillets of lamb, and cook over a fairly fierce heat, turning occasionally, until the lamb is well sealed and nicely pink inside. Remove from the pan and keep warm.

Add herb purée to stock and cream until a deep green colour and good flavour is obtained. Sieve and adjust seasoning and consistency to taste.

To serve: coat 8 large hot plates with the sauce. Slice the lamb into thin medallions and lay these, around the plate. Decorate with vegetables and herb leaves.        Serves: 8

# Hill's
# Restarant

Originally part of a 17th century farm building, **Hill's Restaurant** is to be found near the market place in Stratford-upon-Avon. It is small and simply decorated, seating only thirty persons between the intimate flag-stoned restaurant and the galleried upstairs.

The menus are handwritten almost daily to reflect what is best of the locally available produce: fruit and vegetables from the Vale of Evesham, cheeses from Major Rance's stores in Berkshire, fresh fish from Cornwall.

The wine list is well chosen rather than comprehensive, with 50 wines listed.

Shaun Hill, after extensive training, was executive chef at the Lygon Arms before opening this delightful small restaurant.

## Hill's Restaurant

**3 Greenhill Street
Stratford-upon-Avon,
Warwickshire**

**0789-293563**

**Lunch: By arrangement
Dinner: Tuesday — Saturday 7 to 11 p.m.**

**Proprietor/Chef: Shaun Hill**

# Roulade of Sole

6 scallops

salt and pepper

1 fl oz double cream

6 sole fillets

¼ pt red shellfish stock (see below)

1 lb unsalted butter

¼ pt white wine

1 small piece fresh ginger, peeled and crushed

lemon or lime juice

Process the scallops in a food processor for a few seconds then pass through a sieve. Season with salt and pepper and mix in the cream. Lay the sole fillets alongside and touching each other. Lay the scallop purée on top. Roll the fillets up together and smooth into one "sausage". Cover with buttered paper.

To make the red butter: reduce the red shellfish stock by half and thicken with ½ pound of the butter. To make the white butter: add ginger to the white wine and reduce by half. Add remaining ½ pound of butter to thicken. Finish with lemon or lime juice and strain.

Steam the "sausage" for 2 minutes until just cooked. Slice it into circles and serve surrounded by the two sauces.

Serves: 6

**CHEF'S TIP**

To make red shellfish stock, simmer together some fish carcasses, lobster or crab shells, a little tomato purée, leeks, carrots, onion, and a bouquet garni in water for 20 minutes. Strain.

# Croustade of Veal

1 lb well-rested puff pastry

1 lb veal fillet

1 lb calf's sweetbreads, lightly blanched

1 lb calf's kidney

butter for frying

a little veal stock

1 tsp Meaux mustard

4 oz unsalted butter, cut in pieces

1 tbsp cream

salt and pepper

Roll out the puff pastry to ¼ inch thick. Cut 6 rounds with a cutter, press these into scallop shells or similar moulds to make croustades and bake blind in a hot oven for 5 minutes.

Carefully remove any nerve or membrane from the veal. Cut veal, sweetbread, and kidney into neat ¼ inch dice. Heat some butter in a copper pan and fry all meat quickly until pink. Remove and keep warm. Deglaze the pan with a little veal stock and the mustard. Whisk in the butter, piece by piece, until thick. Finish with the cream and seasoning, then strain onto veal.

To serve: remove croustades from the oven, spoon veal mixture into the centres and serve immediately.

Serves: 6

# Bavarian Creams with Marron Glacé

½ pt milk

½ tsp vanilla essence

4 oz caster sugar

4 egg yolks

2 sheets gelatine, well soaked in water

½ pt double cream, whipped

2 marrons glacés, roughly chopped

½ lb raspberries

1 oz stock syrup

Slowly boil the milk with vanilla essence. Cream together the sugar and egg yolks. Whisk the milk onto the egg yolks and stir over low heat until mixture starts to thicken. Stir in gelatine. Sieve and allow to cool. When nearly set add the whisked cream and marrons. Pour into ramekins and allow to set. Blend raspberries and syrup to a purée in food processor. Turn out cream onto a plate and serve with a little raspberry purée.

Serves: 6

# The Lygon Arms

The stately **Lygon Arms** has been providing hospitality for more than 400 years in Broadway, reputed to be one of the most famous villages in England. Here at the Inn, the old and the new are successfully combined to provide 20th century comforts in a unique 16th century setting that features a wealth of antiques, log fires, and oak-beamed rooms.

The setting for dinner is the Great Hall, with its barrel-shaped ceiling and oak panelling. "Now good digestion wait on appetite and health on both" is written above the entrance to the room. There is a fine cocktail bar, adjacent to the Great Hall, that features canapés and, on cold nights, hot savouries.

The Lygon Arms is situated in the centre of the Cotswolds and on the edge of the Vale of Evesham, and the menu reflects this: Cotswold Lamb and Evesham Vale Asparagus and Strawberries are offered along with choice traditional French dishes and all are complemented by an international and highly selective wine list.

Should you require a meal for a special occasion, Chef Alain Dubois (previously at Hunstrete House) is glad to accommodate.

---

## The Lygon Arms

**Broadway, Worcester**

**0386-852255**

**Breakfast, Lunch, and Dinner
Daily
Reservations**

**Proprietor: Douglas Barrington
Chef: Alain Dubois**

---

# North Sea Fish Soup

½ lb each: turbot, cod, scallops, and monkfish

4 oz peeled prawns

lemon juice, as needed

2 pt fish stock, made from white wine, fish bones, prawn shells, and water

1 oz chopped shallot

1 oz chopped parsley

1 large tomato, skinned and seeded

½ oz potato flour

3 egg yolks

½ pt cream

salt, pepper, and nutmeg, to taste

Skin and fillet fish. Cut into large chunks and turn briefly in lemon juice to keep from discolouring. Poach fish in stock until just done. Lift fish into a tureen, add shallot, parsley, and tomato. Slightly thicken the cooking liquid with potato flour. Mix egg yolks and cream together and add to cooking liquid. Reboil. Adjust seasoning with salt, pepper, and nutmeg. Pass soup onto fish.

Serving suggestion: serve with croutons made from 2 slices of white bread.

Serves: 6

Wine: *chilled Don Zoilo Fino Sherry*

**CHEF'S TIP**

Take care not to test soup for seasoning and texture with a teaspoon or by dipping in your finger. What tastes fine in tiny amounts is often overpowering when you are to take a bowlful. Use a soupspoon or a cup.

# Supreme of Hare with Horseradish

6 fillets of hare

1 drop of vinegar

1 pt good game or veal stock

4 tbsp grated horseradish

1 tbsp mustard

½ pt double cream

1 lb celeriac purée

Remove membrane from fillets. Reserve a little hare's blood mixed with a drop of vinegar. Seal fillets in a copper pan and cook slowly for about 5 minutes until pink. Remove fillets, set aside, and keep warm.

Deglaze pan with stock and allow to reduce. Add horseradish, mustard, and cream, then reboil. Finish sauce with hare's blood. Adjust seasoning. Slice fillets and arrange on top of sauce. Garnish with celeriac purée.

Serves: 6

Wine: *Aloxe Corton, Chanson Père et Fils, 1971*

# Pears in Cider

6 pears

1 pt stock syrup

1 pt cider

6 egg yolks

6 oz caster sugar

juice of 1 lemon

8 leaves gelatine, well soaked

Peel the pears without removing the stalks. Poach in stock syrup and ¼ cider until done. Allow to cool. In a double saucepan or over a bain-marie, whisk the egg yolks, sugar, remaining cider, and lemon juice. When thick, incorporate the well soaked gelatine. Arrange the pears in a crystal bowl or attractive glasses. Coat with the cider sabayon. Serve chilled.

Serves: 6

Wine: *Château Coutet Premier Cru Barsac, 1972*

# Mallory Court Hotel

**Mallory Court Hotel** is a country house hotel set in ten acres of garden-like grounds. Built in 1915, it was once the luxurious home of Sir John Black of Standard Motors. This small private hotel is now owned by Allan Holland and Jeremy Mort who, five years ago, purchased the property and converted the house. Both owners have had prior management experience: Mr. Holland in the retail business and Mr. Mort in the hotel trade in both Switzerland and the U.K.

A main attraction of Mallory Court is its restaurant. Its decor is highlighted by fine oak panelling and enormous open fireplaces, both of which add to the intentional warmth of the place.

Mr. Holland is the chef, and his modest but comprehensive menu reflects his preference for *la nouvelle* French cuisine. Therefore, the accent is on lighter and more imaginative cooking. Chef Holland also goes to great lengths to present each dish in as uncluttered and as appetising a fashion as possible.

There is no bar area, however, there is bar service at the table. There are also 100 bins of carefully selected French and German wines, most priced in the medium to expensive range, from which to choose to complement a most rewarding dining experience.

## Mallory Court

**Harbury Lane, Bishops Tackbrook**
**Leamington Spa, Warwickshire**

**0926-30214**

**Lunch: 12.30 to 2 p.m.**
**Sunday — Friday**
**Dinner: 7.30 to 10 p.m.**
**Monday — Saturday**
**and Sunday for Residents only**
**Reservations**

**Proprietors: Allan Holland**
**Jeremy Mort**
**Chef: Allan Holland, M.C.G.B.**

# Suprême de Volaille Jacqueline

8 oz raw, skinned, and boned duck flesh

1 egg white

½ tsp salt

　pinch of white pepper

8-10 fl oz double cream, chilled

¾ pt chicken stock

6× 6-7 oz chicken suprêmes

4 fl oz red port

½ pt double cream

　lemon juice, as needed

　salt and white pepper, to taste

1 oz butter

2 oz flaked almonds sautéed in butter until golden

6 thin slices truffle

　sprigs of fresh chervil or parsley, to garnish

To prepare duck mousse: purée the duck flesh either in a food processor or by mincing then pounding flesh in a mortar. Slowly beat egg white into the purée. Pass through a fine drum sieve into a basin, put basin on ice, and refrigerate for 1 hour. Lightly whip chilled double cream until it begins to thicken, then gradually beat cream into duck mousse over ice with a wooden spoon until mixture looks light and mousse-like. Season with salt and white pepper. (If mousse seems too firm, add more cream.) Cover the basin and refrigerate.

Make a slit on the top of the breasts lengthways to form a small pocket. Fill pocket with some duck mousse, but do not overfill as mousse will swell during cooking. Place filled suprêmes in a lightly buttered sauté pan and pour cold chicken stock in. Cover pan, bring slowly to simmering point, and poach suprêmes very gently for about 8-10 minutes or until just cooked. Remove suprêmes; cover and keep warm while finishing the sauce.

To prepare sauce: pour port into the pan with the stock and boil down rapidly over high heat until well reduced and syrupy. Add cream and reduce briefly until sauce has a coating consistency. Remove from heat and add lemon juice and seasoning to taste. Swirl in the butter. Pass sauce through a very fine strainer.

Arrange the suprêmes in the centre of a serving dish or on individual plates and coat with the sauce. Sprinkle with almonds and garnish with truffle slices. Surround dish with sprigs of chervil or parsley.

Serves: 6

---

# Crème Brûlée aux Mandarines

6 mandarins

1 pt double cream

8 egg yolks

2 oz caster sugar

2 tbsp Mandarin Napoleon liqueur

　soft light brown sugar, as needed

With a very sharp, small knife, remove rind and pith from mandarins and cut out the segments. Divide segments, without membrane, among 6 small ramekins, arranging them on the bottom of the dishes.

Rinse a heavy saucepan with cold water and leave wet. Pour in double cream and heat to just below simmering point over low heat. In a separate bowl, beat egg yolks and caster sugar together until thick and pale in colour. Slowly pour hot cream onto yolk and sugar mixture, stirring slowly. Blend in liqueur.

Rinse out a saucepan and leave wet. Pour in custard mixture and, over very low heat or a pan of simmering water, cook custard, stirring continuously with a wooden spoon. (Make sure to scrape bottom of pan to prevent custard catching.) Continue stirring until mixture thickens sufficiently (until it leaves a trail when you lift out the spoon) but *do not boil*. Strain custard into ramekins and allow to cool. Refrigerate at least 6 hours or overnight.

An hour before serving, preheat grill and sprinkle an even layer of sugar (about ¼ inch thick) over the top of the custards. Place ramekins in a shallow tin filled with ice cubes and place under hot grill until sugar melts and caramelises (only a few moments). Remove from grill and allow to cool, but do not refrigerate.

Serves: 6−8

### CHEF'S TIP

If mandarins are not available, oranges can be substituted. In that case, add a spoonful of grated rind to the custard and use Grand Marnier instead of the Napoleon liqueur.

# Le Manoir aux Quat' Saisons

**Le Manoir aux Quat' Saisons** opened early in 1984 in Great Milton Manor, a Grade II Historic House, 15 minutes from Oxford. Raymond and Jenny Blanc have converted The Manor into a 10 bedroomed country house hotel, and incorporated their existing restaurant Les Quat' Saisons, which won numerous accolades during its 6 years in Summertown, Oxford.

The Manor is in a beautiful setting, surrounded by 27 acres of landscaped gardens and parkland, with tennis court, swimming pool and an attractive water garden. All bedrooms are luxuriously appointed, each with en suite bathroom (some with jacuzzi). There are 3 delightful interconnecting dining rooms, each with quite individual character, and a large private dining room for functions.

The menu features contemporary seasonal cuisine prepared with Raymond Blanc's unique natural flair and seasoned with his admirable philosophy. His own description cannot be bettered:

"Every happy instant is celebrated at the table, which is such a wonderful symbol of happiness, friendship, love ... the little miracle of the contentment of the guest ... that is the soul of our Team, the real meaning of our work.

'Of course, the stone base is the cuisine, the seasons playing the most vital part in the choice of dishes, bringing new colours, flavours, and taste ... new ideas, teasing your imagination..."

**Le Manoir aux Quat' Saisons**

**Great Milton, Oxfordshire OX9 7PD**

**08446-230**

**Lunch: Tuesday — Sunday**
**Dinner: Tuesday — Saturday**
**Reservations**
**Proprietors: Raymond and Jenny Blanc**
**Chef: Raymond Blanc, M.C.G.B.**

# Escalopes de Turbot

## aux poireaux et saveurs des sous-bois

6 × 150 g turbot fillets

lemon butter to brush turbot

2 tbsp shallots

14 g butter

300 ml Gewürztraminer wine (a dry and fruity wine)

1 handful button mushrooms, finely sliced

12 baby leeks, trimmed, washed, tied up, blanched for 3–4 minutes, then cut into 1½ cm pieces

300 g wild mushrooms, washed (girolles, chanterelles, morilles or mousserons de printemps)

juice of ½ lemon (extra to taste)

2 tbsp truffle juice

2 tbsp Madeira

2 tbsp whipping cream

170 g unsalted butter, cut into small pieces

1 tbsp finely chopped chives

Jersey new potatoes, to garnish

Season the turbot fillets and brush with lemon butter. Heat gently a straight-sided sauteuse (large enough to hold the 6 turbot fillets later). Add the shallots and ½ tablespoon butter, and cook until translucent (not coloured). Add the wine and boil for 1 minute to remove the alcohol. Add the sliced button mushrooms. Place the turbot on this bed. Seal the pan and place in a preheated oven at gas mark 6 (400°F/200°C) for 3 minutes.

Meanwhile, warm up leeks in an emulsion of butter and water. Put a knob of butter in another pan, sauté the wild mushrooms, add a squeeze of lemon and the truffle juice and cook for 1 minute. Remove the wild mushrooms, cover and keep them warm. Pour the juices from the wild mushrooms into a casserole. Add the Madeira and reduce, then add 30 grams of butter. Keep this sauce to one side.

After 3 minutes, remove the turbot and check it is correctly cooked (when pressed slightly the fish should not break, or offer too much resistance). Keep turbot warm. Pass the fish juices through a fine strainer and reduce by ⅓. Add cream, bring to the boil, and the 170 grams unsalted butter pieces and blend together by whisking at full boil. Add the chives, seasoning, and lemon juice to taste.

To serve: place a fillet of turbot in the middle of a plate and arrange around it alternate little moulds of leeks and wild mushrooms. Cover with buttered paper and place back in the oven for 2 minutes covered. Remove, pour the wine sauce over the turbot, and truffle sauce over the wild mushrooms, to give magnificent colour and texture contrast.

Serves: 6

Wine: *Gewürztraminer 1976*

# Nougat Glacé aux Fruits de la Passion

400 g sugar

100 ml water

5 egg whites

250 ml milk

250 ml cream

2 vanilla pods

6 egg yolks

900 ml passion-fruit juice

100 ml orange juice

60 ml mandarin liqueur

250 g whipping cream, whipped

75 g nougatine

1 tsp arrowroot

5 tbsp passion-fruit ice cream

To prepare Italian meringue: mix 300 grams of the sugar with the water and bring to the boil until temperature reaches 120°C/250°F. Whip the egg whites until stiff and pour the syrup gently over them, beating well all the time.

To prepare passion-fruit ice cream: make a vanilla cream by heating together the milk, cream, vanilla pods, egg yolks, and remaining 100 grams of sugar. When cold add 400 ml of passion-fruit juice and the orange juice. Pour the mixture into a sorbetière and when almost set add 150 grams of the Italian meringue. Using a spatula, line the bottom and sides of a terrine with ⅗ of the ice cream, leaving a cavity for the nougat. Place in the deep freeze.

To prepare nougat: mix together the mandarin liqueur, whipped cream, nougatine, and remaining Italian meringue (250 grams). Place this mixture in the cavity of the terrine, and, using a spatula, seal the terrine with ½ of remaining ice cream. Freeze for 8 hours.

To prepare coulis: place remaining of passion-fruit juice in a pan. Warm and bind with arrowroot. When cool whisk in the remaining ice cream. Chill.

To serve: turn out nougat glace onto a serving dish by dipping the terrine in hot water. Pour the cold coulis around it.

Serves: 6

Wine: *Champagne Brut*

# Rookery Hall

**Rookery Hall,** the home of Mr. and Mrs. Peter Marks, is reputedly Georgian in origin but was rebuilt in the early 19th century. It is set in 28 acres of gardens and wooded parkland. Poised on a hill overlooking the green Cheshire plain, it is one of the finest country houses in the area.

The architecture is impressive, in the style of a grand château. Baron Von Schroeder, who owned it at the turn of the century, was responsible for the substantial additions that give it an unusual Continental, baronial character, making it almost unique in Britain today.

In three intimate, panelled dining rooms, Brian Hamilton presents his award-winning French cooking. This talented young chef, ex sous-chef, under Christian Delteil, at Chewton Glen and more recently from the legendary La Réserve de Beaulieu at Beaulieu-sur-Mer, southern France. The emphasis is on many small courses, rather than the conventional three-course meal, so a memorable six-course dinner with sorbet is served nightly. The wine list was previous owner, Harry Norton's special interest; it offers a choice from about 500 bins, with more than 20 vintage ports.

There are 12 individually furnished letting bedrooms, including 3 splendid suites; the atmosphere is one of secluded tranquility and style — more like a luxurious, well-staffed home than a hotel.

Worleston
**Near Nantwich, Cheshire**
**0270-626866**
**Non-residents:**
Dinner: Tuesday — Saturday
**Residents: All meals daily**
**Reservations**

Proprietors: Peter and Audrey Marks
Chefs: Jean Norton, M.C.G.B.
**Brian Hamilton**

# Feuilleté de Foies de Volaille au Madère

1 oz butter

1 large onion, thinly sliced

1 lb chicken livers, cleaned, halved and marinated in milk overnight

½ cup Madeira

½ cup chicken stock

1 tsp thyme, preferably fresh

freshly ground black pepper

pinch salt

1 egg, beaten with a little milk

6 puff pastry lids for 6 ramekins

Melt butter in a saucepan, add onion, then livers and sauté gently for 5 minutes. Add Madeira and stock and bring to boil. Simmer for a further 5 minutes. Stir in thyme, black pepper and salt.

Spoon into small ramekins. Brush the edges with eggwash and place a pastry lid on each. Brush with eggwash and cook in a hot oven at gas mark 6 (400 ° F/200 ° C) for 10 minutes.

Serves: 6

Wine: *Hermitage, Chante-Alouette, 1979, Chapoutier*

**CHEF'S TIP**

Do not overcook livers as this will spoil the dish completely.

---

# Aiguillettes de Caneton sur Duxelles, Deux Sauces

3 × 5 lb fresh ducks, dressed weight

1 lb fresh veal

1 large onion

2 medium mushrooms

2 cloves of garlic

1 tsp thyme, preferably fresh

2 egg yolks

2 tbsp brandy

2 tbsp double cream

½ tsp ground mixed spice

½ tsp salt, ground black pepper

honey for glaze

Remove duck breasts with skin and set aside. To prepare forcemeat: remove remaining flesh and mince finely with veal, onion, mushrooms, and garlic. Add thyme, egg yolks, brandy, cream, mixed spice, ground black pepper, and salt and mix well. Shape the mixture into 6 portions and place each on a small square of tinfoil.

Remove skin carefully from duck breasts. Slice breasts thinly and place over prepared forcemeat. Neatly trim breast skin, removing surplus fat, score and place on top of breasts. Mould foil around portions to form a neat oval, and brush skin with honey. Cook in a hot oven at gas mark 6 (400 ° F/200 ° C) for 15 minutes, then finish off under the grill.

Serve with two sauces: a fruit purée and a Madeira sauce.

Serves: 6

Wine: *Clos de la Roche, 1976, Domaine Armand Rousseau*

**CHEF'S TIP**

Pour surplus fat off during cooking otherwise forcemeat will get soggy.

---

# Syllabub au Gingembre

750 ml double cream

2 tbsp advocaat

1 lemon (juice of whole and zest of ½)

6 pieces of stem ginger, finely chopped, and a little of the syrup

3 egg whites, stiffly whipped

Whip together cream, advocaat, lemon juice, and zest. Fold in ginger and syrup, and egg whites.

Serves: 6

Wine: *Château Coutet 1974, Premier Cru Barsac, C.B.*

**CHEF'S TIP**

If extra sweetness is needed, add a little icing sugar with the egg whites. This syllabub keeps well.

# La Sorbonne Restaurant

The building that **La Sorbonne Restaurant** occupies is better known as Kemp Hall. It was built in 1637. Situated on High Street in the centre of Oxford, it must count as one of the best preserved and least altered examples of 17th century domestic architecture in the city. The exterior of the building is distinguished by five gables of various sizes, a timbered framework, and overhanging upper stories. The interior is still in an excellent state of preservation as well, with its many original fireplaces, doorways, and a fine carved staircase.

The building became the site of La Sorbonne in September 1966, when the lease was acquired by M. André Chavagnon. Since then, it has become one of the finest restaurants in the county, providing a menu of a range and quality with which few others can compare.

André Chavagnon began his apprenticeship at age 14 at the Grand Hotel in Roanne. After three years, he went on to work in Vichy, Cannes, and Paris, gaining experience in all types of cuisine. He came to England in 1956 and has remained here. When he opened La Sorbonne, he had only one waiter; today, there is a large service and kitchen staff to cater to discriminating diners from all over the world. The original waiter, Alain Desenclos, is still serving today.

## La Sorbonne

**130A High Street**
**Oxford, Oxfordshire**

**0865-41320**

**Lunch: 12 to 2 p.m.**
**Dinner: 7 to 11 p.m.**
**Monday — Saturday**
**Reservations**

**Proprietor/Chef: A.P. Chavagnon**

# Le Râble de Lièvre Sauce Poivrade

1 pt red wine

1 French onion

2 carrots

1 bay leaf

1 sprig fresh thyme

½ oz crushed black pepper

1 clove garlic

2 tbsp vegetable oil

salt, to taste

1 tsp natural green pepper

1 tbsp red wine vinegar

1 × 8 lb hare

2 oz fresh butter

2 French shallots, finely chopped

3 tbsp double cream

1 tbsp redcurrant jelly

2 tbsp brandy

boiled new potatoes, to garnish

½ oz finely chopped parsley

To prepare marinade: mix red wine, onion, carrots, bay leaf, thyme, black pepper, garlic, ½ the vegetable oil, salt, green pepper, and vinegar together. Cut legs from hare. Marinate back or saddle (le râble). After 3 days, heat ½ the butter and remaining oil. When very hot, cook saddle for 10 minutes, turning it frequently. Remove meat and drain oil from saucepan. Strain marinade.

To prepare sauce: add remaining butter, shallots, 6 tablespoons of marinade, and green pepper to oiled saucepan. Heat until reduced by ½. Add cream and jelly. Reduce again for 2 minutes.

Bone hare into long thin slices, then replace it in its original form, keeping meat pink. Pour brandy on top and place in hot oven for 2 minutes. Remove from oven and cover with sauce.

To serve: garnish with potatoes and sprinkle with parsley.

Serves: 4

**CHEF'S TIP**

Always give yourself plenty of time when preparing a meal. Always think about what you are doing to make sure you do not make mistakes.

---

# La Tarte aux Pommes Flambée au Calvados

250 g sieved plain flour

120 g caster sugar

3 drops vanilla essence

150 g butter

2 egg yolks

1 egg white

200 ml water

pinch of salt

500 g best cooking apples, peeled and cored

300 g granulated sugar

100 ml water

butter, as needed

200 ml Calvados

Prepare pâté sable by mixing first 8 ingredients together. Refrigerate approximately 4 hours. When chilled, roll out pastry and line a 20 cm dish (about 2.5 cm deep). Prick base with fork. Place a layer of greaseproof paper on base and cover with baking beans. Bake blind for 20 minutes at 350°F (175°C). Allow to cool.

To prepare filling: cook 300 grams apples with ½ the sugar in water. Reduce until purée is a golden colour. Allow to cool.

Slice remaining apples in fan-shaped slices. Fill tart base with cooled apple purée. Decorate top with apple slices. Dot with butter. Sprinkle with remaining sugar and brown under a moderate grill for 2−3 minutes.

To serve: pour flamed Calvados over and serve warm.

Serves: 4

Wine: *Calvados*

# The Bridge Inn

**The Bridge Inn** is a pub/restaurant in a beautiful Durham village. It has a charming dining room and bar, which are separate from the main pub and overlook the village green. Proprietors Nick and Cath Young are dedicated to good food and try to share their enthusiasm with their clientele, who are welcomed with a friendly smile, a plate of fresh crudités, and a dish of garlic mayonnaise. Aided by a willing staff of students, they serve a blend of traditional, new and personal dishes — and positively encourage diners to linger.

The Youngs opened The Bridge 5 years ago, after 2 years at the Wansfell Hotel, Cumbria, which they put into the Good Food Guide. A self-taught chef, Nick cooks every order himself, and loves experimenting — the menu includes Brace of Quail with Black Cherry Sauce and Paddy's Brochette, lamb's kidney and liver wrapped in bacon, skewered, and charcoal-grilled with garlic and herb butter. The humble-sounding "selection of vegetables" is a delight, as are Cath's home-made sweets (and bread), followed by large cups of coffee, with fudge.

The medium-sized wine list is reasonably priced, with some real gems; and cask beers are sold from handpumps in the public bar, where there are some genuine pub-grub bargains.

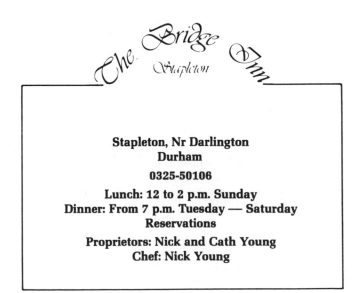

**Stapleton, Nr Darlington
Durham**

**0325-50106**

**Lunch: 12 to 2 p.m. Sunday
Dinner: From 7 p.m. Tuesday — Saturday
Reservations**

**Proprietors: Nick and Cath Young
Chef: Nick Young**

# "Paddy's" Brochette

4 lamb's kidneys, cored and quartered

¾ lb lamb's liver, cut in 1 in sq cubes

8 rashers streaky bacon, derined, flattened, and stretched

½ green pepper, cut in 1 in squares

½ red pepper, cut in 1 in squares

½ large onion, cut in 1 in squares

2–3 cloves garlic

1 dessert spoon fresh thyme, chopped

4–6 oz butter, softened

Wrap each piece of kidney and liver in bacon. Skewer with a piece of pepper, then alternate pieces of liver and kidney, separating each piece with a square of onion or pepper, and finishing with pepper.

Grill over a hot charcoal grill, turning 3 or 4 times, for 5–10 minutes until just cooked. DO NO OVERCOOK. Place on a warm ovenproof dish and spread with ½ the crushed garlic and ½ the chopped thyme. Spread with ½ the softened butter and grill again under a very hot conventional grill until the butter melts and the garlic and thyme just start to sizzle. Turn the brochettes and coat the other side with the remaining garlic, thyme and butter and repeat the final grilling. Serve with the melted herby garlic butter spooned over the brochettes and a little salad garnish, including onion and watercress.

The amounts of garlic, thyme, and butter can be adjusted according to taste — try a little smoked bacon mixed in for variation. A charcoal grill is preferable for this recipe, but a conventional grill can be used.

Serves: 4

Wine: *Côtes du Rhône or Gamay de Touraine*

# Médaillons de Veau Medicis

4 oz good button mushrooms

1 oz butter

good squeeze lemon juice

salt and freshly ground black pepper

1–1¼ lb trimmed veal fillet

1 oz clarified butter

4 tsp ruby port

4 tbsp wine vinegar, rosemary flavoured

4 tbsp veal or chicken stock

4 tbsp double cream

a little butter

Finely slice the mushrooms (reserving 2 or 3 for garnish). Stew them gently with the butter, lemon juice and seasoning until the juices run freely. Strain and reserve liquid. Slice the veal fillet across the grain into ½–¾ inch thick medallions and flatten slightly with the heel of your palm. Sauté in the clarified butter, remove and keep warm.

Deglaze the pan with the port, vinegar, stock, and mushroom *fumet* and reduce until lightly syrupy (about ¾ reduction). Add the cream and thicken slightly by simmering. Add the cooked mushrooms and check the seasoning. If the sauce is too strong add a little more cream; not rich enough, whisk in a little butter.

Arrange the medallions on a dish, garnish with watercress and mushrooms, and spoon over the sauce.

Serves: 4

Wine: *Beaujolais Village or young red Bordeaux*

# Strawberry and Cream Water Ice
## with fresh peach, raspberry and port purée

4–6 oz sugar, ½ pt water

juice of ½ lemon and juice ½, orange

1 lb fresh or frozen strawberries

3 fl oz double cream

½ lb fresh or frozen raspberries

2–3 oz caster sugar

2 fl oz ruby port

4 fresh peaches

Boil the sugar in the water for 10 minutes. Add the lemon and orange juice. Liquidise the strawberries with a little of the cooled syrup and sieve to remove the seeds. Mix the strawberry purée and the rest of the syrup and freeze in a suitable covered container until nearly frozen. Put the cream into the liquidiser and add the frozen strawberry purée gradually, blending well until smooth. Freeze.

Liquidise the raspberries, caster sugar and port. Sieve to remove seeds and set aside. Submerge the peaches in just boiled water for about 1 minute, refresh in cold water and skin them. With a sharp stainless-steel knife, cut towards the peach stone vertically, cutting out ¼ inch thick wedge-shaped segments. Work right round the peach leaving just the stone. Reserve the segments.

Place one scoop of water ice in the centre of a flat sweet plate. Carefully spoon the raspberry purée round the water ice, covering the whole of the plate, and arrange the slices of peach on top of the purée, each slice pointing outwards like the petals of a flower.

Serves: 4

# Farlam Hall

**Farlam Hall** is listed as of historical and architectural interest. In 1826, the property changed hands, and from a 17th century farmhouse, it was enlarged in stages to become a notable border manor house and the centre of a thriving local community.

John Wesley is reputed to have preached in the house. George Stephenson, of steam engine fame, stayed here; his famous "Rocket" belonged to the family, and it spent the last years of its working life on the local line before being presented to the Science Museum.

Farlam Hall stands in four acres of mature grounds with lovely trees, a stream, and an ornamental lake. It is now a country house hotel, owned and personally run by the Quinion family, that offers Cordon Bleu cooking and high standards of comfort and service. Extensive use is made of the prime local meat, game, fish, and dairy produce available. Only fresh vegetables are offered. A modest, but well selected, wine list is available.

A small bar for the use of residents and diners, three lounges, 11 spacious bedrooms, central heating, and open fires all contribute to the feeling of peace and well-being enjoyed in this fine old country house.

## Farlam Hall

**Bampton, Cumbria**
**06976-234**
**Lunch on Sunday, Dinner nightly**
**Reservations**
**Proprietor: Alan Quinion and family**
**Chef: Barry Quinion**

## Hot Savoury Cheese Tart

¾ pt double cream

3 whole eggs

3 oz strong cheese, grated

1 tsp mixed herbs

1 tsp chopped parsley

  salt and pepper

8 in pastry case (uncooked)

Combine together (preferably in a blender) all filling ingredients and place mixture into the pastry case. Bake at gas mark 5 (375°F/190°C) for about 45 minutes in the centre of the oven.

Serve hot, or cold with salad (almost as good).

Serves: 6–8

---

## Supreme of Duckling with Quenelles

2 medium ducklings (to give 6 oz leg meat)

2 egg whites

6 oz double cream

  brandy

  salt and pepper

¼ medium onion

1 tsp mixed herbs

¼ pt red wine

½ pt brown stock

Remove the legs from the ducklings and mince the leg meat 3 times. Blend with the egg whites, cream, brandy, and seasoning, make into quenelles and leave to rest for about 4 hours. Cook the duck breasts on the bone at gas mark 6 (400°F/200°C) for 35–40 minutes, until just pink, and poach the quenelles.

To prepare red wine sauce: reduce onion, mixed herbs and red wine to ½ quantity then add stock and simmer for a few minutes.

To serve: pour sauce over duckling and quenelles.

Serves: 4

---

## Strawberry Cake

½ lb digestive biscuits

4 oz butter

4 oz caster sugar

2 eggs, separated

  grated rind of 1 lemon

½ lb strawberries

½ pt cream, lightly whipped

Crush the biscuits and use ⅓ of them to line a lightly buttered flan ring (with removable base). Cream the butter and sugar together. Add the egg yolks and lemon rind. Whisk egg whites until thick and fold them in. Place the mixture onto the crumb base. Slice the strawberries and lay them on top of the mixture. Pour the cream onto the strawberries and cover with the remaining crumbs. Chill well.

Serves: 6–8

# McCoy's Restaurant

Conceived in 1973, later to be born in November 1976, **McCoy's Restaurant** is the result of three brothers' aspirations, frustrations, and determination to succeed.

The building, which was built originally as a "post-house" in 1804, employs a somewhat eclectic decor, borrowing from almost every decade of the 20th century in furnishings and accessories, all of which add up to, say the owners, "a rather suave hotch potch."

This intentional, informal blend is also evident on their menu, which features selections of French, Italian, English, Indian, and other cuisines. The current owners, Peter and Thomas McCoy, are the self-taught cooks, and it is greatly to their credit that they have achieved the high standards evident at McCoy's. Of course, they did have the advantage of being born into the restaurant business and have lived in that atmosphere all their lives.

You will certainly enjoy your visit to McCoy's, whether for the restaurant or five-room hotel, as long as you can get in. The brothers say, "Steer past the only rubber-toothed labrador bitch, find the door if you can, and hope for miracles when you ring the bell."

---

## McCoy's Restaurant

**The Tontine, Staddlebridge
Northallerton, North Yorkshire**

**060982-207**

**Breakfast, Lunch, and Dinner
Monday — Saturday
Reservations**

**Proprietors/Chefs:
Peter and Thomas McCoy**

# Rough Terrine of Chicken Livers and Pork

7 spoonfuls Armagnac

3 tbsp port

3 tbsp sherry

2 tsp peeled, chopped garlic

¾ oz chopped parsley

1 tsp thyme

　pinch of nutmeg

1 tsp caster sugar

2 heaped tsp salt

12 turns of the pepper mill

18 oz chicken livers, halved

7 oz pork belly, cubed

7 oz sausage meat

7 oz pork back fat for lining

4 sprigs thyme

4 bay leaves

8 oz butter

3 lb onions, thinly sliced

3 tsp salt

2 tsp pepper

11 oz sugar

1 lb dried apricots

¾ lb sultanas

14 tbsp sherry vinegar

4 tbsp grenadine

1 pt red wine

To prepare the marinade, mix the first 10 ingredients together. Place the livers, pork cubes, and sausage meat in a bowl and marinate for about 12 hours. Line an ovenproof dish (6½ by 4 by 3 inches) with pork back fat and fill to brim with mixed marinade. Cover top with fat. Put thyme and bay leaves on top. Bake for 3 hours in a bain-marie in the oven at gas mark 7 (425°F/220°C). Cool overnight in the refrigerator.

Next day, prepare apricot and onion purée. Heat the butter in a saucepan until nut brown, add onions, apricots, salt, pepper, and sugar. Cover pan and allow to cook for 30 minutes. Add remaining ingredients and cook slowly for another 30 minutes. Allow to cool. Serve the purée with the terrine.

Serves: 8

Wine: *Beaujolais, Pierre Ferrard, St. Armour, 1978*

---

# Sole Roly Poly

1 tsp chopped chives

4 heaped dessertspoons small, shelled clams

　salt and cayenne pepper, to taste

4 peeled langoustine or jumbo scampi

4 large fillets of sole, skinned

2 hearts of lettuce cooked gently in butter

¼ pt fish fumet

¼ pt double cream

　lemon juice, to taste

Mix chives and clams with a sprinkling of salt and cayenne pepper. Lay ¼ of this mixture with 1 langoustine or scampi on each piece of sole. On top, place ½ lettuce heart. Roll up the sole around the mixture and secure with cocktail sticks.

Poach fillets gently in fish fumet. When fish are just cooked (firm to the touch), remove from pan, set aside, and keep warm.

Quickly reduce fumet to ⅛ pint approximately. Add double cream, bring to a boil, remove from heat, season with salt and lemon juice. Pour sauce over sole fillets and serve.

Wine: *White Beaune Grèves, 1976*

# Michaels Nook

**Michaels Nook Country House Hotel/ Restaurant** is 15 years old and is, today, one of the most renowned country house hotels in England. It still retains the character and atmosphere of an elegant private home; furnishings, enhanced by an abundance of flowers and plants, reflect the taste and knowledge of the proprietor, Reg Gifford, whose reputation is also long-established in the antique world; the ten bedrooms are charmingly decorated and furnished, each with a character of its own.

Relaxed elegance is matched by no lack of sophistication in food, wine, and service in the hotel's restaurant. This small dining room is very tastefully appointed; the genuine antique wood tables are candlelit and set with silver, porcelain, crystal, and fresh flowers — all of which lend to the overall effect of warmth and comfort.

The menu features mainly traditional English dishes. Subtlety of cooking and good wines (not necessarily the most expensive) are high among Reg Gifford's priorities. Chefs Paul Vidic and Philip Vickery have developed a highly skilled and innovative partnership. They work with the finest fresh produce and provide a table d'hôte menu that offers a choice in all courses. The menu changes every day.

Michaels Nook, as a whole, has attracted consistent praise, and both the food and the wine list have received some of the highest accolades.

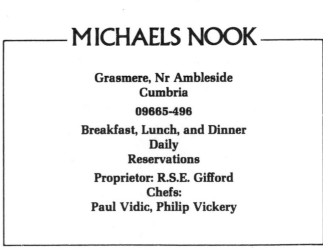

## MICHAELS NOOK

**Grasmere, Nr Ambleside
Cumbria**

**09665-496**

**Breakfast, Lunch, and Dinner
Daily
Reservations**

**Proprietor: R.S.E. Gifford
Chefs:
Paul Vidic, Philip Vickery**

# Scallop Mousse with Saffron

10 fresh scallops without roes

2 oz pike or whiting flesh

   salt and pepper

2 egg whites

2 pt whipping cream, chilled

½ pt Noilly Prat

3 medium shallots, chopped

¼ pt fish stock

   generous pinch of high-grade saffron

   lemon juice to taste

   tomato and watercress to garnish

Soak scallops in water for 1 hour to whiten. Drain and pat dry. Purée in a food processor with whiting or pike flesh, ½ teaspoon salt and a pinch of pepper for 40 seconds. Sieve into a bowl standing on ice. Allow to rest for 30 minutes.

Lightly whisk egg whites into very soft peaks, then, using a spatula, beat together with scallop purée, and gradually add 1¼ pint cream. Check seasoning, and divide among 8 buttered ramekins (2½ inches), tapping down hard to exclude any air. Poach in a covered bain-marie in the oven at gas mark 5 (375 ° F/190 ° C) for about 15 minutes.

To prepare sauce: put the Noilly Prat, shallots and fish stock in a pan and reduce. Add saffron and reduce further to a syrup. Add remaining ¾ pint cream, bring to the boil, reduce by ⅓, and strain into a clean pan. Check seasoning, adding a few drops of lemon juice to bring out the flavours.

To serve: turn out the mousses onto small plates, surround with sauce, and garnish simply with tomato roses and watercress leaves. Serve immediately. Serves: 8

# Guinea Fowl with Blackcurrants

2 × 1½ lb fresh guinea fowl

   salt and pepper

2 oz butter (1 oz clarified, 1 oz softened)

8 oz blackcurrants

3 tbsp water

2 oz sugar

4 capfulls sherry vinegar

2 tbsp blackcurrant jam

1 pt dry white wine

4 tbsp crème de cassis

¾ pt well reduced clear brown game stock

2 tbsp cream

Heat oven to gas mark 7 (425 ° F/220 °C). Truss the guinea fowl, season with salt and pepper. Heat clarified butter in a heavy frying pan and lightly colour guinea fowl on all sides. Transfer birds to the oven for 24 minutes, turning every 8 minutes. They should be slightly underdone to preserve the moisture and tenderness. Untie the guinea fowl, remove the legs and supreme the breasts by cutting closely down each side of the breast bone. Season the joints lightly, and keep warm, but not hot. Chop carcass into 6 pieces and reserve for sauce.

Cook blackcurrants in the water and sugar for 3 minutes. Strain and reserve juice. Keep blackcurrants for garnish.

To prepare sauce: reduce sherry vinegar and blackcurrant jam in a saucepan, deglaze with white wine and reduce by ⅔. Add the crème de cassis, carcasses, game stock, and juice from blackcurrants. Cook gently for 15 minutes, skimming occasionally, and strain through a fine sieve, applying pressure to extract all juice. Reduce sauce again until about ½ pint remains, add cream and season lightly. Remove from heat and add the softened butter.

To serve: slice each guinea fowl breast into 5 long fillets, removing winglets, and arrange in a fan shape on hot plates. Cut the legs into 2 at the joint, and place at the base of the fan. Add blackcurrants to hot sauce, spoon over meat, and serve immediately.

Serves: 4

Wine: *Gewurztraminer, Cuvée Tradition Hugel & Cie, 1978*

# Iced Raspberry Parfait

50 g fresh or frozen raspberries (extra for decoration)

   tiny pinch of salt

4 egg whites

250 g caster sugar

500 ml whipping cream, lightly beaten

To prepare coulis: liquidise raspberries, or rub through a very fine sieve. Sieve again to remove all seeds. (Do not liquidise for too long or the seeds will break up.)

Add a tiny pinch of salt to the egg whites, and whip until stiff. Add ¾ of the sugar and beat again until stiff. Fold in remaining sugar. Fold in ½ the raspberry coulis, then the cream. (The cream will fold in much more easily if left to come to room temperature after it has been lightly beaten.) Place mixture in medium-sized terrine and tap it firmly to remove all air bubbles. Freeze for 4–5 hours.

When frozen, turn out onto an iced board, and slice into portions about ¾ inch thick. Lay each portion on a large chilled plate, and surround with remaining coulis. Place fresh raspberries in coulis for decoration.

Serves: 6

# Miller Howe

**Miller Howe** is an elegant country house hotel, perfectly situated in the heart of the English Lakes. Sitting on the brow of a hill, it looks over Lake Windermere to the Coniston Fells and Langdale Pikes beyond.

But, beautiful though Miller Howe is in its setting and luxurious in the manner of a fine home, it is made, more than anything else, by its people. John Tovey, the internationally famous Chef/Patron, and his staff are people whose pleasure it is to create pleasure. Their unique blend of personalities and skills create, each day, a welcoming, warm atmosphere that will make the most discerning guest feel at home.

Each evening, a different five-course English dinner is served. When the guests are seated, the house lights are dimmed, and the room is transformed into a theatre. The fare is then presented. The panache and élan of the service cooking to produce a brilliant result. The extensive wine list features speciality South African wines.

John Tovey has had no formal training as a chef, but he has most certainly become a professional. After ten years with Miller Howe, his enthusiasm, dedication, and attention to detail have gained him an enviable reputation. Dinner at Miller Howe is a dramatic as well as gastronomic experience.

## MILLER HOWE

**Windermere, Cumbria**
**09662-2536**
**Breakfast and Dinner daily**
**March — December**
**Reservations**
**Proprietor/Chef: John Tovey, M.C.G.B.**

# Spinach and Mushroom Roulade

2 lb frozen or leaf spinach, chopped (not frozen creamed spinach)

½ oz butter, melted

½ nutmeg, grated

4 eggs separated

¼ tsp salt

grated Parmesan cheese

1 lb mushrooms, chopped

1 oz butter

1 pt rich thick white sauce

2 gills Marsala, reduced to 2 tbsp

Cook the spinach in boiling salted water, then leave to drain. Squeeze out remaining water between two dinner plates. Mince the spinach and dry out further with the melted butter in a saucepan over a low heat. Add the nutmeg. Gently beat the egg yolks, beat them into the spinach and turn mixture into a large plastic bowl. Stiffly beat the egg whites with the salt, fold ⅓ into the spinach, then fold in the remainder.

Line two 12 × 8 inch trays (½ inch deep) with oiled silicone paper, and sprinkle with some of the Parmesan cheese. Turn the mixture out into the trays and spread evenly using a large palette knife. Bake in a preheated oven at gas mark 4 (350°F/180°C) for about 15 minutes. Meanwhile, place a piece of tinfoil on the work surface, cover with a sheet of greaseproof paper, lightly brush this with oil and sprinkle with a little more Parmesan cheese.

To prepare the sauce: sauté the mushrooms gently in the butter, drain well on kitchen paper then fold into the white sauce with the Marsala.

Check that the roulade is cooked, remove from the oven and turn out onto the prepared grease-proof paper. Immediately, spread the mushroom mixture evenly on top and roll up.

Serves: 6

# Leg of Lamb Baked in Hay

1 × 6–7 lb leg of lamb

4 oz butter, softened

4 tbsp chopped fresh herbs, sea salt

freshly ground black pepper

fresh clean hay

Wipe the leg dry with a kitchen cloth, then coat liberally with the softened butter mixed with the herbs. Season liberally. Cover the base of a roasting tray with fresh clean hay, lay the lamb on this and cover with clean hay. Cover the whole tray with aluminium foil. Bake in a preheated oven at gas mark 9 (475°F/240°C) for 3 hours. There is no need to baste.

Serves: 8

Wine: *A South African Cabernet Sauvignon*

# Wheatmeal Chocolate Rum Slice

8 oz butter

4 large fresh eggs

8 oz soft brown sugar

5 level tsp baking powder

4 level tbsp cocoa powder (not drinking chocolate)

2 tbsp rum

8 oz wheatmeal flour

1 pt double cream

4 tbsp caster sugar

3 tbsp dark rum

Put first 7 ingredients into a warm bowl and beat until combined (preferably in an electric mixer). Pour into a lined 11 inch square tin and bake in a preheated oven at gas mark 4 (350°F/180°C) for about 30 minutes. Leave to cool.

When cold, turn out, cut in ½, then cut each piece lengthwise to make 4 equal layers. Whip the cream with the caster sugar and rum until stiff, and use to sandwich together the 4 layers.

Serves: 8

Wine: *A Golden Harvest South African*

# Oats
# Restaurant

**Oats Restaurant,** in Skipton, Yorkshire, has long had a fine reputation, but in 1983 a new and talented young team set about improving standards in every department. Proprietor Norman Fullalove has given the 60 seat interior a softening face-lift, including wildlife prints, Victorian photographs, and a huge centre-piece picture of Skipton High Street at the turn of the century. Cordon Bleu trained manageress Jane Bishop presides with a winning but discreet friendliness and ensures that service is always immaculate. Her charm and efficiency are a major part of the Oats' success.

Award-winning Chef Roger Grimes trained at The Old Swan, Harrogate, and in 14 years at Pool Court helped to create that establishment's name for quality and consistent excellence. He is famed for artistic presentation, with a particular love of fish and sauces — though he also recommends the Oats' veal, venison, and traditional steaks. The wide-ranging menu is mainly French and English, with "a touch of the Orient". The table d'hôte menu is reasonably priced and the à la carte changes weekly.

A modest but excellent wine list offers some vintage bottles, and there is draught beer at the bar.

## OATS Restaurant

**Chapel Hill, Skipton, North Yorkshire**

**0756-3604**

Lunch: 12 to 2 p.m.
Dinner: 7 to 9.30 p.m.
Tuesday — Saturday
Reservations

Proprietor: Norman H. Fullalove
Chef: Roger Martin Grime

# Sole Épinard with Hollandaise Sauce

4 fillets of lemon sole

8 spinach leaves (4 medium and 4 small)

2 tbsp butter, melted

1 glass white wine

    salt and pepper

1 egg yolk

½ tbsp lemon juice

    salt and pepper

2½ oz butter, melted over low heat

    small spinach leaves and tomatoes

Skin sole or ask the fishmonger to do it for you. Blanch the spinach by plunging into boiling salted water for 1–2 minutes, and cool under cold water.

Lay the fillets of sole, skinned side up, and cut across the flesh at an angle (not too deeply), to prevent shrinking. Lay 2 leaves of spinach on each fillet, brush with butter, and sprinkle with a little seasoning. Fold into an envelope. Brush an earthenware dish with butter and lay the fish folded side down. Brush each fillet with a little melted butter, pour wine over the fish and add salt and pepper. Cover the dish with buttered tinfoil or buttered grease-proof paper, making sure the dish is well sealed. Bake at gas mark 4 (350 ° F/180 ° C) for 15–20 minutes.

To prepare sauce: put egg yolk, lemon juice, and seasoning in a basin. Boil some water in a pan which the basin will fit into. Lower heat to simmer and place basin on pan. Using a small whisk, gently blend egg yolk, lemon juice, and seasoning together, until the consistency becomes thick and creamy. Then add melted butter.

To serve: place each fillet of fish (well-drained) on a warm serving plate. Cover with the hollandaise sauce and decorate with a small spinach leaf and a tomato rose. Serve immediately.

Serves: 4

*Wine: Chablis Premier Cru Montmains 1981*

---

# Faisan en Filet au Jus d'Orange

4 breasts of young pheasant, skins removed

1 medium onion, finely chopped

½ pt chicken stock (not too strong)

    zest and juice of 3 oranges

    juice of 1 medium lemon

2 tbsp white wine vinegar

1 tbsp caster sugar

1 tbsp marmalade

    salt and pepper and a little melted butter

    chopped fresh mint to decorate

Using a stainless-steel container, marinate breasts of pheasant in onion, chicken stock, orange and lemon juice (not zest), and seasoning for 2–3 hours.

To make the sauce: remove pheasant breasts from marinade. Pour remaining marinade into a pan, bring to boil, then simmer gently for about 15 minutes. In a separate pan cook vinegar, sugar, and marmalade until chestnut in colour. Now add the reduced marinade to the caramelised syrup (be very careful as the caramel is very hot and can soon splash). Simmer gently for about 5 minutes, mixing thoroughly. Allow to cool, then liquidise. Put into a clean pan, bring to boil, and simmer gently for 5 minutes. Add orange zest and cook. Check flavour and if necessary add seasoning to taste.

Place seasoned pheasant breasts under preheated grill and cook to your own requirements, brushing occasionally with a little melted butter.

To serve: place the breasts on plates and coat with sauce. Decorate with orange segments and zest dipped in mint.

Serves: 4

---

# Les Fraises et Pêches Chaudes

1 lb fresh strawberries

2 large fresh peaches

4 oz caster sugar

½ glass white wine

2 fl oz brandy

    zest and juice of 2 oranges

    juice of 1 lemon

    a few red peppercorns, crushed

    vanilla ice cream and chopped fresh mint

Hull strawberries and, if large, cut into halves. Stone peaches and slice thinly. Caramelise sugar and wine until pale gold in colour. Add brandy and leave to flame. Add orange and lemon juice (not zest), then some of peppercorns and simmer for 5–10 minutes. Strain into a clean pan, add zest and remaining peppercorns.

To serve: add fruit to syrup in pan and heat through for 30 seconds. Remove fruit using a slotted spoon and place on appropriate plates. Put ice cream in small ramekin dishes and place on same plates, with fruit. Pour a little of the syrup over the fruit and garnish with mint.

Serves: 4

# Pool Court Restaurant

Michael Gill and his wife, Hanni, opened the **Pool Court Restaurant** some 17 years ago at Pool in Wharfedale, a small village just nine miles from Harrogate, Leeds, and Bradford. Since that time, a combination of elegant surroundings within the Georgian mansion, a balance of imaginative and classical dishes on the extensive menu, and a feeling of genuine, warm welcome have contributed to their success. Today, Pool Court is certainly one of the top restaurants in Great Britain.

Chef Melvin Jordan, who trained extensively in this country and Switzerland before coming to the restaurant 11 years ago, and his team base their cooking entirely on fresh in-season produce. The menu is changed at least weekly, offering guests a four-course meal with a choice of six or seven dishes in each section.

The restaurant is traditionally furnished in the Regency style, and a separate dining area, known as the Cellar Restaurant, is available for private parties. It has a separate bar for informal pre-dinner drinks, an intimate atmosphere, and the same standard of cuisine and service for which Pool Court has become justly famous.

Pool Court also features an extensive wine list that offers a choice from more than 200 bins, with three excellent French house wines available. The latest development is the provision of four magnificent bedrooms with excellent facilities.

**Pool in Wharfedale**
**Otley, West Yorkshire**

**0532-842288**

**Lunch by appointment**
**Dinner: Tuesday — Saturday**
**7 to 10 p.m.**
**Reservations**

**Proprietor: Michael W.K. Gill**
**Chef: Melvin Jordan**

# Trout Fillet with Chives

- 2 lb trout
- 1 small onion, chopped
- 1–2 carrots, chopped
- 2 sticks of celery, chopped
- 1 bay leaf
- ¼ pt white wine
- ½ pt fish stock or water
- 2 oz unsalted butter
- 1 oz fresh chives, chopped
- salt and pepper
- 4 vine leaves to garnish (optional)

Fillet the trout, remove all the bones and skin. Place the onion, carrots, and celery in a saucepan with the bay leaf, wine, and fish stock or water. Bring to the boil and simmer for 20 minutes to form a court bouillon. Poach the trout in the court bouillon for 3–5 minutes. Remove the fish. Strain the cooking liquor into a clean pan. Reduce by ⅔, then whisk in the butter. Add the chives and season to taste.

To serve: arrange the vine leaves on the plates, then the trout, and spoon the sauce over.               Serves: 4

---

# Noisettes d'Agneau des Tournelles

(pan-fried lamb cutlets with onion purée and an onion and Noilly Prat sauce)

- 2 medium-sized onions, peeled and chopped
- 2 oz butter
- 4 fl oz lamb or beef stock
- 1 egg yolk
- salt and pepper
- ¾ lb onions, peeled and chopped
- 1 pt lamb stock (made from lamb bones, celery, carrots, leeks, and parsley)
- ¼ pt Noilly Prat
- 2½ oz sugar
- 3 oz white wine vinegar
- ½ pt double cream
- 12 lamb cutlets, well-trimmed of fat, and bones cut down
- oil and butter for frying

To prepare onion purée: cook the 2 onions lightly in ½ the butter (without colouring) and pour the 4 fluid ounces lamb or beef stock over. Bring to the boil and simmer for 5–8 minutes until onion is soft. Liquidise (or pass through a strainer). Allow to cool slightly and beat in the egg yolk. Season to taste and leave to cool.

To prepare sauce: sweat off the ¾ pound of onions in remaining butter until transparent. Add 1 pint of stock and Noilly Prat and bring to the boil. Simmer for about 20–30 minutes. In a separate thick-bottomed pan, cook sugar and white wine vinegar over a moderate heat to a light caramel. Add the onion mixture and bring to the boil. Liquidise. Pour into a clean pan, add the cream and heat through. Do not boil.

Fry the cutlets lightly in oil and butter (leave quite pink), and drain on absorbent paper. Transfer to a grilling rack, spoon onion purée over each eye of meat and grill until purée is golden brown. Serve immediately, offering the sauce separately.

Serves: 4

---

# Les Fraises Chaudes au Poivre Vert

(Fresh strawberries tossed in orange-flavoured syrup with green peppercorns)

- 4 oz granulated sugar
- 2 fl oz brandy
- juice of 1 lemon
- juice of 2 oranges
- 10 green peppercorns
- 1 lb strawberries, hulled and washed
- homemade vanilla ice cream, to serve

Using a thick-bottomed pan, caramelise the sugar, but do not stir when boiling. When a light caramel is achieved around the sides of the pan (not too dark or it will be bitter) add the brandy. This will flame, so caution is necessary. When the flames stop, add the fruit juice and simmer for 5–10 minutes to dissolve any lumps. Add the peppercorns while simmering.

Add the strawberries to the simmering liquid, leave for 1 minute only, then serve with a small dish of ice cream.

Serves: 4

**CHEF'S TIP**

To be at its best, this dessert should be made seconds before serving.

# The River House

**The River House** was built about 1830 as a gentleman farmer's residence. Up a quiet creek, it overlooks the River Wyre with views of boats and the Bowland Fells. Although only four-and-a-half miles from Blackpool, directions are usually essential for first-time customers.

The house, which was once described as shabbily comfortable, is furnished with antiques, has a cosy bar with a log fire, and is also the home of the Scott family.

There are four guest bedrooms, one sporting a half four-poster bed. The bathroom has a hooded bath — a wonder of Victorian plumbing in regular use.

The River House was opened in 1958 by a Mrs. Scott. Nine years ago, her son, Bill, joined her. Now, with the help of his wife, Carole, Bill runs the business and does the cooking.

"Our aim," says Bill, "is to present freshly cooked food that tastes of what it is; that is, beef of beef. Consequently, I do not cook dishes in sauce, but serve them with sauce. I believe good food presents itself, and these days, too much attention is paid to tarting up food at the expense of quality. In order to achieve this, we ask customers, whenever possible, to order their main course in advance. The last thing you taste is the pudding. It should be freshly made, not frozen or tinned. Better to have less selection."

## THE RIVER HOUSE

Skippool Creek, Thornton-le-Fylde
Blackpool, Lancashire

0253-883497

Breakfast, Lunch, Dinner
Daily
Reservations

Proprietor: The Scott Family
Chef: Bill Scott

# Crab Mousse

½ c bread crumbs

¼ c milk

⅛ c stock

½ lb dark and light crabmeat

salt and pepper, to taste

1 tsp lemon juice

½ tsp chopped fresh parsley

1 egg yolk, beaten

1 egg white, well beaten

lettuce, cucumbers, and lemon wedges, to garnish

Add bread crumbs to milk and stock and leave in a warm place for 5 minutes. Add crabmeat, salt, pepper, lemon juice, and chopped parsley. Cool slightly, then add beaten egg yolk. Fold in well beaten egg white. Pour into 4 well greased cocottes, cover with foil, and bake in a tin of water in a moderate oven for 40 minutes. Serve each garnished with lettuce, cucumber, and a wedge of lemon.

Serves: 4

# Crispy Rare Noisettes with Garlic Sauce

2 middle cut loins of lamb

butter, to grease

½ pt double cream

6 cloves garlic, crushed

salt and pepper, to taste

2 tbsp brandy

Strip off outer layer of skinny tissue on lamb loins (should pull off quite easily). Cut meat off bone in one piece. Trim, leaving enough fat to

wrap around eye of loin. Tie securely with string at 1 inch intervals. Cut between strings to make noisettes. Place flat on a buttered baking dish. Cook for 5 minutes in a preheated oven as hot as you can get it (500–550°F/260–290°C). The fat outside should be crispy and the meat rare.

To prepare sauce: reduce cream and garlic over high heat until it thickens. Add salt and pepper to taste and brandy. Pour over noisettes and decorate with sprigs of parsley.

Serves: 4

# Hungarian Torte

5 egg yolks

8 oz caster sugar

2 tbsp lemon juice

½ lb ground hazelnuts

2 scant oz fine white bread crumbs

3 oz raisins

5 egg whites

sweetened fresh cream, as needed

chocolate butter icing, prepared, as needed

Beat egg yolks, gradually adding ½ the sugar until quite thick. Fold in lemon juice, ground hazelnuts, bread crumbs, and raisins. In a separate bowl, beat egg whites with remaining sugar until quite stiff, then fold in the nut mixture. Divide the mixture between two 8 inch cake tins and bake at gas mark 6 (400°F/205°C) for 30–35 minutes. Cool on a cake rack.

Sandwich the two cakes together with sweetened fresh cream and cover with chocolate butter icing.

# Sharrow Bay Country House Hotel

**Sharrow Bay Country House Hotel** began in 1948 when Francis Coulson found this beautiful early Victorian house superbly situated on the edge of Lake Ullswater. With the support of his father and a few hundred pounds in his pocket, he tackled converting the empty family mansion house into a small hotel. Mr. Coulson was trained formally by a French Cordon Bleu chef and obtained further experience working with colleagues in France.

In the spring of 1949, Sharrow Bay opened with six bedrooms and, as food was still being rationed after the war, a menu that was simple but honest.

In 1952, Brian Sack, who trained at the Westminster Hotel School in London, arrived on the scene, intending to stay for only a short time, but it seemed straightaway that the two men complemented one another, and it obviously was meant to be that a partnership should develop. The success of that partnership was reflected in the gradual development of Sharrow Bay into the cosy, comfortable establishment, with 29 bedrooms, 19 private bathrooms, and a first-rate restaurant, that it is today.

The restaurant features English and French cuisine and specialises in Old English roasts, local fish and fowl dishes, and traditional English puddings. An extensive wine list, highlighting French and German vintages, is also available.

*Sharrow Bay*

**Lake Ullswater
Penrith, Cumbria
08536-301
Breakfast: 9 to 9.30 a.m.
Lunch: 1 to 1.30 p.m.
Dinner: 8 to 8.45 p.m.
Daily
Closed: December — February
Reservations

Proprietors:
Francis Coulson, Brian Sack
Chef: Francis Coulson, M.C.G.B.**

# Special Pâté Parfait

½ lb chicken livers, prepared

Madeira or port, for marinating

1 oz lard

3 oz bacon, finely chopped

1 small onion, chopped

thyme and bay leaf, to taste

1 tbsp sherry

1 tbsp port

brandy, to taste, kirsch preferred

3 tbsp double cream, optional

seasoning, to taste

melted butter, as needed

Marinate livers in Madeira for 1½ hours, turning occasionally. Drain livers. Heat lard in a small frying pan and when hot, sauté livers briefly, just long enough to brown all sides. In another pan, cook bacon and onion, add thyme and bay leaf and cook over low heat. When mixture is cooking, add livers but do not overcook; remove from heat. Put mixture, minus bay leaf, into a liquidiser or through a sieve. Add sherry, port, and brandy to taste, mix well. Add cream if dish is to be served immediately. Season to taste. Place mixture into a terrine dish and cover pâté with melted butter.

---

# Casserole of Rump Steak Eszterhazy

1 × 2 lb rump steak

flour seasoned with black pepper, to dust

1½ oz lard

1 medium onion, chopped

1 clove garlic, minced

2 small carrots, finely chopped

3 tbsp flour, approximately

1½ pt beef stock, fresh or tinned consommé

¼ - ½ tsp allspice

3 medium bay leaves

4 peppercorns

a little thyme

1 strip of lemon peel

4 rashers lean bacon, finely chopped

chopped parsley

3 tbsp white wine vinegar

8 tbsp double cream

1 tsp lemon juice

Cut up steak, trimmed of fat and sinew, and dip pieces in seasoned flour. Heat lard and brown steak all over. Remove to a dish. Add onion, garlic, and carrot to original pan and cook about 8 minutes, stirring frequently until vegetables are lightly coloured. Remove from heat and stir in flour; continue to stir until all flour has been absorbed. Add stock and bring to a boil; stir until completely smooth. Add allspice, bay leaves, peppercorns, thyme, lemon peel, bacon, parsley, and vinegar. Return meat to pan and bring to a boil. Reduce heat, cover pan, and simmer until tender (about 50 minutes), or as desired.

Arrange steak on a dish and keep warm. Strain contents of pan, skim off any surface fat, whisk cream a little and fold in. Add a little lemon juice. Do not let boil again or it will separate.

Serves: 4

---

# Le Gâteau Victoire au Chocolat

7 oz menier chocolate or any good dark chocolate

1 oz cocoa or unsweetened chocolate

½ tbsp instant coffee

3 tbsp boiling water

1 tbsp dark rum

3 large eggs

2 oz caster sugar

9 fl oz double cream

½ tbsp vanilla essence

butter and flour, as needed

icing sugar and whipped cream, as needed

Melt chocolate with cocoa, coffee, water, and rum. Beat eggs with sugar to a thick foam, the consistency of lightly whipped cream. Beat mixture until smooth and shiny. Beat into eggs until smooth. Whip cream to very soft peaks; whip in vanilla. Fold cream into chocolate mixture and pour into a buttered and floured cake tin about 8 inches in diameter. Place tin in a bain-marie of boiling water to come 1½ inches up the sides and bake on rack in lower middle of oven at gas mark 4 (350°F/180°C) for 1½ hours or until cake has risen, cracked slightly, and skewer comes out clean. (Cake will sink to original volume.)

Turn off oven, leave door ajar, and let cake sit in oven for 30 minutes. Remove from bain-marie and let sit another 30 minutes before unmoulding. Dust with icing sugar and serve with whipped cream.

# Tarn End Hotel

The **Tarn End Hotel** stands on the banks of the 60-acre Talkin Tarn in a country park on the outskirts of Brampton, ten miles east of Carlisle. It boasts a Regency-style restaurant, a delightful cocktail bar, and seven comfortable bedrooms.

A family-run business, its air of smooth efficiency reflects the professional experience of the proprietress, Mrs. M.C. Hoefkens, her son, Martin, who is a Paris-trained chef, and his daughter, Carole, who is second chef.

The restaurant boasts the most extensive à la carte and table d'hôte menus in the district, and the Hoefkenses prepare French haute cuisine to tempt the palate of the most discerning gourmet.

Daughter-in-law Jean, who runs the restaurant, will be only too pleased to give you the benefit of her wide experience in the choice of wines available, from a most comprehensive wine list, to complement your meal.

The pleasantly restful cocktail bar, with its open log fire, is run by daughter Claire, who has studied the fascinating art of mixing drinks for 25 years. She will produce "the drink for the occasion" or your own particular mix on request.

The entire hotel exudes the atmosphere of a French-style country restaurant.

**Tarn End Hotel**

**Talkin Tarn, Brampton
Cumbria**

**06977-2340**

**Breakfast: 8 to 9.15 a.m.
Lunch: 12.30 to 1.45 p.m.
Dinner: 7.30 to 9 p.m.
Daily
Closed October
Reservations**

**Proprietor: Mrs. M.C. Hoefkens
Chef: M.J. Hoefkens**

# Grapefruit Soufflé

6 grapefruit

3 oz plain flour

9 oz sugar

2 dessertspoons Madeira

6 eggs, separated

2 tbsp candied peel

Hollow out the halved grapefuits. Squeeze the juice into a saucepan and reduce by ½. Finely chop the flesh. When juice is cool, add the flesh, flour, sugar, Madeira, and egg yolks. Whisk over low heat until thickened.

Whisk egg whites until stiff and fold into the mixture. Fill the half shells and bake in preheated oven at gas mark 6 (400°F/200°C) for about 15 minutes. Dust with icing sugar and garnish with candied peel.

Serves: 6

Wine: *Sercial Madeira or Amontillado Sherry*

---

# Ballantine of Young Grouse

6 oz butter

6 finely chopped shallots

livers and hearts of the grouse

3 level tbsp oatmeal

3 level tbsp bread crumbs

3 dessertspoons heather honey

6 measures of malt whisky

1 pt demi-glace

6 young grouse (boned as for ballantine)

6 short pastry barquettes (each 14 in long)

¼ lb grouse pâté

6 sprigs heather

salt and black pepper

To prepare the stuffing: sweat off the shallots, livers, and hearts in the butter. Add the oatmeal, bread crumbs, half the honey, seasoning, and some of the demi-glace to make a soft paste. Stuff the birds and tie into sealed oval parcels. Roast at gas mark 7 (425°F/220°C) for 20 minutes.

Line the barquettes with the grouse pâté. Place a grouse on each. Deglaze the roasting pan with the whisky, and remaining honey and demi-glace. Check for seasoning, strain over each bird and garnish with springs of heather.

Serves: 6

Wine: *Moulin-à-Vent*

**CHEF'S TIP**

Sauce should be thick enough to coat the birds; if not, reduce and whisk in some butter.

---

# Gooseberry Gâteau with Raspberry Sauce

1½ lb gooseberries

5 oz sugar

1 oz butter

6 drops vanilla essence

6 eggs

6 oz raspberries

4 oz sugar

½ pt water

1 heaped tsp cornflour

whipped cream (optional)

Lightly stew the gooseberries, sugar, butter, and vanilla in a covered pan. Allow to cool. Whisk the eggs and mix into the gooseberries. Pour into a buttered dish (8 inches wide and 2½ inches high) and cover with buttered paper. Bake in a bain-marie at gas mark 4 (350°F/180°C) until set. Allow to cool.

To prepare sauce: boil the raspberries and sugar with the water, and thicken with cornflour. Strain into a sauce boat.

Turn out the gâteau. Serve (warm or cold) with the sauce and a little whipped cream, if desired.

Serves: 6

Wine: *Château Coutel 1976*

# The Wordsworth Hotel

**The Wordsworth Hotel** is a splendid Victorian building dominating the centre of Grasmere Village, Wordsworth's home. Only 4 years ago it was a virtual ruin, but proprietor Reg Gifford (of Michaels Nook) has transformed it into one of the finest four-star hotels in Lakeland. It has all the facilities of a modern luxury hotel, 35 individually designed rooms, 24 hour room service, swimming pool etc., coupled with exquisite antique furnishings and a high degree of comfort and service.

Talented Head Chef Bernard Warne serves ample and imaginative meals in the bright and spacious Prelude Restaurant, cooking high-quality food simply, to bring out the full, natural flavours. His speciality is a traditional, crystallised Wordsworth Daffodil served on a bed of kiwi fruit, with orange or strawberry sauce. Chef Warne moved from Eastwell Manor to open the Prelude, having trained and worked in an impressive selection of first-class kitchens, including Le Talbooth, Thornbury Castle, and the Savoy and Connaught Hotels. He is ably assisted by fellow Master Chef Barrie Garton, and Karen Warne, his wife and pastry chef.

The wine list is extensive, with a predominance of French, German, and Alsace labels, and an excellent house wine. There is an elegant cocktail bar, and traditional ales are served in the lounge.

THE *Wordsworth* HOTEL

**Grasmere, Nr Ambleside, Cumbria**

**09665-592**

**Breakfast: 8 to 9.30 a.m.**
**Lunch: 12 to 2 p.m.**
**Dinner: 7 to 9 p.m. (9.30 Friday and Saturday)**
**Daily**
**Reservations (April — October)**
**Proprietor: Reginald Stanley Everett Gifford**
**Chef: Bernard Warne**
**Barrie Garton**

# Selected Seafood "Wordsworth"

4 eggs

8 oz plain flour

5 fl oz milk

2 fl oz white wine

2 fl oz fish stock

12 oz seafood (salmon, scallops, peeled prawns, halibut, and sole)

4 oz butter

Beat the eggs and flour to a smooth paste. Slowly add the milk, wine and fish stock and whisk into a batter. Leave to rest for 2 hours.

Mix and season the seafood. Add the butter to a preheated frying pan, and allow to turn a light nut-brown. Sauté the seafood for 1 minute, stirring and tossing to ensure that it does not stick.

Distribute the seafood evenly on 4 "sur le plat" dishes (4½ inches) and pour on the batter. Cook in a preheated oven, gas mark 6 (400°F/200°C) for 10–12 minutes. Serve piping hot.

Serves: 4

Wine: *Pouilly Fumé de Ladoucette 1980*

**CHEF'S TIP**

The batter must be poured on to the seafood while it is very hot to ensure lightness.

# A Pocket of Cumberland Veal

6 oz red Windsor cheese

1 egg (size 4)

4 × 6 oz loin of veal steaks

4 oz butter

2 fl oz ruby port

seasoning

Beat together cheese and egg to a workable consistency. Make a small incision at the side of each steak and, using a turning knife, carefully work the blade inside the steak to form a pocket (take care not to pierce the top or bottom of the

steak). Fill the pocket with the cheese mixture.

Flour, egg, and breadcrumb the steaks and shallow-fry on a low heat until golden brown. Remove the steaks and clean the pan of any crumbs or grease.

Mount the butter into the port until the butter becomes soft but not separated. Season to taste. Serve the veal on the port sauce.

Recommended vegetables: roast potatoes with bacon, deep-fried aubergines rolled in oatmeal, and fine French beans.

Serves: 4

Wine: *Santenay Louis Latour 1976*

# Butterscotch and Walnut Mousse

½ lb granulated sugar

¼ lb butter

½ pt single cream

3 leaves of gelatine, soaked in water

juice of 1 lemon

¼ pt softly whipped cream

4 oz chopped walnuts

3 whole eggs

3 oz caster sugar

whole walnuts to decorate

Cook the granulated sugar and butter in a pan until golden brown. Carefully add the single cream, stirring until a sauce is formed. Leave to cool. Dissolve the gelatine in the lemon juice. Fold ¾ of the cold butterscotch sauce into the whipped cream and walnuts.

Whisk the eggs and caster sugar until peaked. Fold in the cooled gelatine and then the cream-and-butterscotch mixture. Spoon into glasses and refrigerate. Decorate with piped cream, remaining butterscotch sauce and walnuts.

Serves: 6

Wine: *Zeltingen Sonnenuhr Riesling Auslese 1976*

# Fairlieburne House Hotel

**Fairlieburne House Hotel** sits in its own grounds, with superb views over the Firth of Clyde to the Isles of Cumbrae and Arran. The house itself has some interesting features, such as a Burmese teak staircase, and though there are only 6 letting bedrooms, the restaurant seats 40 and the function suite can accommodate up to 100 guests for private dinner parties.

Chef-Patron Bill Kerr took over Fairlieburne in June 1983 and has worked hard to build up the restaurant's clientele: not too difficult a task for the talented 1977 and 1979 winner of the title "Chef of the Year, Scotland." He was head chef at Nivingston House for 8 years, and has graced the kitchens of Malmaison, Glasgow, Prestwick Airport, Kyle of Lochalsh — and a luxury yacht. Chef Kerr's menu is mainly French with the emphasis on a back-to-nature simplicity and good presentation. Specialities of the house are pâtés, shellfish, and "soups with a difference," e.g. fresh shellfish bisque laced with Pernod and cream — and they also feature on the superb bar lunch menu.

A modest wine list of excellent quality includes the Austrian St. Leopold as house wine.

## *Fairlieburne*

**Fairlie, Ayrshire**
**Fairlie 246**
**Breakfast, Lunch, and Dinner**
**Closed Sunday evenings and Monday**
**Proprietors: Bill and Diane Kerr**
**Chef: Bill Kerr**

# Apple Farcie, Stilton and Port Wine Pâté

2 oz panada

1 clove garlic

1 glass port wine

2 oz double cream

2 tbsp fresh mayonnaise

salt and pepper

4 oz Stilton cheese, grated

4 whole golden delicious apples

1 stick celery, cut into curls

black grapes

4 slices of bread

Prepare panada. Mix together with next 5 ingredients. Fold in cheese and check seasoning. Pour into a mould to set.

Slice tops off apples and scoop out flesh with a Parisienne spoon. Fill skins with pâté. Decorate with apple Parisienne, celery curls and grapes. Serve with fingers of hot toast.

Serves: 4

---

# Filet Mignon of Beef Sauté de Montford

8 medallions of fillet of beef

knob of butter

2 oz shallots, chopped

8 fresh oysters

2 fl oz malt whisky

4 oz double cream

4 oz beetroot purée

8 oz potatoes

Sauté beef in butter until cooked. Remove from pan. Deglaze pan with shallots. Open oysters and place in the same sauté pan. Flame the oysters with malt whisky. Add cream and simmer until coating consistency.

Place an oyster on top of each fillet, and coat with sauce. Garnish with an oyster shell filled with beetroot purée, and olivette potatoes.

Serves: 4

---

# Swan Lake "Vacherin"

½ pt double cream

1 oz icing sugar

2 fl oz Grand Marnier

12 oz fresh strawberries

4 oval-shaped meringue nests

1 oz walnuts

1 kiwi fruit

4 meringue swan necks (S-shaped)

Whip cream. Fold in Grand Marnier and icing sugar. Gently mix in strawberries.

Fill meringue nests with the mixture. Top with walnuts and a slice of kiwi fruit. Serve on S-shaped meringue necks.

Serves: 4

# Isle
# of
# Eriska

**Isle of Eriska** is housed in an old Scottish baronial country house in Ledaig. It is owned by Robin and Sheena Buchanan-Smith who also own the island and its private vehicle bridge, guaranteeing privacy. The restaurant is ten years old and features traditional country cuisine prepared by Sheena.

Sheena's practical experience includes many years of country house entertaining. Her dishes do not possess the aggressiveness of the impressive giants of metropolitan renown, but rather tend toward the reflection of country house living of an earlier era.

Breakfast with its hot dishes set under silver covers, a lunch concentrating on the delights of a cold table, and the more formally set six-course dinner combine to impart the unique character of the old house, as a whole.

Despite the candlelit sparkle of crystal and silver, there is an informal sense of belonging and of a sharing of the atmosphere with fellow guests.

The service is most attentive, without being stiff, and the silk wallcoverings, light wood panels, and traditional furnishings blend well with the ease of the house and its surrounding countryside.

An extensive wine list and a cocktail lounge are available.

**Ledaig, Connel, Strathclyde**

**063172-371**

**Open Easter to November
All meals served daily
Reservations**

**Proprietors:
Robin & Sheena Buchanan-Smith
Chef: Sheena Buchanan-Smith**

# Venison Terrinc

1 lb haunch of venison

1 onion

butter for frying

4 oz bread crumbs

juice and grated zest of 1 orange

¼ pt port

salt and pepper

¾ lb bacon to line dish

Finely chop the venison. Sauté the onion in butter, and mix with the venison, bread crumbs, juice and zest, port, and seasoning.

Line an ovenproof dish with the bacon, and add the mixture. Place in a bain-marie and bake at gas mark 2 (300°F/150°C) for about 1½ hours until firm. Allow to cool, and press overnight.

Serve thinly sliced with salad.

Serves: 8

---

# Piobaireachd of Chicken

1 × 3–4 lb chicken

8 oz bread crumbs

juice and zest of 2 lemons

mixed herbs

1 onion, chopped and sautéed

1 egg

salt and pepper

½ lb puff pastry

Bone the chicken. Make a stuffing with the next 6 ingredients and stuff the chicken. Roast at gas mark 4 (350°F/180°C) for 30 minutes. Leave to cool.

Roll the pastry out to ⅛ inch thick and wrap it round the chicken, making a fold at the base. Roast for a further 30 minutes.

Serve with a lemon and wine sauce.

Recommended vegetables: new potatoes, French beans, and carrots.

Serves: 8

Wine: *White Burgundy*

---

# Cranberry and Orange Brulée

1 lb cranberries

2 fl oz water

2 oranges

½ pt double cream

Demerara sugar

Stew the cranberries and oranges in the water until soft. Allow to cool. Lay the fruit in a dish. Whip the cream until stiff, and spread over the fruit. Refrigerate until set.

Heat the grill. Sprinkle the Demerara sugar over the cream, and place under the grill until the sugar melts.

Serves: 8

# Kirroughtree Hotel

The **Kirroughtree Hotel,** built in 1719, stands in 8 acres of sweeping grounds giving beautiful views, and it has recently been refurbished to very high standards of luxury. The French reproduction style of the lounge includes onyx and marble-topped tables and fine porcelain; while the 24 individually designed bedrooms have lace and velvet furnishings, draped canopies over the beds and a generous supply of French toiletries. Along with this elegance, proprietor Henry Velt has created a relaxed, friendly, and homely atmosphere throughout the hotel.

He gives pride of place, however, to the flair and dedication of his Head Chef Ken MacPhee, who presents a light and delicate cuisine "so that guests can eat the full meal and enjoy it." His specialities include Poulet sauté Pernod, Terrine de Sole et Saumon, and Brandied Apricot Crêpes. Chef MacPhee was previously head chef at Inverlochy Castle, where, in 1981, he was awarded the only Michelin star in Scotland. He is ably assisted by Brian Webb, an Associate Member of the Master Chefs Institute, and they are likely to be highly rated in the 1985 Michelin and Egon Ronay Guides.

Meals are served in two dining rooms (one for non-smokers), surrounded by watered silk wall-coverings, cut glass, and Wedgwood china, and accompanied by an outstanding, mostly French, wine list.

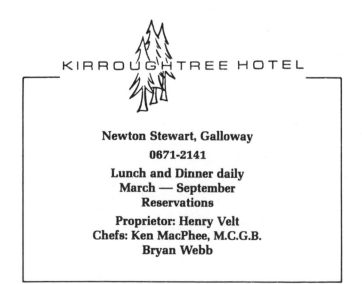

**Newton Stewart, Galloway**

**0671-2141**

**Lunch and Dinner daily
March — September
Reservations**

**Proprietor: Henry Velt
Chefs: Ken MacPhee, M.C.G.B.
Bryan Webb**

# Pâté de Gibier

1 onion

2 oz butter

1 clove garlic

8 oz fatty pork

8 oz venison

   pinch nutmeg

   pinch basil

   salt and pepper

8 oz chicken liver

2 fl oz brandy

1 egg

6 fl oz cream

4 oz bacon

2 oz pistachio nuts

Sauté onion in butter and garlic. Add pork and venison and sauté lightly. Add nutmeg, basil, and seasoning, then chicken liver and brandy, and put mixture through food processor. Add whole egg and cream, and mix thoroughly.

Line pâté dish with bacon. Put half of the mixture in the dish, and place a row of pistachio nuts closely together in the middle of the dish so that each slice will have a nut. Add the rest of the mixture.

Cook in a bain-marie for 1½ hours at gas mark 2 (300 ° F/150 ° C). Serve with Cumberland sauce.

Serves: 4

---

# Suprême de Saumon Finlandia

1 clove garlic

1½ oz butter

2 oz onion

4 darnes salmon

5 tomatoes, skinned, seeded, and chopped

1 pt fish stock

½ pt white wine

1 tsp dill weed

1 tsp tarragon  pinch paprika

   juice of ½ lemon

½ pt cream

   watercress to garnish

Rub sauté pan with garlic. Melt butter and sauté onion. Add the salmon and sauté lightly. Add tomatoes, fish stock, wine, herbs, paprika, and lemon juice, and poach the salmon. When cooked, remove the salmon and keep hot.

Reduce the cooking liquid by ½, add the cream and simmer until the sauce thickens. Spoon sauce over salmon and garnish with watercress.

Recommended vegetables (in a side dish): fine green beans, courgettes stuffed with spinach, buttered celery batons, dauphine potatoes, and parsley potatoes.

Serves: 4

---

# Chocolate Cheesecake

8 oz chocolate digestive biscuits, crumbled

2 oz butter, melted

8 oz cream cheese

4 oz caster sugar

2 eggs, separated

1 bar Meunier chocolate (100 g), melted

¼ pt cream, whipped

Mix crumbled biscuits with melted butter and use to line dish. Blend cheese, sugar, and egg yolks. Add melted chocolate. Fold in whipped cream and whipped egg whites. Add to biscuit base and leave for 2 hours to set.

Serves: 4

# The Peat Inn

**The Peat Inn** is a traditional coaching inn dating from around 1750, near Cupar, Scotland. David and Patricia Wilson bought it in 1972 and, with great dedication over the years, have transformed it into a well-appointed, internationally famous restaurant. They have also created one of the foremost wine lists in Scotland, with over 300 wines from all round the world. Inside the lovely old building, the atmosphere and furnishings are delightful, and the Wilsons preside over it all with refreshing informality.

David Wilson is in charge of the cooking — he is mainly self taught, coming into the business from an industrial marketing background. His outstanding cuisine is soundly based on the best of fresh, Scottish produce, such as beef, lamb, game, fish, and shellfish; all cooked to capture the natural flavours and presented to excite the eye. Try a Little Cake of Lobster and Prawns in a Seafood Sauce, or Tay Salmon in Pastry with a vermouth, dill, and cream sauce. For dessert, Little Pot of Chocolate and Rosemary Cream is a delicious and unusual combination.

## The Peat Inn

Cupar, Fife, Scotland
0334-84206
Lunch: 12.30 for 1 p.m.
Dinner: 7 to 9.30 p.m.
Tuesday to Saturday
Reservations

Proprietors: David and Patricia Wilson
Chef: David Wilson

# Pigeon Charlotte

3 plump Scottish pigeons

2 oz carrots, finely diced

1 oz onion, finely diced

1 oz mushrooms, finely diced

1 oz butter

3 tbsp red wine

½ oz plain flour

¾ pt chicken stock

1 clove garlic, chopped

1 bouquet garni

4 juniper berries

4 large tomatoes (about 12 oz), hashed

salt and pepper

6 green leaves from a spring cabbage or savoy

1 oz bread crumbs

1 tbsp milk

7 tbsp double cream

nutmeg

tomatoes to garnish (optional)

Remove pigeon breasts, and cut meat into small dice about ¼ inch square. Reserve carcasses and legs.

Melt butter in pan. Add diced pigeon breast and brown for about 2 minutes stirring occasionally. Add diced vegetables and continue to brown for another minute. Add wine and reduce for ½ minute. Add flour and cook out for about 1 minute. Add chicken stock, garlic, bouquet garni, juniper berries, and hashed tomato. Cover, bring to boil and cook gently for about 1 hour or until pigeon is tender.

To prepare forcemeat: remove meat from pigeon carcasses and legs (2 ounces required). Place in a bowl with bread crumbs soaked in milk. Refrigerate until ready to use. Liquidise when ready to assemble dish. Add cream and liquidise again. Season and refrigerate.

Blanch cabbage leaves in salted boiling water for about 1 minute. Refresh in cold water.

To assemble: take 6 ramekin dishes, about 3 inch diameter, 2 inches deep, buttered or preferably lined with clingfilm. Place cabbage leaf with centre vein in centre of dish, trim off excess with sharp knife. Divide forcemeat among dishes, spooning on base of cabbage leaf and up sides of dish. Using slotted spoon, divide pigeon meat among dishes, leaving most of liquid in pan. Fold over clingfilm (if used). Place ramekins in ovenproof dish or roasting tray and fill with water until about ¾ way up sides of dishes. Place tray in preheated oven gas mark 2 (350°F/150°C) for 1 hour.

Keep remainder of sauce warm, adjusting consistency with chicken stock if required. Check seasoning. Turn ramekins out on to warm plates, spoon sauce around. Garnish with skinned and halved tomatoes (optional).

Serves: 6

Wine: *Cornas, or Crozes-Hermitage*

**CHEF'S TIP**

To hash tomato: skin (by dropping in boiling, then cold water), squash in palm of hand to remove excess juice and seeds, chop flesh.

---

# Salmon in Pastry

½ lb sole

1 whole egg

1 egg white

¾ pt double cream

salt and pepper

6 × 6 oz slices of fresh wild Scottish salmon

puff pastry (scraps will do) eggwash

3 fl oz Chambéry vermouth

¼ pt fish stock

4 oz butter (extra if required)

fresh or dried dill to taste

To prepare fish mousse: skin sole, chop roughly and liquidise. Add whole egg and egg white and mix again. Refrigerate. When required, mix in chilled scant ½ pint double cream thoroughly. Season.

To prepare salmon: spread the fish mousse (about ¼ inch thick) on top of each slice. Roll out pastry almost paper-thin. Place each salmon portion on top of a piece of pastry, mousse side down. Cut pastry so it just meets when folded over. Press down edges to seal. Brush with eggwash. Place on baking sheet, mousse-side up, in pre-pre-heated oven at gas mark 8 (450°F/230°C) for about 10 minutes, until pastry is light golden. DO NOT OVERCOOK.

To prepare sauce: put vermouth and fish stock in saucepan and reduce by about ½. Add butter in pieces and whisk in. Add dill to taste, then remaining ¼ pint cream. Adjust consistency of sauce by adding a little more stock if too thick or another knob of butter if thin.

To serve: put salmon portions on warm plate. Cut half way through middle and open slightly. Pour sauce around. Garnish with fine julienne of vegetables (carrot, leek celery, mushrooms) on side of plate (optional).

Serves: 6

Wine: *The best white Burgundy you can afford*

# Prestonfield House Hotel

**Prestonfield House Hotel** stands in some 23 acres of its own grounds within the city of Edinburgh. The present house was built in 1687 for Sir James Dick, a close friend of King James II. The architect, Sir William Bruce, had just built the neighbouring Palace of Holyrood House. Today's Prestonfield has been subtly transformed into a country house hotel with five bedrooms and a number of very elegant public rooms, furnished with priceless antiques, Persian carpets, Chinese and Dresden porcelain, and Mortlake tapestries.

Outside, shadows of trees as old as the 17th century house still trace their patterns across its harled walls. Peacocks step diffidently across the paths, whilst pheasants and partridges still feed on the lawns, unaware that they are within a city's limits.

The relaxed and elegant dining rooms at Prestonfield glow with polished wood, silver, and glass, providing the correct setting for the French and classic Scottish cuisine perfectly prepared and presented by Chef Colin Warwick and his team.

Chef Warwick, who has been in the trade for more than 18 years, is particularly pleased to present his Wild Duck with Orange and Ginger, which is a long-standing house speciality. With 24 years experience, Manager Giovanni Fabbroni capably guides the smooth running of the entire operation. His wine cellar, incidentally, features an excellent choice of both European and Californian wines.

---

## *PRESTONFIELD HOUSE*

**Prestonfield Road
Edinburgh**

**031-667-8000**

**Breakfast, Lunch, and Dinner
Daily**

**Manager: Giovanni Fabbroni
Chef: Colin Warwick**

---

# Avocado Stilton

100 ml olive or corn oil

50 g rindless Blue Stilton cheese

juice of ½ lemon

chopped parsley, to taste

100 ml wine vinegar

½ tsp French mustard

salt and milled white pepper, to taste

lettuce, as needed

4 large ripe avocado pears

chopped parsley, to garnish

tomato, cucumber, capsicum etc. to choice

To prepare the dressing: liquidise the first 6 ingredients, then season with salt and pepper to taste.

Form a bed of lettuce on each of 8 plates. Using a stainless steel knife, halve the avocados, remove stones, then carefully peel off skin. Slice at an angle into 8 slices, taking care to retain shape of the pear. Lay slices on lettuce and, with gentle pressure, spread slices slightly. Coat with dressing, sprinkle with chopped parsley, and garnish each plate neatly with optional salad items.

---

# Venison Chop Prestonfield

200 ml red wine

25 ml oil

2 cloves crushed garlic

1 bay leaf

1 blade mace

25 ml wine vinegar

100 g chopped onion

pinch of thyme

pinch of rosemary

½ tsp crushed peppercorns

8 × 150-200 g venison chops

seasoned flour, to dust

100 ml oil

100 g butter

375 ml basic brown sauce

1 small jar redcurrant jelly

125 ml cream

8 small choux paste buns

Mix the first 10 ingredients together to make a marinade. Place the chops in the marinade at least 1 day before required (3 days would be ideal).

Drain venison from marinade. Drain liquid from rest of marinade ingredients and retain both. Season, flour, and sauté chops quickly in a frying pan with hot oil and butter. Take care to keep them frying, not stewing in their own juices. Take out when medium well done and keep warm.

Drain off any excess oil and gently fry the onion, garlic, and herbs saved from the marinade. Do not scorch. When the onion is soft, add liquid from the marinade and reduce almost completely. Add brown sauce and a dessertspoonful of redcurrant jelly and boil. Add cream and check seasoning and consistency. Add any juice or blood that has drained out of the chops being kept warm. (Optional: to increase gloss and enrich sauce, add 50 grams butter in pieces, mix in and do not re-boil.)

To serve: coat the chops with the sauce and decorate with the choux buns which have been slit and filled with redcurrant jelly.

Serves: 8

Wine: *Barolo D.O.C. Fontanafredda, Justerini & Brooks*

---

# Chocolate Mint Mousse

350 g plain chocolate

25 g butter

60 ml water

5 eggs, separated

1 small measure brandy

50 g caster sugar

125 ml whipped cream

2 measures chocolate mint liqueur, or to taste

To prepare mousse: melt 250 grams chocolate with the butter and water and cook. Let cool. Whisk the yolks, brandy, and ½ the sugar together in a double boiler on a slow fire until light and thickened. Remove from heat and beat until cool. Beat whites with the remaining sugar until stiff. Mix the yolk mixture into the cooled melted chocolate. Fold in the whites thoroughly. Divide between 8 wine glasses and allow to cool in the refrigerator for at least 4 hours.

Meanwhile, melt the remaining chocolate. Place a little at the bottom of 10 or 12 (to allow for breakage) small petits four cases. Using your finger, spread chocolate around the sides as evenly as possible. Repeat process to build up a cup with walls strong enough to withstand removing paper case by careful tearing.

Decorate top of mousse with whipped cream. Fill 8 of the chocolate cups with chocolate mint liqueur and place on top.

Serves: 8

# Turnberry Hotel

The **Turnberry Hotel** offers all the luxuries of four-star comfort on the beautiful Ayrshire coast — plus world-famous golfing facilities. Guests can try their game on the Ailsa course, site of the 1977 Open, or the Arran, a more leisurely, though still testing, par 69. Also on offer are an indoor swimming pool, sauna, solarium, tennis courts, gym, and billiards. The decor is elegant, the cocktail bar suitably sophisticated, and the service throughout the hotel is experienced and attentive.

The restaurant, which seats 200, is rightly considered one of Scotland's finest, with the inspired cuisine of Head Chef Duncan Cameron, who was previously at the Station Hotel, Perth and Central Hotel and Malmaison, Glasgow. His cuisine is traditionally French, but adapted to modern tastes, and he specialises in fish and game. Naturally, therefore, Highland venison, local salmon and lobster feature prominently on the menu, along with Scottish oatcakes and shortbread. The emphasis is on fresh ingredients, presented simply to make the most of their natural colours.

There is a well-balanced and comprehensive wine list, with a range of French bottled house wines from the Turnberry's excellent cellar.

He is now ably assisted by an Associate Member, Jim Anderson who was with him at Malmaison before a short stay at The George, Edinburgh.

*Turnberry Hotel Restaurant*

**Turnberry, Ayrshire**
**06553-202**

**Lunch: 1 to 2 p.m.**
**Dinner: 8 to 9.30 p.m.**
**Reservations**

**General Manager: C.J. Rouse**
**Chef: Duncan Stewart Cameron M.C.G.B.**

# Cailles Grillés au Citron Vert

8 quails

2 oz honey

1 glass Madeira

4 limes

caramel sauce to cook limes

a little butter

½ pt jus lie

seasoning

sprig parsley

Split the quails, removing and reserving back bones. Brush the split quails with honey and marinate in the Madeira overnight. Cook lime zest in caramel sauce and drain overnight.

Sauté the bones and trimmings from the quail in a little butter. Add the marinade, jus lie, and a little lime juice. Cook to the right consistency, then pass through a fine conical strainer. Finish with butter, and season to taste.

Grill the quail quickly and place on sauce-covered plates which have been garnished with warm lime segments. Sprinkle with drained lime zest. Garnish with parsley.

Serves: 4

# Coronne de Homard Belle Maison

2 oz shallots

2 oz butter (extra for frying)

1 glass white wine

1 pt double cream

2 oz Gruyère cheese

salt and pepper

12 scallops, poached and sliced

2 lobster tails, cooked and sliced

2 oz each carrot, turnip, leek, celery cut into julienne and blanched

1 truffle, lobster leg to garnish

Sauté chopped shallots in butter, and add white wine, cream, and Gruyère cheese. Season to taste. Pass the sauce through a fine conical strainer and add a knob of butter. Sauté the scallops and lobster tails in a little butter till hot but not browned.

Coat the plates with the sauce and place the scallop and lobster in a circular crown shape. Place the heated julienne of vegetables and the truffle in the centre of the crown. Garnish the rim of the plate with the lobster leg.

Serves: 4

# Mousse de Chocolat à la Menthe Brouillés

3 egg yolks

3 oz sugar

¾ pt double cream, lightly whipped

½ oz chocolate, melted

measure of crème de menthe

4 oz caster sugar

1 tbsp golden syrup

2 oz butter

2 oz flour

1 tbsp brandy

Cream yolks and sugar over bain-marie until cooked. Fold in cream, chocolate and crème de menthe.

For brandy snaps: place all remaining ingredients in a bowl and mix to a smooth paste. Weigh off 1 ounce portions and cook in a hot oven, gas mark 8 (450°F/230°C) until golden brown. Allow to cool slightly before shaping over the back of a teacup.

Serves: 4

# Index of Recipes

# Directory of Restaurants

L'Arlequin, London **10**
*Chef:* Christian Delteil

Bagatelle, London **12**
*Chef:* Osamu Ono

Bell Inn, The, Buckinghamshire **130**
*Chef:* Jack Dick

Boulestin Restaurant Francais, London **14**
*Chef:* Kevin Kennedy

Bridge Inn, The, Durham **158**
*Chef:* Nick Young

Capital Hotel, London **16**
*Chef:* Brian Turner, M.C.G.B.

Carved Angel, The, Devon **102**
*Chef:* Joyce Molyneux

Castle Hotel, The, Somerset **106**
*Chef:* Christopher Oakes

Chewton Glen Hotel, Hampshire **74**
*Chef:* Pierre Chevillard

Chez Moi, London **18**
*Chef:* Richard Walton

Chez Nico, London **20**
*Chef:* Nico Ladenis, M.C.G.B.

Count House Restaurant, Cornwall **108**
*Chef:* Ann Long

Dorchester, The, The Grill Room, London **22**
*Chef:* Anton Mosimann, M.C.G.B.

Dormy House, Worcestershire **134**
*Chef:* Roger Chant

Drangway Restaurant, The, Swansea **110**
*Chef:* Colin Pressdee

Eatons Restaurant, London **24**
*Chef:* Santosh Kumar Bakshi

Elms Hotel, The, Worcestershire **138**
*Chef:* Nigel Lambert

English Garden, The, London **26**
*Chef:* Paul Brooks

English House, The, London **28**
*Chef:* Paul Rigby

Escargot, L', London **30**
*Chef:* Martin P. Lam

Fairlieburne House Hotel, Ayrshire **180**
*Chef:* Bill Kerr

Farlam Hall, Cumbria **160**
*Chef:* Barry Quinion

Fox and Goose Inn, The, Suffolk **140**
*Chef:* A.P. Clarke

Français, Le, London **32**
*Chef:* Jean-Jacques Figeac

Frederick's, London **36**
*Chef:* Jean-Louis Pollet

Gavroche, Le, London **38**
*Chef:* A.H. Roux, M.C.G.B.

Gavvers, London **40**
*Chef:* Denis Lobry

Gidleigh Park, Devon **112**
*Chef:* Kay Henderson

Gravetye Manor, Sussex **76**
*Chef:* Allan Garth, M.C.G.B.

Greenway, The, Gloucestershire **142**
*Chef:* William Bennet

Hambleton Hall, Rutland **144**
*Chef:* Nicholas Gill

Hill's, Warwickshire **146**
*Chef:* Shaun Hill

Hole in the Wall Restaurant, The, Avon **114**
*Chef:* A.T. Cumming

Homewood Park Hotel and Restaurant,
Avon **116**
*Chef:* Antony Pitt

Horn of Plenty Restaurant, The, Devon **118**
*Chief:* Sonia Stevenson, M.C.G.B.

Hotel Inter-Continental, Le Soufflé Restaurant,
London **42**
*Chef:* Peter Kromberg, M.C.G.B.

Hunstrete House, Avon **120**
*Chef:* Martin Rowbotham

Hyatt Carlton Tower Hotel, London **44**
*Chef:* Bernard Gaume, M.C.G.B.

Interlude de Tabaillau, London **46**
*Chef:* Jean-Louis Taillebaud

Isle of Eriska, Argyll **182**
*Chef:* Sheena Buchanan-Smith

Ivy Restaurant, London **48**
*Chef:* Guiseppe Pedri

Kirroughtree Hotel, Galloway **184**
*Chef:* Ken MacPhee M.C.G.B.

Kundan Restaurant, London **50**
*Chef:* Aziz Khan